The Savvy Investor's Guide for Doing Business in China

Other titles from Marquette Books

James Gillett, *A Grassroots History of the HIV/AIDS Epidemic in North America* (2011). ISBN 978-0-9826597-7-9 (paperback)

John Markert, *The Social Impact of Sexual Harassment: A Resource Manual for Organizations and Scholars* (2010). ISBN 978-0-9826597-4-8 (paperback)

John C. Merrill, *Farewell to Freedom: Impact of Communitarianism on Individual Rights in the 21st Century* (2011).
ISBN: 978-0-9826597-5-5 (paperback)

John W. Cones, *Introduction to the Motion Picture Industry: A Guide for Students, Filmmakers and Scholars* (2009).
ISBN: 978-0-922993-90-1 (paperback)

John Schulz, *Please Don't Do That! The Pocket Guide to Good Writing* (2008).
ISBN: 978-0-922993-87-1 (booklet)

Global Communication Association and the Global Fusion Consortium, *Global Media Journal: Volumes 1-3 and 3-5* (2008). ISBNs: 978-0-922993-69-7 and 978-0-922993-70-3 (paper)

Héctor Luis Díaz, Johnny Ramírez-Johnson, Randall Basham and Vijayan K. Pillai, *Strengthening Democracy Through Community Capacity Building* (2008). ISBN: 978-0-922993-95-6 (paper)

John W. Cones, *Dictionary of Film Finance and Distribution: A Guide for Independent Filmmakers* (2008). ISBN: 978-0-922993-93-2 (cloth); 978-0-922993-94-9 (paper)

Hazel Dicken-Garcia and Giovanna Dell'Orto, *Hated Ideas and the American Civil War Press* (2008). ISBN: 978-0-922993-88-8 (paper); 978-0-922993-89-5 (cloth)

Mitchell Land and Bill W. Hornaday, *Contemporary Media Ethics: A Practical Guide for Students, Scholars and Professionals* (2006). ISBN: 0-922993-41-6 (cloth); 0-922993-42-4 (paperback)

Stephen D. Cooper, *Watching the Watchdog: Bloggers as the Fifth Estate* (2006). ISBN: 0-922993-46-7 (cloth); 0-922993-47-5 (paperback)

David Demers, *Dictionary of Mass Communication: A Guide for Students, Scholars and Professionals* (2005). ISBN: 0-922993-35-1 (cloth); 0-922993-25-4 (paperback)

The Savvy Investor's GUIDE for Doing Business in CHINA

Gary Bonvillian
Editor

Marquette Books
Phoenix, Arizona

Printed in the United States of America

Library of Congress Cataloging Number
2018957225

ISBN for this edition:
978-1-7327197-0-5

Marquette Books LLC
16421 North 31st Avenue
Phoenix, Arizona 85053
509-290-9240
books@marquettebooks.com
www.MarquetteBooks.com

Dedication

This book was inspired by

Dr. Michael T. C. Hwang

A visionary in international business and education

Table of Contents

Introduction

By Gary Bonvillian

The goal of this book is to help people — especially investors, business executives and college students in America and other Western countries — learn about, invest and do business in the People's Republic of China. Although other books and publications have offered good advice on this subject, none are as comprehensive, nor do they benefit from the extensive knowledge provided by the expert team of seasoned writers and scholars assembled here, all of whom have worked in China.

No nation in recent history has gained political and economic power at the rate of China. A serious investor or businessman must take into account the extraordinary transformation of this ancient society and how its business practices function both in public and behind the scenes.

Since becoming a member of the World Trade Organization in 2001, China has influenced not only its own advancement as a developing nation, but also the advancement of many other countries. As a consequence, China is now the topic of study in many colleges, universities and corporate training centers around the world. Even powerful nations cannot ignore what is unfolding.

A mistake outsiders commonly make is to think of the Chinese people in simplistic terms. China's historically isolationist policies have contributed to this misconception. But the Chinese are anything but simple. Seasoned investors with international experience understand the complexity of China and how easily one can falter without access to knowledge about its government, people and culture.

China's influence in the world economy cannot be overstated. Whether examined from the perspective of exporting or importing, China's actions have a ripple effect that influences the economic well-being of many other nations, including the United States and Western Europe. Experts predict that this influence will only become stronger as China's burgeoning middle class grows. In five to six years, three-fourths of China's urban population is expected to achieve middle-class status. Accompanying those increased wages is the expectation of China's continued low prices. When wages and prices are compared, China's middle class should have buying power within its borders that is comparable to other nations. (Iskyan, 2016)

Beyond economic matters, experts also believe that China will take the lead in many aspects of world affairs. China's ambitions and resources have positioned the nation to have an equal place at the table — and, some believe, the most important leader in select initiatives. Several of those topics, from technology to sustainability, are discussed in this book.

Many outsiders also fail to understand China's strategy of seeking partner nations to fortify its own interests. Examples abound of China capitalizing on mutual interests and initiatives. This phenomenon is strongly influenced by the Confucian philosophy of harmony. Like so many other elements of this ancient society, a better understanding of the vast and rich culture of China can lead to more productive and promising experiences. For investors this is not merely a matter of understanding the Chinese — it is a matter of how to engage the Chinese on their own terms.

China's heritage can be traced back nearly 5,000 years and stands among only a select few others that can claim to have histories well beyond that of Western nations. At the center of China's history is its enduring culture. The Chinese view that history with a genuine sense of pride, although in reality the actual physical evidence of these first several thousand years is rather scarce. One element of history generally accepted among historians is that around 2500 BC the area now called China began its long journey toward unification and the ten dynasties. The influence of this period cannot be ignored. (Swaine, 2015; Morton, 1995) Historians can also point back to advances toward a civilized society and the discovery or creation of fire, metallurgy, house construction, farming, medicines, and a working calendar. (Morton, 1995) These milestones influence how the Chinese see themselves today.

Ten dynasties ruled China until the collapse of the Qing Dynasty in 1912, which was the last to see imperial rule. For purposes of this body of work, the dynasties and their place in Chinese history begins with the self-proclaimed *First Emperor*, Qin Shi Huang Di, around 246 BC. Qin is actually the root of the modern word, China. Under Qin's rule, China broke down internal borders and set into motion a centralized ruling structure. For the next two thousand years, this attempt to unify would expand China's borders and create a much more powerful social force than had ever been seen before. (Morton, 1995)

Also worth mentioning in this brief retrospective are the First and Second Opium Wars. These events, taking place in the mid-1800s, proved to be devastating for China, as they revealed a weakness of power to the super nations of the time. Unprepared for the sea power of Britain, the warriors of the Qing Dynasty faced a series of devastating battle losses that led to many concessions on the part of the Chinese, including the loss of Hong Kong Island. At the same time, these losses set the stage for the eventual decline of the dynasties and ushered in a unified governing system. (Szczepanski, 2017) This included Sun Yat-sen's formation of the Kuomintang (the Nationalist Party) in the early 1900s and Chiang Kai-shek's later assent to the leadership of the party. This centralization of power not only set the stage for the rapid advances of China's society but also provided a benchmark for the outside world to judge what might be in its future.

Confucianism also has played an important role in the development of Chinese culture. The backbone of China is composed from Confucianism's basic values of rite, justice, honesty, shame, humanity, love, loyalty and filial piety. (2013, Chang) While China does not formally recognize organized religions and is officially an atheist state, there is no shortage of evidence that Confucius philosophy has endured and even today plays a critical role in national affairs.

One might speculate that China's renewed interest in ancient Confucius philosophy is outdated and unfitting for a modern society. In recent years there has been a growing concern over superficiality amongst the Chinese people, who are driven, in part, by new-found wealth and independence. This contradicts the government's relentless effort to maintain order, obedience and respect for hierarchy and authority; consequently, Confucianism is now taught in the school system. (2015, Worrall) In other words, the Communist government has found a way to actually capitalize on the ancient philosophical tenets of what many would say is not merely a religion.

Over the past century, one of the most influential and controversial events in China's modern history was the Cultural Revolution, which occurred during Mao Zedong's oppressive rule between 1966 and 1976. Mao Zedong was a soldier in China's Revolutionary Army in 1912, when, under the leadership of Sun Yat-sen, the final monarchy rule in China ended. The new nation would be the People's Republic of China. Mao rose relatively quickly through the political ranks of the new government but was torn between beliefs for China's future when Sun died and was replaced by Chiang Kai-shek. Mao, who by then had adopted Communism, led a group of rebels for many years that rejected Chiang Kai-shek's conservative political philosophy and government. (Biography.com Editors, 2017)

Mao saw profound change for China on the horizon through communist ideology, and his message resonated with the people. Although Mao and Kai-shek were united against the Japanese during World War II, this alliance would not endure. Mao dominated the political scene after the war and in 1949 established the People's Republic of China as Chiang Kai-shek fled with his loyalists to Taiwan and established the Republic of China. (2012, Kraus)

Mao's control of the Communist Party, arguably more compelling than his efforts to lead the nation itself, would define his legacy. Although he is still recognized as China's greatest leader, it is widely accepted that Mao failed in attempts to cleanse the nation of those who opposed his ideology. The Cultural Revolution, as it was known from 1966 to 1976, was a setback for China's positioning among other leading nations of the world. There is universal agreement that the Cultural Revolution did more harm than good for modern China. Isolating China from the rest of the world and oppressing education, the arts, and intellectual activity hindered its potential as a modern nation. Today people of China look back on these times as simply one error in judgment by Mao, who will forever be seen first and foremost as a great leader and the man who fully unified China under Communist rule.

Perhaps even more important when examining Mao's legacy — and germane to the purpose of this book — is the advent of state capitalism and its eventual influence on the purest of communist ideology. The movement toward today's modern economy in China is rooted in the principles of state capitalism, whereby the government would have controlling interest in commercial enterprises. Set in motion in the early and mid-1900s, state capitalism was embraced by Mao and subsequently redefined by each ruling leader since. (2015, Holmes)

Many historians argue that during the years in which Deng Xiaoping held office within the Communist Party, decisions and actions on economic reform had a profound influence on China's future positioning as a world power. Although Xiaoping was not always popular with select groups, he did open China to the rest of the world, which provided the economic stimulus to increase Gross Domestic Product. (2011, Vogel)

Xiaoping's legacy was marred by the 1989 uprising on Tiananmen Square, when a group of mostly educated young people protested that their lives were not improving as much as other constituencies within China. The West has often portrayed this uprising as a call for greater democracy; however, there is ample evidence the protesters were more focused on economic inequality. (2017, Chiu)

The next most significant influencer on the changing fortunes of China came with its entrance to the World Trade Organization in 2001. This event signaled the beginning of China's influence on the economies of many countries throughout the world and cleared the way for it to become the major player that it is today. China has been able to successfully blend the best qualities of Communist ideology with a free enterprise philosophy. Whether this mix will continue to work has yet to be seen, but there is no denying that China is now an economic superpower.

Within this general framework, each of the chapters that follow will expand on various aspects of Chinese culture, history and business.

Chapter 1 looks in-depth at how Chinese culture affects all aspects of society, including the practice of business. While there was a brief period when China did not embrace its long held beliefs and deep-rooted cultural heritage, such is not the case today. Today there is a conscious initiative to better understand and appreciate China's history. The many elements of Chinese culture examined in this chapter are daunting to say the least. However, understanding the most elemental of protocols when facing the subtleties of Chinese culture can literally make or break a business deal.

While it is tempting to look at China's transformation as adaptation to Western lifestyles, this would be shortsighted. Xi Jiping uses Chinese history and heritage to promote national pride with an emphasis that China should never fully embrace Western values. Visiting any modern city in China might tempt one to challenge this assertion, particularly when surrounded by familiar high-end international and commercial business enterprises, goods and services. But the Chinese people today celebrate and embrace their past, a practice that produces an intense pride and the expectation of higher positioning in the world order.

There is still a much tempered view of organized religion in China, except when it comes to Confucianism. More than an ancient religion, Confucianism is a way of life — a belief system that guides daily living for many. To an outsider the nuances of Confucianism can be subtle, which makes it all the more important to understand when engaging with the Chinese people.

Some would argue that there is nothing more important for a prospective business person to understand than the notion of *guanxi*, or social connections. Simply put, without *guanxi*, no one in business will advance. In concert with *guanxi* is the Chinese emphasis on stature or hierarchical position of those you are dealing with, particularly within the context of doing business. To ignore the expectation of your Chinese counterparts that they will be dealing with an outsider of equal stature runs the risk of a monumental insult — an insult that can cause your Chinese counterpart to lose face.

Finally, this chapter will examine acceptable social behavioral expectations for visitors when engaged with the Chinese people. The Chinese people are outwardly friendly, light-hearted and enjoy social gatherings. However, clumsy behavior on the part of a visitor who does not understand social protocols is not easily forgotten and often carries over into negative consequences while trying to close business deals. Deals have been known to shut down over a single misstep in social protocol.

Chapter 2 discusses the reality of attempting to introduce Western-influenced free enterprise principles into a country that still embraces Communist ideology. Some would say there is no model, anywhere else in the world, quite like that which is unfolding in China. At the heart of the debate is whether China can be a leader among the innovative nations of the world without removing the shackles of Communism. One might argue that China's growth curve has been impressive. Clearly the country is taking the lead on many new breakthroughs in science and technology. But some question whether its economic prowess can be sustained without far more positive steps toward breaking down centralized controls.

China's emergence as a global powerhouse is an undoubted fact. However, the country's path-dependent business system may hinder the transformation China hopes to achieve. Given China's status as a superpower, it is imperative that comprehensive study is undertaken into the intricacies of the business system, as well as the problems such a system might cause for sustainable growth. As a result of its more segregated past, Chinese business systems are still somewhat uncovered to the rest of the world, the Communist Party having only a small interest in improving the development of modern enterprises. A lack of integration with the rest of the world, coupled with an absence of formal or informal institutional structures, could threaten to curtail the rapid growth of the Chinese economy.

Chapter 3 will examine Chinese technology and its implications. There is clear and compelling evidence that the introduction of new technologies has opened the door for extraordinary discoveries that touch virtually every aspect of human life. At the same time, technology is gradually changing the landscape of employment as people are being replaced by machines throughout the world. China has not escaped this reality.

While the data presented in this chapter provides a sobering picture for all, not just for the Chinese, there are messages of opportunities for investors worldwide. What is not clear at this stage of technological evolution is the ultimate impact the world will feel as a result of its own creations. China, like all industrial nations, has been under increasing pressure to produce more with less and a call for efficiencies further advances new discoveries in technology. This is of no small consequence for a nation as large as China, with hundreds of millions of people requiring gainful employment to improve their lives. Of course, new technologies are not all about executing processes. They are also about breakthrough innovations in health care, environmental protection, military defense, social services and a myriad of other central elements of humankind's everyday life. Herein may lie the best opportunities for foreign investors, as China has made it clear that technology advancement is a central element of their long-term strategic growth and prosperity as a nation.

Finally, this chapter will reflect that China is not only cognizant of the opportunities and challenges of an increasingly digitized world, it is vigorously seeking to be a leader among all nations. Leading Chinese scholars and economists are well aware that technology will play a key role in China's economic advancement strategies. Early indicators of this point would suggest China is making genuine progress.

Chapter 4 examines an element of China's pursuit of social and economic development that requires serious consideration but may not be as apparent to an outsider as the other subject areas of this book. It is widely known that China, for all of its modern successes, still lags behind other developed nations in attending to the needs of their disenfranchised citizens, including those who are living in extreme poverty, the elderly and the undereducated.

Today, China has a self-imposed mandate to improve social conditions for its people, and data presented in this chapter will indicate that it is making progress. The challenge, however, is formidable given the enormity of China's demographics. Most relevant to this chapter, and the book as a whole, is the manner in which the challenge will influence the exploration, investment and conduct of business enterprises. The Government has an expectation that both internal and foreign investors will play a role.

This chapter examines China's political commitment for accelerated social development and the implications for business conduct in the coming years. Corporate social responsibility (CSR) — as a business response to the Chinese Government's development priority for social inclusiveness and eradication of extreme poverty by

2020 and achieving moderate prosperity for everyone — will not be sufficient to satisfy this political objective. Instead, it will be necessary for businesses to strengthen partnership arrangements with non-traditional stakeholders, to leverage business engineering and technological breakthroughs, and to contribute to other social innovations.

Access to quality education, health, social protection, clean drinking water and sanitation, and caring for the elderly are some of the basic tenets of development in China. They present novel business opportunities for the creation of additional values and possible new frontiers for business success. Foreign multinational companies that are investing or plan to invest in China need to take into consideration this broader policy shift from the quantity of economic growth to qualitative aspects of development.

Chapter 5 covers one of the more complex topics in this book but perhaps most critical to the outside investor. There is no denying the major impact China has made on the world economy. This impact can be felt on many levels, both positive and negative. The trajectory that China has been on in terms of growth and development could lead to its overtaking the United States as the most influential economy in the world. This, of course, has yet to be played out but there is ample data to suggest it is possible. Of particular note for outsiders attempting to understand the Chinese economy is that it is unlike anything else in the world. China's economy is not driven by autonomous business entities, as is more commonly seen in Western nations. Rather, China operates as a large, integrated nation driven by the Communist Party.

The chapter will present information and data that support the assertion that China's economic decision making and actions have a disruptive impact on the economies of other nations. Like other disruptive forces in business and industry, such as the introduction of ground breaking new technologies and products that sweep world markets, China's economy has the same effect. That impact can be either positive or negative for investors, given China's intent and the ability for other nations to react. The Chinese economy, when examined as a disruptive force, drives home the reality that nations throughout the world are nearly all interconnected — if not ideologically, then most certainly through their dependencies on markets, goods and services.

This chapter will further focus on the facts, and not speculation, of modern China's disruptive economy and how it impacts virtually the entire world today. Rather than approaching the oftentimes academic and even philosophical theories of economics, the information and data in this chapter is presented to ready foreign investors and business people for the reality of the underlying economic strategy and decision making by the Chinese government and leading business enterprises.

The data illustrate China's rise as a behemoth economy. Although Communist government control and occasional interference in both home-grown and foreign-investment enterprises may appear to be overwhelming and threatening to investors, this is not always the case. This chapter offers suggestions and opportunities for foreign investors if they understand what to look for when attempting to make a deal with this complex nation.

Chapter 6 addresses one of the most challenging of social and economic issues that has significant implications on business enterprises for internal and foreign investors: neglect of the environment. Prior to the collapse of the Cultural Revolution, there is ample evidence of this problem on the part of the government and the Chinese people. Of course, it could be argued that most other countries around the world, including the leading Western nations, were also neglectful of growing environmental concerns up until that point in time. The difference was that China was about to launch the most rapid and comprehensive buildup of industry ever seen by humankind. The data in this chapter, at least on the surface, could be seen as overwhelmingly negative for foreign investors. It should not, though, as there are many opportunities for educated investors interested in environmental enterprises.

The effects of China's rapid economic buildup on environmental issues were immediate, with implications for the health, safety and sustainability of the Chinese environment and economy. To their credit, the Chinese people did not fail to respond. However, the task for them, post-Cultural Revolution, has been attempting to maintain that same pace of industrial buildup while also implementing new and aggressive environmental protection initiatives. Anyone of the contributors to this book, all of whom have traveled and conducted business in China over the past twenty years, would report profound changes underway to attend to this social and economic dilemma. The question that still cannot be fully answered is whether the actions taken are going to be successful. Like many other aspects of this great society, the sheer volume of initiatives necessary to tackle a nation-wide environmental crisis is staggering.

This chapter will share the contents of influential legislation that has come forth from the Communist government to address this situation and report on its progress. In addition, and for the expressed purpose of this body of work, the chapter will not only present the challenges for foreign investors in China enterprises but also real opportunities. It is in these opportunities, and the efforts of the government and the people themselves, that we may begin to see the worldwide leadership in environmental protection and sustainability that some expect to emerge from China. What both internal and foreign investors would likely agree upon today is that environmental protection and sustainable economic growth are inseparable.

The **Conclusion** will provide a glimpse, albeit a somewhat cloudy one, into China's potential future in its journey to world leadership. Scholars and practitioners agree that it is difficult to predict just exactly how China will fare, long-term, as there are simply too many variables at play to accurately determine the success they will have with their many initiatives.

Paramount to China's effort will be its ability to transform from an economy that is dependent upon export to one that is more influenced by consumerism. In order to do this, China must continue to build on its economic model that strengthens the buying power of its citizens. The data would suggest this is possible given the rate of increasing middle-class status many of its citizens are achieving. One looming challenge, however, is the disparity that is growing between the rural and urban populations. The migration to urban centers has fueled this increase of standard of living but has done little for those left in the vast rural regions of China.

Current demographics and expected changes over the next twenty to thirty years will also play a significant role in China's advancements. A rapidly growing elderly population with a diminished younger generation, due to the one child policy, places a tremendous burden on families and social structures which, today, are not fully adequate to meet the needs. The conclusion will illustrate the reality of the Chinese family unit being pulled apart in modern times due to the necessity for an educated citizenry to be more mobile.

The constant tug between a Communist ideology and a purported embrace of free enterprise has yet to be reconciled. Can any country legitimately have and support both? Many would argue it is not possible. There is ample evidence, at least today, of government intrusion and out-right interference in the affairs of businesses that are supposedly operating under free-enterprise rules. This fact, perhaps more than any other variable, should carry much weight in the decision-making of foreigners as they decide how, when and where to invest.

Several unmistakable factors of the social and political landscape that could easily turn the tide of progress in China will be shared and close out this body of work. However, like so many other aspects of China's rise and now obvious powerful position in the world there is still no clear predictive future. It is cloudy to say the least. As such, China will remain a work in progress until many of the initiatives cited in this book are fully played out.

In spite of these and other challenges for foreign investors that will be covered in this book, there is no denying the great potential that China offers investors, if for no other reason than the sheer size of the market itself. That said, the challenge would seem to be in knowing how to navigate these challenges. Without exception, those who have contributed to this book could point to their own successful entry and enterprises in China. They would say, it is worth the risk.

References

Biography.com Editors (2017). *Mao Tse-tung*. Retrieved from https://www.biography.com/people/mao-tse-tung-9398142.

Chang, Chi Jun. (2013). *Confucianism: A modern interpretation*. Singapore: World Scientific Publishing Company.

Chiu, Lisa. (2017). The root of the student protests in Tiananmen square. *ThoughtCo*. Retrieved from https://www.thoughtco.com/root-of-the-tiananmen-protests-688411

Holmes, Frank. (2015). How China went from communist to capitalist. *Business Insider*. Retrieved from http://www.businessinsider.com/how-china-went-from-communist-to-capitalist-2015-10

Iskyan, Kim (2016). China's middle class is exploding. *Business Insider*. Retrieved from www.businessinsider.com/china-middle-class-is-exploding-2016-8

Kraus, Richard, Richard C. (2012) *The cultural revolution: A very short introduction*. New York: Oxford University Press.

Morton, W. Scott. (1995). *China: its history and culture*. New York: McGraw-Hill.

Swaine, Michael D. (2015). China: The influence of history. *Diplomat*, 15(1). Retrieved from https://thediplomat.com/2015/01/china-the-influence-of-history

Szczepanksi, Kallie. (2017). The first and second opium wars. *ThoughtCo*. Retrieved from https://www.thoughtco.com/the-first-and-second-opium-wars-195276

Vogel, Ezra F. (2011). China under Deng Xiaoping's leadership. *East Asia Forum*, Retrieved from https://www.eastasiaforum.org/2011/09/27/china-under-deng-xiaopings-leadership

Worrall, Simon. (2015). Why is confucius still relevant today? His sound bites hold up. *National Geographic*. Retrieved from https://news.

nationalgeographic.com/2015/03/150325-confucius-china-asia-philosophy-communist-party-ngbooktalk

Chapter 1

How to Navigate Chinese Culture

By Gary Smith and Yang Zhao

Culture is a complex whole in which each part is related to every other part. This interdependence includes the customs, traditions, language, religion, values, and other important aspects that are associated with a way of life. Culture also encompasses the behaviors and beliefs that are learned and shared by a group of people. (Zhao, 2012) The term Chinese culture is used here to refer broadly to that which is mainly associated with the Han Chinese, the majority ethnic group in modern China. It is important to note, however, that Chinese culture varies across regions and ethnicities and that this chapter is designed to provide a broad overview.

Chinese President Xi Jinping gave an address at the celebration of the 95th anniversary of the Chinese Communist Party on July 1, 2016. Zhang (2017) summarized that one key point in Mr. Xi's address was the need to promote cultural self-confidence. This address has marked a climax of the discourse and debate among Chinese intellectuals on the revitalization of Chinese traditions. Zhang (2017) further stated that through a long process — the establishment of the Republic of China (1912), the New Culture Movement (1915-23), and the Root-Seeking

Movement in the late 20th century, Chinese culture finally seems to have returned to its roots, and many people have regained cultural self-confidence.

Although the concept of cultural self-confidence has been widely used in China over the last several decades, it primarily refers to national pride in Chinese history and tradition. What has remained unclear in this discourse about cultural self-confidence are the specific traditional beliefs, values, or customs that comprise the roots of this pride and how to revive them. (Zhang, 2017) This chapter points out such cultural roots and mechanisms. Our goal is to assist people from other countries as they try to navigate Chinese culture and do business in China.

The Origin of Chinese Cultural Thought

Chinese traditional culture is influenced by three systems of thought: Confucianism, Daoism and Buddhism. The first two are indigenous to Chinese culture while Buddhism is a foreign religion introduced from India, and thus is quite different from the former in thought, tradition and beliefs. Since the introduction of Buddhism in the Han dynasty, there were sometimes conflicts among the three systems of thought. It's important to note that harmony and integration are key elements in the development of Chinese cultural thought. Thus, Chinese culture has developed into a united system of the three religious thoughts with Confucianism at the center and supported by Daoism/Taoism and Buddhism. (Guang, 2013)

The concept of Dao is more often associated with the figure Laozi and the classic Dao De Jing (*The Book of the Way and Its Power*) than with Confucius. It is not certain whether they were contemporaries. Their philosophies, though, are like two sides of a coin. Laozi emphasized harmony with the Dao, a way of doing things in order to achieve balance in life. To assist this process, Laozi taught his followers the concepts of non-action (*wu wei*) and shade and light (yin/yang-

primordial, dynamic balancing of opposites). (Foy, 2018) Foy explained that the principle of non-action meant that one should discern the natural course of things and cooperate with that movement. Thus, if a person was good at making clothes, he or she shouldn't become a cook. The concept of yin/yang (to be discussed later) reminded Laozi's students to look for the balancing forces of opposites and learn how to cooperate with and embody them. The teachings of Laozi and Confucius were not incorporated into a religious movement until the Han dynasty (206 B.C.E. to 220 C.E.). The result was a mix of philosophy and religion. Over the centuries that followed, both Confucianism (Rujiao—the teachings of the scholars) and Daoism (Daojiao—the teaching of the way) developed elaborate rituals and sacred writings. (Foy, 2018)

Chinese cultural values are based on a blending of the teachings of Confucius and Daoism. Rank and hierarchy continue to be important. Although Chinese society has become more egalitarian, much reverence is still given to superiors and the elderly. (Lang, ct al., 2012) Confucius believed that humanity should behave in a princely way and could be characterized by five virtues. In Chinese, they were *ren/jen, yi, li, zhi/chih,* and *xin. Ren/jen* represented benevolence and humanism. *Yi* stood for righteous or morality. *Li* signified proper conduct. *Zhi/Chih* meant wisdom and understanding. *Xin* represented trustworthiness. (Zhao, 2012)

The teachings of Confucius have a high regard for education and learning, harmony, family, and collectivism. Of these, harmony is the most important. According to this virtue, one puts his or her own concerns and wishes behind those of the whole society. More than anything, Confucianism is seen as a way of living and conducting business rather than a religion. Harmony is considered playing a vital role in this process. (Lang, et al., 2012)

The principle of Yin and Yang also reinforces the concept of harmony. Yin/Yang dates from the third century B.C.E. or earlier. The principal proponent of the theory was the cosmologist Zou Yan (or Tsou Yen) who believed that life went through five phases (*wu xing*) — fire, water, metal, wood, earth — that continuously interchanged. (Cartwright, 2018) Thus, when Feng Shui speaks of balance, this is referring to the tenuous presence of both types of energy in optimum quantities and relative to each other. Yin stands for the female force and reaches its height of influence with the winter solstice. Yang stands for the male force and reaches its height of influence with the summer solstice. (Zhang, 2014)

In Chinese mythology yin and yang were born from chaos when the universe was first created and they are believed to exist in harmony at the center of the Earth. When there is balance between the yin and yang, the wholeness of the universe is represented. (Zhang & Zhou, 2014) There is good balance, which then brings prosperity, health, well-being and happiness. Chinese philosophy uses the two forces to explain all phenomena, including those concerning human beings and nature. While the Western perspective normally identifies independent and dependent variables on the basis of which causal relationships can be theorized, the Yin–Yang perspective does not advocate such explicit causal relationships. (Cartwright, 2018)

Thus, in the long history of Chinese civilization, harmony has always been a highly valued virtue. Chinese people have always put an emphasis on harmony. It encompasses the fundamental principles of nature, society and humanity. It is also a prerequisite for cultivating morality, protecting family, doing business, governing the nation and stabilizing the world. Harmony is at the core of Chinese traditional culture. (Kilarski, 2017)

Confucius Merchants in China

In the Chinese business world, there is a word that used to be very popular and now has started to regain public attention. That word is *rushang*, meaning Confucius Merchants. Some Chinese scholars prefer to translate *rushang* into English as *Confucius Entrepreneur*. This term may have a better echo to the contemporary Chinese business reality, but is not what *rushang* originally meant in China. (Awen, 2015) Historically, there were four occupations or four hierarchical social class categories developed by either Confucian or Legalist scholars. This goes as far back as the late Zhou Dynasty and is considered a central part of the fengjian social structure. In descending order, these were the *shi* (gentry scholars), the *nong* (peasant farmers), the *gong* (artisans and craftsmen), and the *shang* (merchants and traders). (Four occupations, 2018) This system of social order was adopted throughout the Chinese cultural sphere.

In the classic Chinese era, elite households were the families with a member who passed a state examination, hence obtaining a title of scholar, or those with a royal connection. Merchants, no matter how rich they might be, occupied a status that was considered beneath that of the peasants. (Awen, 2015) These people were prevented from working at government office, and their sons were ineligible to participate in scholarly examinations to become a government official. It was a desperate measure to insulate Chinese society from the influence of a profit-chasing mentality, and it was also a policy designed to encourage the development of a real economy. To improve their social status, the merchants arranged for some family members to be peasants, and educated themselves and some of the sons working in commerce with Confucius teachings in order to become ethically more conscious and, therefore, more acceptable by society. (Awen, 2015) By the late Ming Dynasty, elites often needed to solicit funds from powerful merchants to build new roads, schools, bridges, pagodas, or engage in essential industries, such as book-making, which aided the entry class in education for the imperial examinations (Four occupations, 2018). Merchants began to imitate the highly cultivated nature and manners of scholar-officials in order to appear more cultured and gain higher prestige and acceptance by the scholarly elite. They even purchased printed books that served as guides to proper conduct and behavior and which promoted merchant morality and business ethics. With the

Analects (Confucius classics) in one hand and an abacus (a traditional Chinese calculator) in the other, came the motto of the Confucius Merchants. (Awen, 2015)

Today, successful entrepreneurs in China are recognized as those who thrive in an environment where they have a high degree of autonomy. To society, being your own boss means having the highest degree of power or control over your own organization, which further translates into a higher sense of career success. However, being socially successful does not necessarily lead to increased pay or promotion, but gaining fame, recognition, popularity and status in a socially approved manner plays a paramount role in motivating Chinese entrepreneurs to climb up the career ladder because of the emphasis on collectivism in the Chinese society. (Hansen, 2013) In fact, the desire to gain *mianzi* or face (to be discussed later) is a concept that succinctly captures one of the most influential factors that motivate Chinese entrepreneurs to strive for higher achievements.

Chinese Social Organization

According to Hofstede's cultural dimensions, the most important characteristics of Chinese culture are its high level of collectivism and power distance, with the Chinese having a relatively low level of uncertainty avoidance and relatively high levels of long-term orientation. (Hofstede, 2001) Hofstede defined collectivism in terms of the extent to which individuals are integrated into groups and form their judgments based on group norms. Members of a collective acknowledge their interdependent natures and obligations to the group. They place relatively greater importance on the group's needs and norms than on their own needs. Chinese people are often motivated by norms and duties imposed by the in-group, and try to emphasize their connectedness with the in-group. (Kragh, 2012) The tendency to focus on group preferences and group harmony leads to an ability to repress internal (personal) attributes in certain settings. (Wei & Li, 2013) Collectivists prefer to be the same or similar with others in the group. They are easily impacted by consensus or public voice, and care a lot about others' opinions of them.

Chinese culture is characterized by high levels of embeddedness, hierarchy and mastery. In terms of communication, China is recognized as being a high-context culture, which means most of the information is either in the physical context or initialized in the person, while very little is in the coded, explicit, transmitted part of the message. (Hofstede, 2001) These studies provide a stylized overview of Chinese culture in comparison with others. However, for a better understanding of Chinese values, beliefs and behaviors, we need to understand the roots of the culture and how they influence its social organization.

Business Practice and Tips

Most Western people know business relationships are important, but it is even truer in China, as a great part of contracts one signs come from these relationships. In many cases, one will find it hard to conclude a good deal only by e-mail. Instead, one may have to spend hours, maybe days, with a potential client, talking about unrelated topics, dining or joining other activities. In Chinese culture, as well as in many others in Asia, one is defined by his or her relationship to the larger group. (Wei & Li, 2013) All actions, whether positive or negative, don't just reflect on oneself, but on the group as a whole. Also part of Confucian thought is to subject one's own desires to the needs of the group and the good of society. A good example was given in the *Harvard Business Review* by Graham and Lam. In preparing for a business trip to China, most Westerners like to arm themselves with a handy, one-page list of etiquette how-tos. Tipsters say to carry a boatload of business cards. Bring an interpreter; speak in short sentences; wear a conservative suit. Such advice can help get you in the door and even through the first series of business transactions, but it won't sustain the kind of prolonged, year-in, year-out associations that Chinese and Western businesses can now achieve.

All too often, Americans see Chinese negotiators as inefficient, indirect, and even dishonest, while the Chinese see American negotiators as aggressive, impersonal, and excitable. Such differences have deep cultural origins. The writings of Confucius served as the foundation of Chinese education for some 2,000 years. During those two millennia, knowledge of Confucian texts was the primary requisite for appointment to government offices. (Graham & Lam, 2003) Confucius maintained that a society organized under a benevolent moral code would be prosperous and politically stable and therefore safe from attack. It is communal, not individualistic; survival depends on group cooperation and harmony. (Zhao, 2012) Loyalty and obedience to social hierarchy binds people together. These moral values express themselves in the Chinese negotiating style. Consider what happened when an American company neglected to pay attention to the importance of social status in Chinese culture. The company sent a relatively young and low-level sales representative to a high-level negotiation. The Chinese executive remarked, "Ah, you're about the same age as my son." The Chinese felt insulted by the Americans' failure to send an executive whose rank at least equaled theirs. They doubted the Americans' sincerity, and the deal died before it began. (Graham & Lam, 2003)

While a new, market-driven China has been emerging fast in the global marketplace, Western companies have often reported frustration and confusion when negotiating in China. Chinese negotiators are more concerned with the means than the end, with process more than the goal. The best compromises are derived only through the ritual back-and-forth of haggling. This process cannot be cut short, and a compromise allows the two sides to hold equally valid positions. While Americans tend to believe that the truth, as they see it, is worth arguing over and even getting angry about, the Chinese rely on haggling to settle differences. Chinese negotiators are taught a large variety of communication techniques for negotiation arrayed along a continuum from the relationship-based win-win strategy to the pure competition-based win-lose mentality; however, the win-win techniques are taught and used far more frequently. (Graham & Lam, 2003) According to Confucius philosophy, Chinese education clearly reflects China's foreign trade and economic cooperation negotiation principles: equality, mutual understanding, mutual trust, mutual benefit, and long-term cooperation.

In examining the negotiation process with Chinese business people, Westerners wouldn't be surprised to see that in many circumstances most important pre-negotiation contacts came from requests from China and from regular sales calls. The Chinese negotiating team typically was twice as large as the Western team and one-third of the negotiation time was spent on talking about technical specifications and another third was spent on price. Although both sides tended to use a cooperative strategy, the Chinese team could make sudden demands, apparently to put the Western team in a disadvantageous position. (Neidel, 2010) One famous strategic book, written by Sun Tzu's (256 B.C.E.), is called *Art of War*. The book taught the Chinese long ago the value of unsettling the mind and upsetting the plans of one's opponent. Therefore, they conclude that negotiating processes in China are likely to continue to be full of surprises. The Chinese negotiators tend to ask many more questions and to interrupt more frequently than their Western counterparts. Such subtle differences point to a potential problem: When the Chinese do not reciprocate with cooperative behavior, their counterparts' economic returns are diminished. By knowing this, Western business managers could develop appropriate strategies when negotiating in China. (Graham & Lam, 2003)

Family Influences and Expectations

Both Confucianism and Daoism/Taoism focus on the family's value to an individual. Being educated in this way, Chinese people have a very deep concept of family, which is also reflected in their purchasing behaviors. (Luo, 2009) For a typical Chinese family, the most important focus is on those who are older, such as parents. The older family members/parents have contributed most of their lives for the family. As a result they get the most respect in a family. But on the other hand, Chinese culture also emphasizes on root-generation continuation. Children are looked to as the future of the family and have placed on them a variety of expectations. In China, other than old parents, children gain a crucial position in a family. As a result, during the process of identifying needs, age and kids have extreme priority.

Confucius said, "When walking with two other people, I will always find a teacher among them. I focus on those who are good and seek to emulate them, and focus on those who are bad in order to be reminded of what needs to be changed in myself." (Lunyu 7.22) Confucian ideas are an important component of the fundamental beliefs and values in Chinese culture. Confucius emphasized principles for self-guidance. The key to producing a harmonious life, he wrote, is in how we treat others — our ancestors, leaders, parents, spouses, neighbors, and friends. To Confucius, a person becomes noble not by birth but by developing the five virtues of humanity. (Zhang, 2013) The most important Confucian virtue is filial piety (*xiao*), the respect and obedience of children toward their parents — for when all relationships between family members are in order, then society will also be orderly. (Foy, 2018) The mainstream of the elite have come to realize that total Westernization is not the path for China because it is against China's inherent cultural logic, and that only localization and harmonization can be constructive for the future of Chinese culture. (Zhang, 2017) Zhang further explained that the substantial transition from stage to stage is usually gradual, with internal or external forces precipitating or enabling the changes. Each transformation is not simply a repetition of earlier stages, but brings forth new cultures in certain forms or contents. This transition is reflected in family influence and expectations. The younger generation has been educated to learn how to derive from deep awareness of one's own culture: being able to distinguish and hold onto the roots and to find paths to grow amid cultural conflicts and interactions with foreign cultures.

Business Practice and Tips

There are two Chinese sayings: A man without a smile should not open a shop, and sweet temper and friendliness produce money and speak volumes about the importance of harmonious relations between business partners. While respect and responsibility are the glue that binds hierarchical relationships, family, friendships and positive feelings or harmonious society (He Xie She Hui) hold relationships of equals together. (Graham & Lam, 2003) The key element of Chinese culture reflecting this aspect of family or reference group is one's *guanxi* or social connections. In fact, social connections don't do justice to the fundamental and complex concept of *guanxi.* While Americans put a premium on networking, information, and institutions, the Chinese place a premium on individuals' social capital within their group of friends, relatives, and close associates. Though the role of *guanxi* is fading a bit against the backdrop of population mobility and the Westernization of some Chinese business practices, it remains an important social force. Having the right *guanxi* is vital to getting things done in China and moving up in Chinese society. (Graham & Lam, 2003) One could even say this is the single most important factor in a person's success. In China, everything is done through one's connections, be it finding a job, making business relationships, or even meeting a potential spouse.

A person's *guanxi* includes one's family, relatives, former classmates, coworkers, plus all the people you meet through them. All the people in a particular group are connected to each other through a system of mutual obligation. (Wei & Li, 2013) The relationships between group members are nurtured by giving and receiving favors. Everyone keeps a mental checklist of all the people who owe them a favor and everyone to whom they are indebted. Even if years have gone by, someone to whom one owes a favor can show up and ask for a favor out of the blue.

Foreigners who have just arrived in China naturally do not have any *guanxi*. It's important to try to build up this network of connections as quickly as possible, both professionally and personally. This will help one navigate through the many layers of Chinese bureaucracy and get things done faster. (InterNations, 2018) However, be wary of accepting big favors unless one is willing and/or capable of returning them. Foreigners are often surprised to be asked for favors for things over which they have no control, such as visa applications and university admissions.

In Chinese culture, the concept of face refers to personal dignity, prestige, and status and serves to maintain harmony in social relationships and hierarchies. (Müller, 2012) The fear of the loss of face permeates Chinese society. It takes another dimension and one had better keep this in mind. One of the safest rules is to avoid criticizing anyone or any project in public as it could result in insulting someone, and one may lose potential clients or partnerships. Stay focused on positive aspects until one is in private. In business, face loss may disrupt deals and harm goodwill. Saying no or refusing to help can be considered in some situations as disrespect and can lead the other person to lose face. Therefore, Chinese people will often say no in an indirect way, like "I agree with what you said, but … " At this point, one is almost sure the other person disagrees with you, while in the West some will add a "but" for more precision. (Upton-McLaughlin, 2014) One of the most annoying situations one can face in China is asking for directions in the street, and nice people without any clue will answer with different responses. Westerners frequently find it difficult to understand the formality of Chinese business people. American-style casualness does not play well in a country where the Confucian values of obedience and deference to one's superiors remain strong. (Graham & Lam, 2003) The formality goes much deeper to many Westerners.

Here is another example.

Mr. Wang, a top-level executive working in China, explained how the laid-back manner of an American boss had made him feel he had no face, but that he became accustomed to this type of behavior with a little more exposure to Americans. He would often come into my office, and we'd talk together. He'd put his feet up on the table. From his perspective, this didn't matter. From the Chinese way of thinking, this was not respectful. Even though you're my boss and I'm your subordinate, we should still respect each other. You make me feel I have no face. It shows me that I hold no status in your eyes. To you, I'm nothing. After working together, we made some adjustments, and slowly we understood the American way of thinking and the American way of doing things.

The Role of Education

Higher education is viewed internationally as an institution to promote national development and political stability through fostering political and technical elites for the modern state. (Liu, 2012) This is especially true for China because it has a long history of selecting elites for governing through civil service examinations. (Brie & Yi, 2014) In Chinese traditional values, educated people are above every other human being in social standing. For thousands of years, education was almost the only way in which people could climb to the elite classes. (Tao, Berci & He, 2006) In China, many people still believe that academic success is the only way to get rid of poverty and advance in social class. This idea stems from Confucianism. Education is an important source of social and economic mobility in China so Chinese families invest heavily in their children's education. (Bodycott & Lai, 2012) At a societal level, education was a mechanism to select elites for governance in imperial times, and this function has been further extended to training administrative and technical elites to promote national development in modern China. (Liu, 2012)

Another more important reason for Chinese parents and students to choose studying abroad is that they are motivated to study abroad in an attempt to seek a better educational experience, follow their true academic interests, and explore the new Western culture. (Bodycott & Lai, 2012) According to the China Daily, 98 percent of Chinese workers want more education, and they want more education in order to improve their professional skills, make themselves more competitive and enrich their life experience. (Zhou, 2017) Globalization has played an important role in impacting Chinese students' perceptions of what it means to study in the Western cultural environment. Chinese students are attracted by the freedom to choose from an array of educational programs, explore the Western world, and learn new culture (Chen & Jordan, 2016). They also seek the prestige of obtaining a degree from a higher-learning Western institution and the potential to join a highly competitive global market of educated adults upon graduation.

This phenomenon has resulted in the Chinese overseas education market becoming the largest in the world. More Chinese students study abroad than any other country. Overseas education is an expensive option and reflects the emerging Chinese middle/upper class family's desire to send their children abroad for the best education, despite the higher costs. It also reflects the increasing demand Chinese youth have for international experiences, ideas and culture. (Zhou, 2017) As a result, the country is less insular and more receptive to foreign influence than it has historically been with overseas institutions of education. China's global economic power entices younger generations to develop a global view and depart from the traditional Chinese system of college education.

Under these circumstances, highly educated people in China have a very high work ethic and look to succeed by developing a wide array of professional skills. As a result, those doing business in China will nearly always be dealing with highly committed and competent individuals who are keen to excel not just for their personal gain, but also for the larger aims of their company as well as their family. This combined with the high level of organization and discipline within Chinese companies, makes doing business in China not only profitable, but also highly rewarding.

Business Practice and Tips

Youthful Chinese people with higher education degrees are more open to Western culture. They celebrate many Western festivals and holidays, such as Halloween and Christmas. They have their favorite Western brands, sports team and music. Some American TV series or highly-anticipated Hollywood movies are quite popular as well. Young Chinese are more comfortable than previous generations with living in a global village. (Buckley, 2015)

Although Chinese people born in the '80s and '90s came of age amid a clash between traditional collectivist culture and the emergence of individualism, humility, trust and honesty, openness, doing things meticulously and carefully as required by Confucius are still highly valued. (Fish, 2017) Foreign partners must maintain their credibility at all times by being well-prepared and being able to answer questions satisfactorily. Chinese culture is goal-oriented, emphasizing doing and results. There is a high level of flexibility in Chinese culture to adapt ethical codes so as to achieve a goal — a utilitarianism in practice. This is an important feature for better understanding the logic of doing business in China. Influenced by Confucianism, Chinese people respect social norms and make efforts to create harmony. (Zhang, 2013)

Western business organizations are continually seeking to differentiate themselves from their competitors in today's increasingly competitive, global business climate. Providing consistent and reliable customer service in China has become an important component in the differentiation strategies of many organizations in the Chinese market.

(Zhang, 2013) As such, Western business people who have certain kinds of skills that allow them to manage professional relationships successfully with people of diverse cultures and patterns of socialization will be more successful in China. What is customary to one group of people may be interpreted negatively by people of different backgrounds and culture. This clashing of behaviors can damage interpersonal relations in the workplace. Westerners must be aware of these differences in order not to destroy relationships before they begin.

Language Transformation and Business Etiquette

Many new business words and expressions came out of the decades of economic and cultural development in China. One of the dilemmas that China has had to deal with after the economic reform of the 1980s is balancing the relationship between tradition and modernity. This balancing act is fundamentally a cultural issue, rather than an economic one. In other words, it is about the interplay of Chinese fundamental beliefs and values versus modernity. (Yu, 2012)

As of 2016, a key topic of discussion and debate on economic development at international forums is the assumptive China Model (*Zhongguo moshi*), which assumes that China's economic development presents a different model from any previous economic models, or a secret recipe. (Zhang, 2017) However, most Chinese experts relate the economic development in China to Chinese culture and history, as well as political policies. The difficulties of cultural influences are determined not merely by economics and politics, but rather arise from myriad linguistic and cultural differences. (Zhang, 2017) While English-speaking business people may have difficulty learning Chinese, they can improve communication skills with Chinese people by placing more emphasis on body language and etiquette. This knowledge can supplement limited verbal skills in Chinese and promote communication in all-English conversations.

Business Practice and Tips

Many expressions of cultural inspiration have emerged in all aspects of everyday life in the past century or so. Penetrating the Chinese market is no longer easy, even on the digital platforms, partly because translating word-by-word may not necessarily give you the right meanings. For example, names referring to Westerners have shown such a transformation: from foreign devils (*waiguo guizi*) or anything fearful at initial encounters, distinguished guests (*guibin*) or foreign guests (*waiguo pengyou*) or anything admirable during the self-denial century, and finally, at the beginning of the 21st century, to foreign persons (*waiguoren*) or old foreigner (*lao wai*, as in Old Wang, a casual way among people for the same status in everyday life) or simply old American (*lao mei*), old French (*lao fa*). (Zhang, 2017)

Understandably, many Westerners consider the 40,000 different Chinese characters to be one of the biggest obstacles to learning Chinese. Only 3,000-4,000 are required for full literacy. However, verbal communication isn't everything in China. Most difficulties in intercultural encounters between well-meaning parties do not arise from what is said, but from implicit assumptions and non-verbal signals. (InterNations, 2018) In order to navigate the Chinese business world, Westerners do not only need to re-learn some basic etiquette and courtesies, such as the correct way of giving a toast, they also have to examine much of what they take for granted, like attitudes towards seniority, hierarchies, and the relationship between the group and the individual as we discussed earlier. Much of what is communicated in Chinese is contextual.

Food presentation is a very important part of Chinese culture. Chinese people love to eat. The meal is a very important moment for them because it is a moment of sharing which can sometimes last several hours. Chinese cuisine is generally a good topic since many Chinese people are keen on educating western people about it. It is a perfect icebreaker and will help create a deeper connection. If you know enough about it, you can also discuss Chinese ancient history or various aspect of Chinese culture like tea or the best *baijiu* (Chinese traditional liquor) in the country. In any case, it is better to avoid any political issue as it is not the most relaxed topic, and cuisine is the safest as you will not find many Chinese who do not like food. (Olivier, 2016)

If you are invited for a meal by a colleague or acquaintance in China, you will most often eat in a restaurant, rather than at that person's home. When you arrive at the restaurant, wait for your host to tell you where to sit. At formal events, according to Chinese customs, age and seniority determine the seating arrangements. Your host will usually order many dishes. A good rule of thumb is to order one or two dishes more than the total number of guests. These dishes will be put in the middle of the table and shared among all the guests. The total number of dishes should be an even number, as odd numbers symbolize death. It is a Chinese custom to order an odd number of dishes at a funeral meal. This has to do with the yin-yang balance of life as mentioned earlier, where yin is associated with cold, dark, death, and odd numbers, and yang is associated with heat, light, life, and even numbers. Once the food has been served, each person fills their bowl from the dishes in the center of the table. Sometimes your host or other guests will put food in your bowl for you to try. It's polite to try a little bit of everything. (InterNations, 2018)

If you are invited to a Chinese person's home, a wedding, or some other event, you should bring a present. Presents should always be given with both hands. This shows that you are offering the fullest extent of yourself. If you receive a gift, open it later or risk appearing greedy. Good gift ideas include imported alcohol, tea, or fancy gift baskets with food. Toys and sweets are good choices for children. If you wrap your gift, good colors are red and gold. Never wrap a present in white paper, as this color is associated with death and funerals. This tradition is also reflected in Chinese weddings. However, the Western custom of wearing a white wedding dress is becoming more and more common. In general, never give someone a present that has to do with the number four, as this sounds too similar to the word for death in Mandarin. The number eight, on the other hand, is considered very lucky. It's not a coincidence that the opening ceremony of the Olympic Games in Beijing took place on August 8, 2008. (InterNations, 2018)

Festival Celebrations and Traditional Customs

China is famous for her rich and ancient cultural tradition. Many colorful Chinese festivals with long-standing traditions are celebrated in China throughout the year. Eleven days are celebrated as public holidays in the People's Republic of China and employees don't have to work on these days. These holidays are New Year's Day (1 January), the Spring Festival, Tomb-Sweeping Day, Labor Day (1 May), the Dragon Boat Festival, the Mid-Autumn Festival, and National Day (1–3 October). Some of thcsc holidays have fixed dates, while others move depending on the lunar calendar. The Spring Festival and National Day are celebrated with three days of public holiday each; every other public holiday is for one day only. The Chinese government decides on the schedule for the next year's public holidays in December of the preceding year. If possible, public holidays are usually scheduled before or after weekends to create long weekends. Of course, the festival celebrations and traditional customs are always related with family gatherings and their cultural roots. (InterNations, 2018)

According to Chinese culture, hospitality is defined as unlimited openness to and acceptance of others, allowing others to enter one's space — that is, to welcome others. This sentiment is expressed in the Chinese expression, combining thousands of little rivers makes the sea great. There are many Chinese customs which revolve around festivals and traditional celebrations. For example, during Chinese Spring Festival, there are firework displays and parades featuring dancers dressed as dragons. Children receive new clothes and money in red envelopes — red is for good luck. Although foreigners are generally forgiven for their faux pas, it is best to learn some basic etiquette to avoid making embarrassing blunders. On the other hand, you may be surprised to find that some practices that would be considered rude in your home country are perfectly acceptable Chinese customs. (InterNations, 2018)

Business Practice and Tips

When Westerners are doing business in China, they have to be aware of the flexible vacation time taken by the whole nation. Spring Festival, also known as Lunar New Year, is the grandest Chinese festival of the year. It ushers in the beginning of the New Year and is celebrated for the first 15 days of the first lunar month. Employees have off work for the first three days of the festivities. Many people take a few extra days to have off an entire week. A similar schedule could happen on National Day which is observed on October 1 each year to celebrate the formation of the People's Republic of China in 1949. Employees have off work from 1–3 October, but many Chinese people take off the entire week. This week is also known as Golden Week, as it is a very profitable week for the domestic tourism industry. As all tourist sites and public transportation will be extremely crowded during this week, it is probably advisable to arrange your business or trade accordingly at that time of the year. (InterNations, 2018)

In terms of festival celebrations, localization is one of the expressions of Chinese cultural vitality, as seen in the transformation of Chinese Christmas or Christmas in China. During the Chinese Christmas, apple (*pingguo*) becomes a unique symbol because it is homophonous of peace (*ping*), and thus a must gift for the festival to the family and friends. The Christmas evergreen tree is now transformed into a money tree (*yaoqianshu*), which also has a long history of practice in China, by making it golden in color or decorating it with gold coins.

It is a very popular gift for family and business organizations. (Zhang, 2017)

Critical Differences from Western Cultures

From the standpoint of appreciating difference, process philosophers or constructive postmodern thinkers remind Westerners to keep an authentic sensitivity to Chinese culture, but also practice what they preach by exploring and appreciating the uniqueness of Chinese culture. (Fan & Wang, 2015)

Fan and Wang point out that David Hall and Roger Ames have identified five critical ontological (the nature of reality) and epistemological (how one comes to know reality) differences between Chinese and Western culture, challenging people to maintain a real sensitivity to the nuances of the Chinese experience:

1. The Western worldview prioritizes substance or fact over process (i.e., it prizes stillness and changelessness). The Chinese worldview elevates process over substance.
2. The West prefers rationality or objectivity of experience over sensory experience and the presumption of a duality between reason and sensory experience. The Chinese prefer to use correlative thinking to know things, with no presumed conflict between reason and sensory experience.
3. The West prefers logical reasoning, abstract speculation, and pursuit of rational harmony. The Chinese prefer to know concrete things through direct experience and value pursuit of aesthetic harmony by reconciling differences and particularity.
4. Western thought prefers definition and seeks certainty, while the Chinese depend, for the most part, upon exemplary models or instance rather than strict definitions to evoke understanding. Knowledge under these conditions has an

element of rich, unbounded vagueness which contrasts rather starkly with the Western quest for certainty.

5. The West defines human nature in terms of universalistic transcendental principles like the image of God, where China emphasizes the exemplary role cultural and moral elites play in shaping personality and cultivating human nature.

In terms of learning the differences between Chinese and Western culture, there is a term called *Yelangism*. This term derives from a Chinese story. There was a small country named Yelang in the Han dynasty, located near the southwestern border of China. The king of Yelang, who thought of his country as the center of the world, asked the diplomatic envoy from China which country was bigger, China or Yelang? This story later became the basis of a new Chinese idiom, *Yelangzida*, meaning ludicrous conceit and parochial arrogance (I already have all the truth and there is nothing left to learn). Although Yelang's king has been dead for more than two thousand years, the parochial arrogance of Yelangism has lived on. In China, varieties of Sinocentrism, China centrism, or Han chauvinism are the manifestations of Yelangism. Likewise, in the West, Western-centrism, European centrism, and human centrism are also manifestations of Yelangism. (Fan & Wang, 2015)

Business Practice and Tips

But the Chinese are open to many Western ideas and lifestyles, including its cuisine. The Chinese enjoy cuisines or gourmets from different places, a practice of diversity within unity in ideology and in everyday practice. As seen today, foreign foods or drinks are treated from fashionable to normal, just like other Chinese regional styles. They have simply enriched the diversity in Chinese cuisine and lifestyle. But local and traditional cuisines and drinks are also enjoying a renaissance. Once again, Chinese practices prove that it is wrong to entertain the following dualistic reasoning: That the widespread availability of foreign food, traditional cuisine will be in danger; to maintain traditions, we must drive away the foreign stuff. (Zhang, 2017) As a matter of fact, the vitality of Chinese culture lies in the integration of all cultural elements. As seen everywhere in China today, for example, tea cultural events and sales are increasing and widespread while coffee culture and shops (e.g., Starbucks) are also spreading widely.

Meanwhile, International companies also try to localize their products or adjust their interior design to fit in the local market. For example, Starbucks stores are bigger with more seating space in China. Unlike Americans, who can't cope without a morning cup of joe, most Chinese customers don't just grab and go. Instead, coffee shops here are a destination. People sit back and chat with friends and family. Some come to meet with clients or do business. (Law, 2014)

Influence of Chinese Culture Around the World

Chinese communities have expanded around the world as China's economy has expanded, and these communities incorporate elements of both the homeland and Western culture. The structure and operation of Chinese communities in the Western world can be observed and followed very well through the so-called Chinatowns. The U.S. Census (2010) indicated that Chinese Americans are often broadly defined to include not only immigrants from Mainland China, Hong Kong, Macau, Taiwan, and their descendants, but also immigrants and descendants of overseas Chinese people who migrated to the United States from places as diverse as Malaysia, Singapore, and other countries in Southeast Asia.

According to the U.S. Census (2010), the three metropolitan areas with the largest Chinese American populations are the Greater New York Combined Statistical Area, with about 666,000 Chinese Americans; the San Jose San Francisco-Oakland Combined Statistical Area, with about 562,000 Chinese Americans; and the Greater Los

Angeles Combined Statistical Area with about 495,000 Chinese Americans. New York City was home to the highest Chinese American population of any city proper (446,714), while the city of Monterey Park, California, in Los Angeles County had the highest percentage of Chinese Americans of any municipality: 43.7%, or about 26,700 people.

Among these Chinatowns, the traditional culture about Confucianism is well imbedded. Confucianism emphasizes the harmony and mutual consensus between human and nature and between persons. One of the greatest goals of Confucianism was the achievement of social harmony, because the continuation and maintenance of harmonious relationships of members ensures the stability and solidarity of civil society. Confucian virtues are conducive to the achievement of harmony and social stability. To achieve a harmonious social relationship, it is extremely important for every individual to observe and perform virtues, according to Chinese norms. (Zhang, 2013)

Creation and Development of Confucius Institutes

Confucius Institutes are a major program for the overseas dissemination of Chinese culture: starting with the establishment of the first Confucius Institute in Seoul, South Korea, in November, 2004. The institutes are designed to advance country-to-country cooperation between the United States and China. The Chinese Ministry of Education opened its first Confucius Institute in the United States in 2005. (Hanban/Confucius Institute Headquarters, 2013) The Confucius Institute Charter stipulates that the institutes are nonprofit educational institutions with the aim of advancing the understanding of people around the world of Chinese language and culture, developing friendly relations between China and other countries, promoting the development of diverse world cultures, and contributing power toward building a harmonious world. (Lei & Chang, 2016) Their main functions are providing Chinese education to all sectors of society, training Chinese teachers, giving Chinese exams and Chinese teacher qualifications, providing consulting on Chinese education, culture, economics, and society, and conducting research on contemporary China. (Hanban/Confucius Institute Headquarters 2013)

More than 70 Confucius Institutes were in operation in the United States by 2017. In international cultural communication, nearly 500 Confucius Institutes and 1,000 affiliated Confucius classrooms have been established in 134 countries and regions, 18 Chinese Cultural Festivals are being held regularly all over the world. (Zhang, 2017) This Chinese investment in U.S. education has generated research interest in Confucius Institutes as a form of China's foreign policy. They have gradually formed education models with various features and have become important sites for the people of all countries to learn Chinese language and culture and understand contemporary China (Hanban/Confucius Institute Headquarters 2013). Since the establishment of Confucius Institutes, they have made remarkable achievements in terms of quantity, promotion of Chinese language, and China-foreign language and cultural exchanges, but they still face some problems in their development. (Lei & Chang, 2016) Lin (2016) suggested that Confucius Institutes should actively interact with the overseas world of Chinese studies as a beneficial external support for promoting Chinese. The selection and compilation of teaching material contents should both conform to the rules of the Chinese language and traditional Chinese culture and also conform to the thinking methods and learning customs of the local students.

New Trends of Chinese Culture

Instead of following a long-term goal-oriented culture, Chinese people are moving toward more short-term thinking. The birth control plan in China from 1979 until recent (new birth control policy has been issued in 2015) shapes a new generation – *Dushengzinv* generation (the only child in a family). (Buckley, 2015) Compared with their parents and people who were born earlier than them who had at least one brother or sister, this new generation has a totally different living situation, and as a result builds a unique perspective of the world and behavior principles. (Sun & Wang, 2010) The Chinese are subjected to strong parental pressure toward their success in their studies from a very young age. They must join the best school, have the best grades, and attend evening classes. All of this is to get the best job and, of course, the best salary. Observers have commented that they are a bit spoiled, have almost no idea of sharing and are often self-centered. But at the same time, they bear a heavy responsibility and burden that their ancestors never experienced. (Luo, 2009) As a result, they are more individualistic and want to be seen as special. They are not as sensitive in terms of following business etiquette in a traditional Chinese cultural way. (Sun & Wang, 2010)

There are now many internal migrations in China. Urbanization is arguably the most important phenomenon shaping modern China. (Seto, 2018) According to statistics, more than 300 million people have moved from the country to cities in the past 30 years, and an additional 350 million are on the way. China has 160 cities with populations of more than one million and 14 with more than five million. Increasingly, these cities are becoming linked, creating urban areas with 30 million people or more. (Population of Cities in China, 2018) While the country has grown very rapidly, this modernization has affected the country's culture in many ways, such as social organization, network (*guanxi*), family structure, and pollution.

The coastal regions have benefited greatly and the rest of China has started to move away from its poorer and underdeveloped conditions. (OECD, 2011) Many Chinese cross the country to settle in the big cities and find a job. All of these movements have brought about change to the traditional Chinese culture. For example, according to one of the training programs in China, the Chinese were more focused on face-to-face interaction and communication in order to gain trust among business partners. Now, it is unthinkable to conquer the Chinese market without being massively present on the Internet. China is one of the most connected countries in the world. It will inquire about your brand online before trusting you, will check the reviews of users, and pay online if they are seduced. However, Chinese business people are also more suspicious and sensitive about online content from Western business. They will always know if your content is not written by a Chinese native. As an outsider, you must pay attention to Chinese expectations and trends, and tailor your strategy to the Chinese culture; otherwise there will be no attraction to your platform. For example, Chinese and Western people display different behaviors when browsing online. Chinese users prefer reading a page with a lot of content from the center-top to the center-bottom, compared to Westerners who eye-track a pages layout from left to right. It has also become known that Chinese users hate seeing blank spaces online. (Marketing to China, 2018)

To be successful, Westerners need to know what is happening in China. Knowing which sectors of activity are clogged and which are promising are the key to make a successful start. For example, 20 years ago, China's main growth came from its four major cities — Beijing, Shanghai, Guangzhou and Chengdu. Today, that number has expanded to more than 80 cities. In the past ten years, the main growth has come from tier-2, tier-3 or even tier-4 cities. (Keely, 2015) In tier 1 cities: Beijing, Guangzhou, Shenzhen, and Shanghai, the consumer behaviors are much more similar to the Western, as they are influenced by Western culture, styles, fashion, and trends. The consumers in these cities are more aware of luxury and premium products; therefore, don't be surprised if they understand more than you on what you're trying to advocate. Tier 2 and Tier 3 cities are the places you will need more knowledge of Chinese consumer culture, as they are unlike Tier 1 cities. They do not always fancy Western products, and they are more focused on their localized products, and remain loyal to them. Other than looking professional, you will need to be knowledgeable on their consumer culture and behaviors and identify with their trends. (Qian, 2016)

Knowing that the second tier cities in China are developing at a faster speed promises a lot of opportunities for the future. China is a large and diverse country. It is also a country with a long history of traditions that have gone through extreme changes in the past 40 years. (OECD, 2011) Even people from Beijing are different from those living in Shanghai, and they are very different from those living in Guangzhou. Understanding Chinese culture and adapting as much as possible without judgment will be the key to conquering China and develop a lasting business relationship.

These new trends have already been challenging the traditional Chinese business culture. Traditionally in China, the leader is whoever has authority or power. The leader can influence people and his or her decisions are seldom criticized. (Cheng, 2011) Although it is becoming less true in recent years, leaders are sometime less respected for their skills than for their title and attitude, and that is a point worth to be considered in some situations. However, influenced by its long history and rich culture, Chinese are still more collective, paying much more attention to harmony and the relationship with others and how others think about them. They tend to focus more on family values, compared to Western countries. (Luo, 2009) For example, despite the rapid development of the Internet, Chinese people are still very reliant on advice and suggestions given by family and friends. When they require information regarding social network platforms, or other online applications, they inquire with people in their own circle before making decisions. (Kragh, 2012) Therefore, when companies try to develop Chinese market, it is necessary for them to understand this before they start.

Globalization has changed the way people do business, demanding new levels of expertise in dealing with diversity in people and environments. (Lang, et al, 2012) China exercises an enormous influence on the global economy today. The American middle class was the world economy's growth engine throughout the 20th century. Now, the engine is the Asia–Pacific region, which will account for two-thirds of the world's middle class by 2030. (HDR Report, 2013) However, as many philosophers have noted, it is culture that truly has a profound influence on humanity. Despite the variety of business styles and practices, globalization and localization of traditions and values call for proportionate advancement toward a more cooperative, more adjustable and more equitable world of nations and communities in order to sustain everlasting peace and harmony. (Tang, 2016) The Chinese market is heavily influenced by its state policy. Local partners are more in tune and familiar with government agendas — both explicit and unspoken just as its culture. Business people should explore business practices in both Western and Eastern cultural contexts in order to advance the knowledge of global business environment and inform the implication for multicultural organization. So East and West might meet and from which different nations and cultures might benefit.

Reference

Awen. (2015). China's Confucius Merchants. Retrieved from http://viewofchina.com/confucius-merchants/

Bodycott, P. & Lai, A. (2012). The Influence and Implications of Chinese Culture in the Decision to Undertake Cross-Border Higher Education. *Journal of Studies in International Education* 16(3) 252–270

Brie, D-r. & Yi, M-c. (2014). The context of higher education development and policy response in China. *Studies in Higher Education*, 2014, Vol. 39, No. 8, 1499–1510

Buckley, C. (2015). China Ends One-Child Policy, Allowing Families Two Children. Retrieved from https://www.nytimes.com/2015/10/30/world/asia/china-end-one-child-policy.html

Buckley, C. (2015). Chinese Embrace America's Culture but Not Its Policies. Retrieved from: https://www.nytimes.com/2015/09/29/world/asia/china-united-states-culture-policy.html

Cartwright, M. (2018). Yin and Yang. Retrieved from https://www.ancient.eu/Yin_and_Yang/

Chen, T. & Jordan, M. (2016). Why so many Chinese students come to the US? *The Wall Street Journal.* U.S. Edition. Retrieved from: https://www.wsj.com/articles/why-so-manychinese-students-come-to-the-u-s-1462123552.

Cheng, C-Y. (2011). Confucian global leadership in Chinese tradition: Classical and contemporary. *Journal of Management Development*, 30 (7/8), 647-662

Fan, M. J. & Wang, Z. H. (2015). Toward a Complementary Consciousness and Mutual Flourishing of Chinese and Western Cultures: The Contributions of Process Philosophers. *Philosophy East & West* Volume 65, Number 1, 276–297

Fish, E. (2017). China's Youth Admire America Far More than We Knew. Retrieved from https://foreignpolicy.com/2017/02/09/chinas-youth-admire-america-far-more-than-we-knew-surprising-survey-results-ideological-university-crackdown/

Four occupations. (2018). In Wikipedia, The Free Encyclopedia. Retrieved from https://en.wikipedia.org/w/index.php?title=Four_occupations&oldid=819574446

Foy, G. (2018). Laozi: The Old Master. Retrieved from https://asiasociety.org/education/laozi-old-master

Graham, L. J. & Lam M. (2003). The Chinese Negotiation. *Harvard Business Review* 81(10):82-91, 137.

Guang, X. (2013). Buddhist Impact on Chinese Culture. *Asian Philosophy*, Vol. 23, No. 4, 305–322

Hall, D. L. and Ames, T. R. (1995). *Anticipating China: Thinking Through the Narratives of Chinese and Western Culture.* Albany: State University of New York Press.

Hanban/Confucius Institute Headquarters. (2013). Kongzi xueyuan fazhan guihua (2012–2020) Confucius institute development plan (2012–2020). http://www.hanban.edu.cn/article/2013-02/28/content_486129.htm

Hansen, W. L. (2013). The Chinese Profile of Success. Retrieved from https://cbk.bschool.cuhk.edu.hk/the-chinese-profile-of-success/

Hershock, P. D., & Ames, T. R. (2006). *Confucian culture of authority.* NY: State University of New York Press.

Holstede, G. (2001). *Culture's Consequences, Comparing Values, Behaviors, Institutions, and Organizations across Nations* (Thousand Oaks, CA: Sage).

Human Development Report. (HDR, 2013). The Rise of the South: Human Progress in a Diverse World.

InterNations. (2018). The InterNations Expat Guide for working and living in China. Retrieved from https://www.internations.org/china-expats/guide

Keely, L. (2015). The Problem With Ranking Chinese Cities. Retrieved from http://fortune.com/2015/12/05/china-cities-tier-system-problem/

Khairullah, H. Z. D. & Khairullah, Y. Z. (2013). Cultural Values and Decision-Making in China. *International Journal of Business, Humanities and Technology* Vol. 3 No. 2.

Kilarski, S. (2017). Harmony: One of the Most Precious Elements in Chinese Traditional Culture. Retrieved from https://www.theepochtimes.com/harmony-chinese-culture_1528988.html

Kragh, S. U. (2012). Preindustrial patterns in Chinese organizational culture. The *International Journal of Human Resource Management,* Vol. 23, No. 11, 2354–2373

Lang, L. L., Irby, B. J., & Brown, G. (2012). An Emergent Leadership Model Based on Confucian Virtues and East Asian Leadership Practices. *International Journal of Educational Leadership Preparation*, v7 n2

Law, V. (2014). Starbucks storms China with its most aggressive overseas expansion yet. GlobalPost. Retrieved from https://www.pri.org/stories/2014-08-07/starbucks-storms-china-its-most-aggressive-overseas-expansion-yet

Lei, Qili. & Chang, Dong. (2016). The Difficulties and Possibilities of Cross-Cultural Communication: A Case Study of the Global Development of the Confucius Institutes. *Chinese Education & Society*, 49: 402–410, 2016

Lin, Jeng-Yi. (2016). A Study on the State of Development of Higher Education Confucius Institutes from Mainland China. *Chinese Education & Society,* 49: 425–436

Liu, J. (2012). Examining massification policies and their consequences for equality in Chinese higher education: A cultural perspective. *High Education* 64:647–660

Luo, Y. (2009). Analysis of Culture and Buyer Behavior in Chinese Market. *Asian Culture and History,* Vol. 1, No. 1.

Marketing to China. (2018). The Training Programs in China: A Market on the Rise. Retrieved from https://www.marketingtochina.com/training-programs-china-market-rise/

Müller, E. (2012). The Meaning of Harmony in China and its Importance in Business Life. Munich, GRIN Verlag, https://www.grin.com/document/296059

Neidel, B. (2010). Negotiations, Chinese Style. Retrieved from https://www.chinabusinessreview.com/negotiations-chinese-style/

OECD Contribution to the China Development Forum. (2011). China's Emergence as a Market Economy: Achievements and Challenges

Olivier. (2016). 6 keys to perform on Chinese market. Retrieved from https://www.tailormadechinese.com/tag/chinese-market-business/

Population of Cities in China. (2018). Retrieved from http://worldpopulationreview.com/countries/china-population/cities/

Qian, R. (2016). Take advantage of China's tier 2 and 3 cities. Retrieved from http://tradecommissioner.gc.ca/canadexport/0000806.aspx?lang=eng

Seto C. K. (2013). What Should We Understand about Urbanization in China? Retrieved from https://insights.som.yale.edu/insights/what-should-we-understand-about-urbanization-in-china

Sun, Jiaming. & Wang, Xun. (2010). Value differences between generations in China: a study in Shanghai. *Journal Of Youth Studies,* 13(1), 65-81

Tang, Zheyuan. (2016). Implications in the Era of Building Confucius Institutes from a Global Perspective. *Chinese Education & Society,* 49: 385–390

Tao, Liqing., Berci, M., & He, W. (2006). Education as a Social Ladder. Retrieved from https://archive.nytimes.com/www.nytimes.com/ref/college/coll-china-education-004.html

Sean Upton-McLaughlin, (2014) "The many faces of suzhi in the Chinese organization and society: Implications for multinational HRM practice", Journal of Chinese Human Resource Management, Vol. 5 Issue: 1, pp.51-61, https://doi.org/10.1108/JCHRM-01-2014-0004

Wei, Xiaohong & Li, Qingyuan. (2013). The Confucian Value of Harmony and its Influence on Chinese Social Interaction. *Cross-Cultural Communication,* Vol. 9, No. 1, pp. 60-66

Yu, Keping. (2012). The Transformation of Chinese Culture since the Launching of Reform: A Historical Perspective. Retrieved from http://en.theorychina.org/xsqy_2477/201306/t20130611_270481.shtml

Zhang, J.W. (Spring 2017). Intangible Cultural Heritage and Self-Healing Mechanism in Chinese Culture, *Western Folklore* 76.2 197-226.

Zhang, J. W. (2015). Chinese American Culture in the Making: Perspectives and Reflections on Diasporic Folklore and Identity. *The Journal of American Folklore*, Vol. 128, No. 510 (Fall 2015), pp. 449-475

Zhang, J. & Zhou C. (2014). Understanding Chinese Culture and Business from the Yin-Yang Perspective. In: Blomme R.J., van Hoof B. (eds) *Another State of Mind*. Palgrave Macmillan, London

Zhang, Lihua. (2013). China's Traditional Cultural Values and National Identity. Retrieved from https://carnegietsinghua.org/2013/11/21/ china-s-traditional-cultural-values-and-national-identity-pub-53613

Zhao, Y. (2012). "Exploring Career Aspirations of Chinese-American Faculty Members at Selected Higher Education Institutions in New York State" (2012). Education Doctorate. Paper 14.

Chapter 2

How China's Business System Works

By Rui Torres de Oliveira and Sandra Figueira

The rapid growth of China is unprecedented. No country has shifted as many people from a position of poverty to financial stability in such a short period of time (Lin et al., 2003; Ravallion and Chen, 2007). The figures are staggering:

- China is the second largest beneficiary of inward foreign direct investment (IFDI) with US $171 billion (OECD, 2018).
- China is the largest exporter in the world with US $2.26 trillion in exports (Customs, 2018).
- China holds the largest amount of foreign exchange reserves in the world, about US $3.14 trillion (CIA, 2018; SAFE, 2018).
- China has US $217 billion in outward foreigner direct investment (OFDI), which means Chinese multinational corporations (MNCs) are second amongst all countries, superceded only by the USA (OECD, 2018).

Despite China's rise as a global economic superpower, many question whether or not the country's growth model, currently still supported by public investments and exports, is sustainable. In apparent concordance with the claim that the growth model is unsustainable, the Chinese government has opted to shift its focus to enlarging both domestic consumption and the services sector, while fostering innovation within their internal enterprises. The question remains: How successful will China be in transforming its economic model to adapt to its dependence on services and internal consumption?

The intricacies of Chinese institutions, coupled with the influence of Confucianism, have significantly shaped the way in which economic agents and individuals interact in China. In comparison to Western firms and other surrounding Asian nations, Chinese firms have different objectives, incentives, rationales, contracts and internal cultural factors that impact their unique business system (Torres de Oliveira and Figueira, 2018; Torres Oliveira et al., 2017).

Hence, it is important to evaluate the Chinese business systems from a multidisciplinary perspective and from different units of analysis. After gaining a comprehensive understanding of the organizational system in place in China, it will be easier, and arguably possible, to assess the types of changes that need to take place in order to advance the central government's objective of advancing internal consumption and service activities and the firms that are predisposed to be successful. Since the business system is eminently path dependent (Whitley, 1999), a brief historical snapshot is required.

Business System

Nations have the ability to influence firms through central institutions (Hall and Soskice, 2001). In 1992, British sociologist and institutionalist, Richard Whitely, formalized the concept of a *business system,* suggesting that institutions and external agents implemented through the economy create business systems. Firms develop within a relational center of forces. These forces are economic agents and interest groups such as labor, shareholders, management, government, communities, agencies and clients. An evaluation of the forces that create business systems can be used to justify the behaviors and actions of firms at particular times.

Given different countries have unique institutions, a firm may utilize alternative strategies when operating within specific nations. Across different countries, the impact of institutions varies immensely. In some states, institutions play active roles as economic agents, directly or indirectly impacting the allocation of investments, production and resources (Amable, 2003). Compared to other states, Chinese institutions act as market arbitrators, influencing through encouragement or protection, investment in specific industries (Whitley, 1999). At a basic level, a common feature of institutions among different states is that institutions formally and informally influence the transaction costs between agents (Williamson, 1979). Furthermore, industrial pressures and accepted norms shape the business system in place in a specific context. Following Whitley (1999), the areas that influence and shape economic activity and business systems to the greatest extent are: the state, the financial system, skill development, control systems, inter-firm relations, norms and values governing trust authority relationships and scale.

For someone who visited regions or lived in China it is not difficult to perceive that this country has many different ways of operating. Local institutions often behave differently; there are industrial specificities; firms' work with varying operational dynamics; and individuals are imbued with unique cultures, ethnics, dialects and values. Without refuting the importance of provinces, regions, local governments' autonomy, or industrial sectors, we believe that there are commonalities in China that are worthy of study. Keeping in mind that the end level of analysis is the firm, we need to understand on a national level the constraints that are imposed on firms.

Based on the definition and main areas of influence within business systems as previously described, we developed each of them here for a better understanding of the Chinese business system and how each area is influenced by institutions and shape a firms strategic capabilities:

The Financial System

The financial system in China is unique for a number of reasons. Based on the previous conjectures about how the Chinese state centralized system works, financial institutions are expected to fully cooperate with the directions of the government (Lin, 2011). The 2008 financial crisis is a good example. When the central government asked banks to increase their loans, the banks responded with unanimity by releasing large credits throughout the economy. A more recent example happened with the stock exchange *shock* in June and July of 2015, where the central government demanded a group of state-controlled enterprises (SCE) to intervene in the market by providing financial support and by imposing stock sells restrictions, in a clear sign of tight control.

Contrary to what we would expect in a developed economy, the central bank of China, the most important guarantor of the financial system, does not have autonomy from the central government, nor from the main financial institutions. This inevitably creates a sense of fragility, impunity, and lack of control in the financial system that in turn creates an important potential brittleness.

Another important characteristic of the Chinese financial system is related to taxation being decentralized but with central government *principles*. Nevertheless, local authorities frequently negotiate with firms on the rates, as described in a 2014 interview with a managing director of one of the companies of CITIC group, the biggest and an older Chinese SCE. "Tax rates (sic) is always a negotiation process with local authorities, since they want to attract investment but at the same time they know that we need discounts to invest in such town." This adds a dynamic as well as competition among local governments in the attraction of investments.

Added to this, the financial system is not immune to corruption (Allen et al., 2005a; Transparency International, 2014), especially in regards to financial loans. The Chinese institutionalized financial system is also characterized by large, dominant institutions, but with an underdeveloped banking system (Johnson et al., 2002; Lei, 2012) and with a lack of expertise in the analysis of investment projects.

In China there are three main types of organizations: SCEs, stock exchange enterprises, and private firms. Each of these types of enterprises has very different access to capital, as well as differences in price. On one hand, we have the SCEs, in OFDI for example, being accused of dumping in terms of capital interest and having an abundance of capital (Rosen and Hanemann, 2011); on the other hand, we see private firms with very low access to capital, and when this happens it is with high levels of interest rates. The SCEs are highly privileged when compared with private firms, with the government pressuring local banks to provide preferential bank loans to SCEs in prejudice to private firms (Zhang and Keh, 2010).

This happens because the institutionalized financial system is controlled by the state and, as in many other dimensions, is highly imperfect (Buckley et al., 2008; Child and Rodrigues, 2005), not transparent, with high transaction costs (Nolan, 2001), and does not follow market rules of competition. Even with high levels of liquidity (Lei, 2012), the allocation of such liquidity is far from being egalitarian and balanced by different agents. In fact, this is not a unique problem for China, but a common issue in emergent economies (Chen, 2008).

Nonetheless, and because of the high rate of savings of firms and of the population (Kuijs, 2006), access to capital for Chinese entrepreneurs and private firms is possible in non-institutional markets, known as *shadow banking.*[1] A good example was given by Liu and Li (2002), when Haier, at an earlier stage (1984), needed money to pay salaries and borrowed it from farmers in villages because the

1. We would define it as all the credit not regulated by standard and conventional financial institutions. For a thoughtful discussion, please refer to Harutyunyan et al. (2015).

institutional capital market was not available. In fact, it is such alternative financing channels[2] that are supporting the real economy and are the principal factors of growth (Allen et al., 2005a). These channels are particularly important to private firms and tied very closely to trust, reputation and relationships. *Shadow banking* is estimated to represent, following GF Securities, Citi Research, and Barclays, around 50% or more of the Chinese gross domestic product (GDP) in 2012 (Li, 2014). More recently, Elliott et al. (2015) reported that this value can go as high as 80%. It is ruled by lending to higher-risk mortgagors such as property developers or small or medium enterprises (Allen et al., 2005b) that usually have difficulties accessing the current financial markets in China.

Another central financial mechanism of any economy is its stock exchange. China presently has two locations – Shanghai and Shenzhen. The stock exchanges in both locations are highly regulated by Chinese authorities, as explained before, and place many restrictions on listing companies. The majority of them belong to or are controlled by the Chinese government, which results in lack of information, transparency, and future orientations that are important for investor decisions. Furthermore, many of the firms in these stock exchanges are partly listed, which hurts minority interests and the investor relations are weak (Liu and Woywode, 2012). Moreover, Chinese listed firms often switch auditors in order to manipulate their work (Lin and Liu, 2009).

The Chinese stock exchange is not completely open to foreign markets and investors, which substantially reduces its purpose as a way to allocate resources into the economy. Redding and Witt (2007) argue that the suspect stock exchange market is the result of China's poor institutions, such as lack of press coverage and flow of information in a general way, reliable accounting and control systems, and a trustworthy

2. Following llen et al. (2005a, p. 3) such informal channels are "informal financial intermediaries, internal financing and trade credits, and coalitions of various forms among firms, investors, and local governments."

financial system. We agree that the lack of institutional grounds are a principal reason for an underdeveloped stock market and add that there are important groups of interests that have high levels of earnings based on this underdeveloped stock exchange. These are all obstacles for change. Furthermore, the lack of alternatives from the population in the allocation of their savings — allied with their lack of knowledge and cultural characteristics — lead millions of Chinese individuals to invest in the stock exchange without any kind of rationality. Even if the data is not available and transparent, it is well known that many stock-exchange firms are using their own shares as loan collateral to subsidize the purchase of other stocks or even their own stocks in a dangerous financial snowball.

Another principal factor when we discuss the Chinese financial system is the reserves that the country holds. In 2012, China had US $3.31 trillion (SAFE, 2018); by November 2014 it had already surpassed US $3.95 trillion (PBC, 2015) and by the end of 2017, even with all the outflow of private and corporate capital, China had US $3.14 trillion (SAFE, 2018). In 2017 the National Security Fund presented US $300 billion (Reuters, 2018) that combined with the China Investment Corporation, with US $900 billion (Xinhua, 2017) and by the middle of 2017 China had, by far, the biggest reserve in the world in USD that is ready to be used. Another dimension in which Chinese authorities hold control is the outflow of capital from China. The fear of asset-stripping and capital flight are still present and used by Chinese authorities for the non-authorization of capital exchange without governmental permission.

All these restrictions have pushed many private investors to create offshore holdings. Furthermore, private investors do not rely on the domestic financial market, and placing their capital elsewhere is a way to circumvent Chinese institutional pressures and restrictions, such as OFDI approval procedures (Ning and Sutherland, 2012). Another motivation of the shareholders and top managers of private firms for creating holdings outside China is to seek legal protection for their stocks (Globerman and Shapiro, 2009). Not only private firms do this, the majority of Chinese OFDI into off-shores are done, curiously, by the SCEs (MOFCOM, 2014). The 2018 example when the Central Government took over one of China's largest insurance company, Anbang, is a clear example of why many firms still see foreigner markets as a way to protect their interests.

Another important part of the financial system has to do with the forms of capital allocation by firms. In Chinese private firms, the allocation of capital is essentially done by the *lao ban,*[3] depending on where such allocation would bring more returns. This authority over capital brings about elevated levels of reputation, income, and power that go unchallenged because it is used as identity differentiation.

In conclusion, the financial system in China is highly institutionalized and is known for its lack of knowledge in risk assessment of investment projects, which leads to support for SCEs and non private firms unless very high levels of *guanxi* exist. Based on that, private firms need to find support with relatives and friends or in the non-institutionalized financial system – shadow banking.

Skill Development and Control System

In relation to the control systems in China, we need to contextualize that capitalism in China is about two major interest groups that are predominant and prevalent in society — family businesses and SCE (state-controlled enterprises). If the importance of the family business is related to their large number, the importance of SCEs is related to their power, weight in the economy (OECD, 2009, 2017), and their direct connections to the legislative and other institutions in China. Another important note is the fact that it was only in June of 1988 that the Chinese central government ruled private ownership, *saying qiyie,*[4] as a for-profit organization.

---

3. The Chinese word for the *big boss* that usually is the owner of the typical family owned firms in China.

4. Chinese name of the private law.

In both groups, the decision makers are at the very top of the organizations. The roots of this are associated with the path-dependency of recent Chinese history, both its centralized authority and its fierce punishment system. Redding and Witt (2007) argue that the lack of qualified human resources is itself a factor of the non-proliferation of decision making across firms. Even today, the *lao ban* is the common word in the daily business of a firm and is part of the Chinese route to respect. Because of this, there is always a reluctance of Chinese workers (blue and white collars) to challenge, provide ideas, or disagree with the *big boss*.

As explained before, the control system of managers in state owned or state controlled enterprises is in the end done by the central or local government or party. This is based on a punishment and incentive system (Lin, 2011). Top managers serve the government or party leaders without much question. However, with such a system the employees enjoy security but diminished negotiating power. In this kind of organization, authority structures are unclear and complex; there is a high resistance to change and usually not many incentives for staff in terms of performance (Desvaux et al., 2004).

The pool of skilled talent in China is poor and the best ones tend to work for international firms where pay is higher and where they have more flexibility and more *voice*. Even so, and based on recent interviews with senior managers of international firms,[5] we realize that skilled labor is reduced even for them. Chinese workers accept strong personal leadership as well as systems of control. When such strong leadership does not exist, the staff feel worried and unsafe because they believe competitors will surpass them. This is an important characteristic of the Chinese business system.

It is very common to see that middle and senior managers across a firm are not sharing any kind of ideas or communication horizontally.

---

5. The companies were Sonae Sierra, Morgan Stanley, Blackstone, and Macquarie.

Their role is to receive orders from above and verify that they are being followed (Redding and Witt, 2007). This creates firms that are good at doing mass production with highly standardized and specialized tasks allied with disciplined and low-cost labor. With such a system, it is not foreseen that Chinese firms will enter into more complex systems of management that are required for multi-national firms or for firms in which the required exchange of ideas flows not only horizontally and vertically but in both directions. Furthermore, the integration and coordination of variety is an important asset of complex firms and is yet to be seen in Chinese organizations. This reminds us of Thompson (1967, p. 132) "The 'pyramid' headed by the single, all-powerful individual has become a symbol of complex organizations, but through historical and misleading accident. The all-powerful chief can maintain such control only to the extent that he is not dependent on others within his organization; and this is a situation of modest complexity, not one of a high degree of complexity."

The personal control of firms, because of ownership structure, will continue to block the growth of professional and autonomous management structures. The large majority of private firms in China are family-owned where one person controls the full operation. Because of that, the decision makers are at the very top of the organization and the control system is highly vertical, stratified, and highly path-dependent. This leads to a common reluctance of Chinese workers to challenge, provide ideas or disagree with their superiors. This fosters firms that succeed at mass production but do not incentivise firms to enter into more complex and non-specialized tasks.

The structure of education in China is still very constrained by the education system created under Mao Zedong during the Cultural Revolution. The education system is fully controlled by the state, and even today foreign schools and universities are not allowed to open and manage facilities without the chancellery of a Chinese school and are under the tight control of local authorities. This can be seen in the example of Nottingham University in Ningbo where the Communist

Party has staff to control overall activity.

Usually, students are divided into university-educated individuals and the others, with a clear separation between both groups in terms of expectation, recognition, and future progression. All the educational systems in China are based in Mandarin[6] and this is one of the most important unifications of China as a nation. The crown jewel remains in the primary school where the free education system is working well and the government wants to introduce it until grade nine.

In China there is no system of recognition of skills and the technical and vocational educational system is very feeble. When it exists, it is organized poorly by the state. Moreover, unions and other agencies of employees do not participate in the organization or certification of competencies. In fact, unions in China are defragmented and decontextualized in relation to the real problems of the workers, and many times are merely pro-forma. In a recent interview, a CEO of a Chinese industrial firm that is a world leader in its industrial segment and employs more than 2000 workers explained that in his firm there is a union, since it is mandatory. Nevertheless, the union is composed of "my father, uncle and other people that are highly controlled by the central management." This is an extraordinary example of how Chinese managers circumvent Chinese institutions and their rules and how unions do not have the power and the strength that we would expect in a Communist Country. It is no surprise that Nichols and Zhao (2010) found that workers in Hubei Province were dissatisfied with their unions.

In China, the labor market is very volatile with workers changing jobs on a regular basis. Firms can, up to some degree,[7] easily dismiss

---

6. Guangdong Province remains an exception essentially because of the pressures of Hong-Kong as we could see in 2013 when the Central Government tried to establish Mandarin in the region. However, students learn Mandarin.

7. If workers are less than five years from retirement, more than 15 years in the company, and pregnant, firing can become more complicated. Otherwise the market presents a flexible human resources policy based on financial

workers based on the current rules-of-law[8] and normal practice. This does not give firms any incentive to invest in training workers since this type of investment can easily be lost and the results enjoyed by competitors. In fact, firms expect that workers will come with the necessary skills that they would need to perform their tasks. Usually, in societies like China, the educational system is the provider of the development and canvassing of such skills. Due to its poor level of education, at least from a practical point of view, workers are available to have a first opportunity at almost any price and conditions since it would be the only way to earn the necessary skills that the market place values.

To conclude, the education system in China does not incentivize the learning of technical skills and students are pushed to the university. Furthermore, the institutions in China, namely through the law, do not assure a low volatility in the labor market. Because of that, firms do not have the incentive to invest in their workers, and do not create jobs that depend highly on people's skills and originality. Instead, it resembles Fordism with its high task mechanization and control, and low level of specialization.

Norms and Values Governing Trust and Authority Relationship

The importance of *guanxi* is the result of the lack of trust in the existing institutions that is extrapolated from the relationships between individuals, organizations, and government entities. The institutions are not the guarantee of exchange between the different economic agents and do not generate trust between relative strangers.

Being that legal systems are one of the most important aspects of an institutional framework (Merryman, 2007), we realize that the legal system in China does not provide the assurance of a free and fair trial (Peerenboom, 2001). The same author clarifies: "The biggest obstacles

---

compensations.

8. Labor Contract Law of PRC

to a law-based administrative system in China are institutional and systemic in nature: a legislative system in disarray; a weak judiciary; poorly trained judges and lawyers; the absence of a robust civil society populated by interests groups; a low level of legal consciousness; the persistent influence of paternalistic traditions and a culture of deference to government authority; rampant corruption; and the fallout from the unfinished transition from a centrally planned economy to a market economy, which has exacerbated central-local tensions and resulted in fragmentation of authority" (Peerenboom, 2001 p. 168-169).

When compared with the USA, for example, the Chinese institutional legal framework is at a much lower level of clarity and market-orientated protection (Peng, 2003). The lack of clear definitions of property rights from the laws, combined with a poor judicial system that does not defend contracts (Li et al., 2011), are the basis for a general lack of confidence in the legal system and its outcomes.

Using the language of North (1990), we could say that business transactions are not based on contracts and rule-of-law since the costs are very high and this is due to an institutional failure. Consequently, this led the economy to a situation of trusting more in interpersonal ties, *guanxi*, than in formal and institutional rules that are usually found in a market-orientated economy. Such situations happen frequently with the entities that possess the capability of influencing the *results of the game* such as governmental officials. Because of that, it is common to see Chinese managers cultivating ties with officials in order to increase the probability of advantages over their competitors, or because of a government bid, a court case, political prestige (Li et al., 2011) or personal favors. This can be seen as governmental void. Khanna and Palepu (2000, p.270) coined these lack of institutional foundations as "institutional voids." Chinese consumers, for example, do not trust the different governmental agencies for food control or baby products. Furthermore, the lack of institutions, or at least the lack of those that individuals trust, remains the main factor for such a high level of savings since the Chinese population still does not rely on social benefits.

Inter-Firms Relations

Independent institutions were never allowed to grow in China due to the risks that they may present to the Communist Party. We cannot find in China an independent central-bank, professional association, or free press (Redding and Witt, 2007). In many economies, such independent institutions are crucial for the inter-firm relations that in some, as the case of Germany, are one of the most important features of their business system (Whitley, 1999).

On one hand, inter-firm relations cannot be held in market relationships because agents do not have the grounds for it, namely due to lack of trust in contracts. On the other hand, agents cannot trust inter-firm strategic interactions because there are no industrial associations or other institutions that would support, regulate and incentivize them. Such industrial associations neither exist nor are allowed, and there is no institutional ground for their development. Inter-firm relations are, because of this, almost non-existent in the Chinese economic coordination system, and the transference of technology and know-how usually happen with the transference of individuals.

Some may ask whether firms collaborate or cooperate with each other in China. They do. And they do so especially in their *comfort zone* and without the transfer of know-how among themselves. In fact, it is well accepted that the Chinese economy had a significant growth pattern in the last decades because of the private family firms, with many of them interacting with each other to build their products. Whilst it is a fact that family firms interact among themselves, they do it usually at an arm's length transaction where there is no risk-sharing, no sharing of product or services development, nor exchanges or transfer of know-how.

This *comfort zone* exists in order to try to decrease uncertainties. The Chinese totalitarian system created a sense of mistrust among individuals that sifted down to the different economic agents and led to a generalized lack of security. Based on this, the individuals who are the only ones trusted are the ones that are in your circle of knowledge. It is important to notice that two very different types of *guanxi* exist and many times are confused. There is the *guanxi* amongst family and close friends,[9] and there is the *guanxi* that comes from the relationships that you establish during the working period that are much less strong. To have a better understanding, we can divide it into layers by importance. The first, and most important layer, is the family that can be truly trusted. Then, you have your close friends that usually come from school, or someone with whom you developed a friendship over the years or did business with and became trustworthy. In the third layer we have the so-called *external guanxi,* which is all the agents with whom you interact in a reciprocal way that are usually in a position to help you in some fashion — officials, bankers, and others (Redding and Witt, 2007). If the latter brings important transaction costs on the cultivation of such relations and risks since it is not based on *firm contracts*, the former presents very low costs of transactions due to the high level of trust that already exists but presents a high spatial limitation.

If you trust in a very limited number of individuals, and the institutions are not the guarantee of a low-cost transaction due to the lack of reliable information and trust between agents, the result will be a considerably decreased number of potential economic agents making transactions. This, in turn, will be a major obstacle for economic development because it does not allow for efficient resource allocation. This stifles competition and innovation, and it diminishes the relationships among firms for the development of joint projects, as *guanxi* is not significant enough. With the development of the economy, the power of *guanxi* is doomed to decline if, at the same time, the Chinese institutions enforce its rules and applicability successfully to counter-balance the necessity of using it. Because of the importance of *guanxi*, in the majority of the cases, the leader holds authority and the most valuable contacts. *Guanxi*, therefore, is not a dimension of Chinese

---

9. Usually neighbourhood, high school, or university friends.

development success as many believe (eg., Peng and Heath, 1996; Peng and Luo, 2000), but is only the result of institutional voids (Khanna and Palepu, 2000).

Due to the lack of trust and applicability of the rule-of-law, that is well revealed in the low level of reliance in contracts, allied with the lack of associations that could ground inter-firms strategic interactions makes the inter-firm relations almost non-existent. The existent relations are arm lengths' transactions. However, the knowledge transference among a firm and the use of resources from other firms are well known to be critical premises for the development of innovative firms.

The State

From the Chinese authorities' perspective, only a strengthening central authority can maintain stability and prevent chaos in a country with so many differences, as Deng Xiaoping had demonstrated in the incident of Tiananmen Square (Yang, 2004). In fact, control by the state has always been the principle of statecraft, and the loss of control is genuinely intimidating from the state perspective (Redding and Witt, 2007). In China, the Communist Party has supremacy over personnel selection and a well-organized rotation system of officials at all levels, undoubtedly signing local officials as subordinates of a strong central governance (Nolan, 2001; Yang, 2004).

Excluding Taiwan, Hong Kong, and Macau, and looking solely at Mainland China, we have the following administrative divisions based on the Chinese constitution: central, provincial, county and township. Moreover, there are two main structures in the administrative divisions — the Communist Party and Governmental Leaders. The former is not an executive division and usually acts as a controller and as an identifier of deviations from the higher levels. The latter are the executive officials responsible for the implementation of the directives of the superior levels. The National People's Congress elects the central government for a period of 10 years, and all the other levels are appointed by the central structure and easily replaced by the same structure that has appointed them. Such a structure is highly permissive within the execution of the guidelines issued by the mutually-dependent central structures because of the desire to delight the superiors who are responsible for promotions. As Lin explained, "The party-state can and does swiftly remove local officials who are deemed disloyal," which suggests a stratified, vertical and top-to-bottom structure (Lin, 2011, p. 73).

This vertical, top-down authority is a good example of path-dependence since it is the result of Chinese history. In the majority of cases, even in state owned or SCEs, the managers ultimately respond to the central (Lin, 2011) or local government, depending on the firm, and not the board of directors as would be expected in the West.

Nevertheless, we can observe that the central government delegated much of its fiscal and administrative authority to provincial or even local governments (Zhang, 2006). With government decentralization, and after the reforms in the 1970-80s, some provincial and even local government agents were allowed to sponsor firms, as collectives or as stockholding firms (Oi, 1995), using them as a way to penetrate into a market where there was a strange, uneasy relationship between politics and the economy. With such a move, the central government was trying to follow the practice of *think central, act local.* Because of this, local governments possess an important incentive to leverage growth since the fiscal decentralization allows them to benefit from it (Montinola et al., 1995).

Another influence on growth is the fact that many officials will be promoted if they are doing better than their peers, which stimulates a naturally competitive environment that can be seen in the local governments and SCEs (Li and Zhou, 2005). Still, the relationship between local authorities and firms is a "fuzzy relationship" as Lin (2011, p. 80) described, but is also a way of keeping "their flexibility to compete in the market place" and to match official interests with their own. Some authors (e.g. Lin, 2011; Redding and Witt, 2007) defend that this was one of the most effective characteristics that allowed Chinese firms to explore and exploit all the corners of the Chinese market, as well as internationally, and one of the reasons for such internal high growth.

In China, the central, provincial and local governments play a crucial role in determining economic activities, not only from a bureaucratic point of view, but also with regard to the overall cohesion of institutions (Deng, 2004; Ren et al., 2012). The government also has the autonomy to circumvent laws, company legal structures and personal legal rights (Lin, 2011). Moreover, the Chinese state shares investment risks with private economic interests. In fact, the state shares risks, creates dependencies, and is an important player directly and indirectly in the daily business activities on the generality of firms in China. An example of the state's power is the constraints that exist in terms of IFDI and OFDI, where many industries are still closed to foreign capital, and Chinese firms have to perform extensive bureaucratic processes before internationalizing (Buckley et al., 2008; Luo et al., 2010; Ren et al., 2012). Another example is the *Countries and Industries for Overseas Investment Guidance Catalogue (duiwai touzi guobie chanye daosiang mulu)*, known as the *Catalogue*, that was issued in 2004 by the Ministry of Commerce of China (MOFCOM) in conjunction with the Ministry of Foreign Affairs (MoFA), with the specific purpose of orienting firms for industries and countries.[10] As an example, Germany is seen as a preferable host country for the manufacturing of high-technology machinery and equipment (Schüler-Zhou et al., 2011). Other examples exist, such as the SCEs and the highly supported solar glass panel industry that led recently to anti-dumping and anti-subsidy investigations by the United States and the European Union.

As Farh et al. (1997) described, this led to important investments from various economic agents in the cultivation of relationships, and *guanxi*, with officials because they have the discriminatory power of decision. Moreover, state directives legitimize public property rights

---

10. See Schuler-Zhou et al. (2011) for a more thoughtful discussion on this matter.

against the restraints on private property rights (Li et al., 2011), and frequently support laws and regulations that favor specific economic agents (Scott, 2002). However, it is recognized that state-directed industrial policy fuels corruption, as Adam Smith in *Wealth of Nations* alerted us to at the end of the eighteenth century (Nolan, 2001). If we tie this to *guanxi*, we begin to understand the position of China in the world corruption index. But the state does not solely influence institutions or organizations. The state in China also plays an important and direct role over individuals (Boisot and Child, 1999; Li et al., 2011; Lin, 2011) by providing such things as supervision, selective support, capital control (Lin, 2011), control of the media and birth, imposition of high levels of bureaucracy and control, and constraints on and control of information.

Through the highly bureaucratic system that exists at the different levels of government, or through more direct means, the Chinese government acts as an *active hand* over individuals and organizations (Lin, 2011), contrary to what Walton (2008) defended. A good example was the state takeover of Mengniu, a Chinese food company, due to a scandal. It was immediate and without any enforcement of the law (Lin, 2011). Such involvement of the state into the economy contributes negatively to its development by increasing inequality, reducing transparent information between different agents, and decreasing efficiency, which inevitably leads to higher costs of transactions.

To review, if on one hand, there is a state that is highly geographically spread out and attempts to have vast control over individuals and economic agents; on the other hand, there is a generalized lack of confidence in the state and its institutions. This lack of confidence in Chinese institutions leads to a discouragement of the establishment of associations between individuals, enterprises, and the state. When a contract has almost no value in the Chinese context (Boisot and Child, 1996; Zhou et al., 2008), we can only expect that strong personal relations, *guanxi*, would encourage the establishment of inter-firm cooperation, alliances, or cartelization. Interactions among economic agents often happen within their *guanxi*, many times without any type of contract. This is a factor of streamlining the interaction and can be seen as a competitive advantage (Teece et al., 1997), especially since discussion of the contract — which does not itself have much value — is not necessary. This is true if the interaction remains in the sphere of *guanxi*, which itself limits the development of economic agents into modern and professional enterprises.

Currently, the Chinese central government is attempting to develop a market economy. However, even with all the new market-orientated policies coming from the central government, two important economic restrictions to production inputs remain: *land ownership* and *business credits*. All the land ownership remains in the state's possession as a single supplier, and law forbids private land ownership. In fact, the sales of land-use rights have been the main source of income from local governments in recent years, which indirectly contributes to the increase of living costs in all Chinese cities.

Another key limitation from the market economy perspective comes from the business credits in the financial sector, which will be explored in the next section. Nevertheless, it is important to clarify at this stage that the Chinese government has sole control of the financial system, such as bank loans, bond issuing, corporate equities and other financial products. All the banks, including international ones, are kept in state hands.

In conclusion, the state in China incentivizes the private firms and in particular its managers to enter into personal ties with the different officials. This happens due to three main reasons: 1) the high bureaucratic system in place that firms try to circumvent; 2) the fact that officials have the discriminatory power of decision that can bring high benefits to the firm with the classic example of the rate of taxes that a firm will pay; and 3) the fact that the state share investments with private firms in a direct or indirect way with the classic example of real estate.

The Factor Scale

The massive manpower and still average low-cost labor that China offers (The World Bank, 2015) shapes its business system in a unique way. Chinese labor presents high levels of geographical fluctuations, in particular from the more rural areas to the cities where it is not uncommon to be discriminated against (China Development Research Foundation, 2014). This led the Chinese economy to prefer to use and rely on individuals, essentially because of a financial perspective, and much less in technology, which would need a scarcer type of human resource. Similarly, the scarce quantity of service companies in China reveals that firms still prefer to be in the industrial sector due to the large availability of unskilled workers and low complexity that is requested. This scale factor influences, for example, the lack of incentive for technological upgrade or human resources development and skills. Another factor of scale is in market dimension. The Chinese home market dimension, due to its population, is in fact a distinctive and idiosyncratic characteristic that shapes its country and firm-specific advantages (Ramamurti and Singh, 2009).

What to Expect from Chinese Private Firms

Based on the above, we may expect that the economic actors in China would behave differently not only from the liberal market economies, but also from the control market economies, using Hall and Soskice (2001) terminology. In this section we discuss what to expect from a typical Chinese firm based on their business system.

Ownership and Control

It should not be a surprise the results of Schlevogt (2001) who found that more than 85% of the private enterprises are family controlled. Within the so-called family-firms, and based on a survey from the Asian Development Bank, the largest individual shareholder holds, on average, more than 59% of the shares (Liao, 2008) in a firm. With such a structure, it is easy to predict that the decisions are centralized on a person, the *lao ban*, with the shareholder structure having the power and the legitimacy for all kinds of resolutions. This causes the main owner to pursue an aggressive strategy toward profitability. Due to the firm's structure and human resources configuration, we may predict a lack of managerial incentives aligned with the firm's results. At the same time, the boundaries of the firms are very well-defined and the top management has full control over the firm that includes hiring and firing. Since the decisions are usually made by the owner, some may expect that firms will only be involved in areas where the owner dominates or can have access to specific knowledge through her/his *guanxi*. Furthermore, having a small number of people managing a firm means the level of complexity that the firm can accomplish is usually trifling. We can expect, then, that Chinese firms will usually have small, tight centralized control, low levels of complexity in their organization, processes, and production, and be based on the *lao ban* network, characteristics, and objectives.

Employer-Employee Relations and Control

Very similar to a market economy (Hall and Soskice, 2001), the governance structure of Chinese firms are based on market relations where the development of long-term relationships is not encouraged. The mobility of workers among firms is considerable, which produces narrow assignments so that they can be easily replaced. This is one of the reasons why job specialization skills are narrow and why there is no incentive from companies to develop such aptitudes. A substantial difference exists between salary rates among different company levels.

Authority in the firms is expected to be vertical and highly hierarchical but with a unique person to make the majority of the decisions, the *lao ban*. Chinese firms rely almost totally on the *lao ban's* experience, *guanxi*, financial capability, and expertise. Middle and senior levels are expected to transmit the *lao ban*'s instructions and expectations and assure that the results are achieved. No horizontal know-how or idea transfers are expected to be seen in Chinese firms.

Blue-collar workers are expected to perform given tasks and be controlled, and no ideas of upgrading the firm or improvement of the products or services are expected. This is an important difference from a typical market economy as described by Hall and Soskice (2001). There is a high level of mistrust between the different levels of the firm, and there is a low level of communitarian responsibilities between labor and capital.

Similar to a market economy, the Chinese workers would tend to pursue an investment in general training instead of company specific-skills. This happens due to the high volatility external labor market that China presents allied with the weak unions since lay-offs can be done without risks or high costs. The external labor market is quite elastic but the internal labor market is very static with low internal transferences.

The lack of strong unions, contrary to what would be expected, produces a lack of collective actions between the employee and the employer. Weak unions, allied with workers mobility, do not encourage the discussion of wages and would not support and encourage industry-specific training, also known as technical education, as we explained.

Inter Firm Relations

Inter firm relations in China are not encouraged. They are not encouraged because inter firm relations cannot be executed within the market due to the lack of the enforcement of the rule-of-law and more specifically formal contractors. The relationships among producers and suppliers are highly opportunistic but made over relational contacts. The cooperation between producers and suppliers is very low and it is typical to observe mistrust and instability between them. This is the result of one of the many institutional voids (Khanna and Palepu, 1997, 2000) that China has, and it is the result of the high profitability that Chinese private firms are pursuing that are a product of their ownership and managerial structure.

The deficit in the quality, transparency, enforcement of the rule-of-law and the non-allowance of independent associations produces a lack of collaborative research and development for products and services among economic actors. Even cooperation between competitors or client-suppliers is infrequent.

The different agents do not see the market as the primary arena for transactions and prefer to use *club deals* based on *guanxi*. This leads the economic agents to use high levels of non-market financial and industrial coordination. This happens because the institutions cannot decrease the uncertainty to a level that would make agents use the market as the platform for transactions. Because of this, and because such *club deals* do not foster the flow of information, when Chinese firms have an expected increase in costs, we see it reflected in the customer price in order to maintain a firm's profitability. Likewise, the lack of guarantees from the market lead firms to develop as far as their contacts may go and does not support interactions with relative strangers.

Financing Pattern and Performing Criteria

In China, banks and other financial institutions do not support private firms (Tam, 2004). With no other way than relying on self-financing and informal credit arrangement (*shadow banking)*, Chinese firms are pushed to short-term maximization of profits and are managed beneath rigid budget restraints. Because of this, Chinese firms are not provided with incentive to pursue long-term development strategies.

The Chinese stock-market exchange is a trusty reflection of the Chinese institutionalized market. Without having absolute certainty, due to weak output data, it is estimated that SCEs count for approximately 70 to 80% of the number of listed companies in both the Shanghai and Shenzhen stock market exchange (Chen et al., 2008; Fan et al., 2011). Therefore, the Chinese institutionalized financial system does not support or encourage new ventures or small and medium enterprises (SMEs). However, after a private firm grows into a certain dimension and/or becomes listed in the stock-exchange market, the institutionalized finance capital starts to open to give support. Nevertheless, new ventures and SMEs have emerged at the expense of personal loans as well as informal credit arrangements.

We have seen that private firms operate under optimal combinations of financial instruments and resources that inevitably lead them to sub-optimal financial conditions. The deficiency of market features in the finance system, and more specifically in capital allocation, have led to much market deregulation. The result of this being, for example, the unnecessary manufacturing installed capability, as well as a lack of real estate planning, and therefore over-capability.

The Chinese financial system has the foundations to cause a disrupted allocation of capital into the economy. Such disrupted allocation brings risks to the financial system as well as increased transaction costs into the economy that will necessarily be reflected in the price of goods or service. This is a clear sign of how poor the information in the market is and how the institutions continue to avoid solving the problems even though it destroys economic value and creates noticeable distortions in the proper allocation of capital into the market.

Competitive Capacity

Many competitive advantages emerged, even with all the institutional voids that the Chinese market, in particular, and the economy presents (Torres de Oliveira and Rotting, 2018). The first competitive advantage is in regards to its cost structure, namely in raw materials and human resources. Second, it has a stable political and social system that produces one of the lowest criminal rates worldwide, which has been important for IFDI. Third, it is a country with flexible labor relations where a different unit of labor produces a different unit of capital.

This business system has been working since the country has been betting on producing simple low- and middle-end products that do not require the following: 1) specialized human resources capabilities; 2) high-level of R&D; 3) managerial complexity; and 4) elevated financial requirements. Due to the lack of highly-specialized human resources allied with the lack of above average levels of complexity in Chinese firms, it is not expected that we would observe high-quality and reliability in the outcome of firms.

Because of the tight control from the owner in the typical family firm, along with the pursuit of increasing the family name's recognition and reputation, many people in China started independent family businesses. Within here lies one of the secrets of China and its elevated levels of growth that we have been observing in the past decades. In fact, being the *lao ban* in China is a very significant way to build up a personal reputation that reflects family's respectability through the generation of wealth, and which buys stability and security for the future. Another reason why many start their own company is the level of income inequality and the much fewer working hours that are expected. Furthermore, being a *lao ban* will allow one to have a *voice*. If many believe that the Chinese propensity for entrepreneurship is its greatest advantage, we may not forget that its achieved by "cutting corners without a conscience" (Redding and Witt, 2007, p. 220). Different agents in China are using the market's faults to avoid suboptimal outcomes many times to surpass other agents' outcomes. It is arguable, however, whether this is a competitive advantage since it may not be sustainable.

Competition in China is very fierce among firms (Redding and Witt, 2007), and business people worry about hard (production) rather than soft skills (marketing, innovation, branding, design, or reliability) because addressing those dimensions would require levels of complexity that Chinese firms are not able to handle. This situation leads to *de facto* employment and business flexibility with rapid changes in firm strategy that are important characteristics of the Chinese business system.

Innovation

In terms of innovation, which is one of the most important factors of economic success (Lundvall, 2010), we can only expect a country to have low levels of innovation that are reflected not only in incremental but radical innovation. This expectation is the result of the distanced relationship that exists between workers, clients, and suppliers as well as the type of educational system that China has with the *unique thinking* path that remains from Mao's era. The lack of property rights protection is another cause, which does not encourage risk-taking activities. The non-existence of institutional financial support, a critical feature for new-ventures, or R&D is another very important problem within the Chinese business system. Finally, the lack of inter-firm cooperation among businesses can be seen as a major cause for the lack of innovation, because it is one of its fundamentals (Lundvall, 2010). As a consequence, if China is appropriating technology, namely by reverse engineering in different ways,[11] it is lacking in the majority of the remaining dimensions that are necessary for fostering innovation in the country.

Following the analysis of the Chinese business system and what we should expect from its firms, we proceed with the understanding of the different strategic choices that firms have.

Opportunities in China

Despite the challenges that firms face in China, the Chinese business system presents several opportunities for local and international firms and entrepreneurs.

The first opportunity relates to the fact that Chinese consumers are open and in fact looking to try new products and services. Because of that, China is an excellent market to introduce new products or services as it is a good place for companies to test creative ideas.

Another important opportunity in China relates to the financial system that it is still very much underdeveloped, as previously explained. If in China it is very easy to leave home without a physical

11. Through JV, M&A, copying, or simply buying it.

wallet (money, debit, and credit card), because a cell phone is enough for daily activities, the reality is that all the remaining financial systems that an economy needs are still built in non-efficient systems. International and local modern financial institutions have a very good opportunity that could be pursued.

The third large opportunity that we identify in China relates to the education system. Even if the central and local governments incentivize the unique thinking and control international institutions present in China very seriously, we believe that it is possible to build a new paradigm based on creativity and critical thinking. Chinese parents are eager to provide an out-of-the-box education to their children, and currently this means send them abroad.

Finally, health and senior-care are areas where the opportunities are just incommensurable. We would argue that the health system in general, and the senior-care in particular, have not been able to catch-up the general development that other sectors have enjoyed in the last 30 years. There is an enormous need for competent, private, and state of the art health systems in China. From a senior-care perspective, and if today is normal that parents take care of elders, the reality is that this happens due to cultural and historical reasons but in large scale happens as well due to the lack of services available. Chinese educated and medium- to high-income couples that both work and are successful will not consider staying home to take care of their parents if a good alternative exists.

Concluding Remarks

While China aims to transform its economy to depend on internal consumption and services, significant flaws still remain that will hinder its development. These include:

- The availability and reliability of information;
- The lack of enforcement of the rule of law;

- The reliance on personal, subjective and biased judgment as opposed to rationality;
- The inefficient allocation of capital;
- The lack of support for innovation;
- The lack of an educated population that is willing to change, challenge and distribute knowledge;
- The lack of independent industrial and professional institutions that enable regulation.

In order to continue its rapid growth, China must adapt its business system to reflect the need for modernization and development. Frameworks must be established that foster innovation and institutional voids must be filled in order to balance the economy.

In spite of the many challenges candidly presented in this chapter, we close by saying there are many opportunities for foreign investors in China. The road to success in China is not made without risks, holes, and hazards, but after investors are educated and understand the system they are about to enter, a paved highway is awaiting.

References

Allen, Franklin, Qian, Jun, & Qian, Meijun. (2005a). China's financial system: Past, present, and future. *Present, and Future (March 28, 2007).*

Allen, Franklin, Qian, Jun, & Qian, Meijun. (2005b). Law, finance, and economic growth in china. *Journal of financial economics, 77*(1), 57-116.

Amable, Bruno. (2003). *The diversity of modern capitalism*: OUP Oxford.

Boisot, Max, & Child, John. (1996). From fiefs to clans and network capitalism: Explaining china's emerging economic order. *Administrative Science Quarterly, 41*(4), 600-628.

Boisot, Max, & Child, John. (1999). Organizations as adaptive systems in complex environments: The case of china. *Organization Science, 10*(3), 237-252.

Buckley, Peter J., Cross, Adam R., Tan, Hui, Xin, Liu, & Voss, Hinrich. (2008). Historic and emergent trends in chinese outward direct investment.

Management International Review, 48(6), 715-748. doi: 10.1007/s11575-008-0104-y

Chen, Gongmeng, Firth, Michael, & Xu, Liping. (2008). Does the type of ownership control matter? Evidence from china's listed companies. *Journal of Banking & Finance, 33*(1), 171-181.

Chen, Yuanquan. (2008). Chinese economy and excess liquidity. *China & World Economy, 16*(5), 63-82. doi: 10.1111/j.1749-124X.2008.00130.x

Child, John, & Rodrigues, Suzana B. (2005). The internationalization of chinese firms: A case for theoretical extension?[1]. *Management and Organization Review, 1*(3), 381-410. doi: 10.1111/j.1740-8784.2005.0020a.x

China Development Research Foundation. (2014). *Demographic developments in china*: Routledge.

CIA. (2018). Retrieved March 2018 https://www.cia.gov/library/publications/the-world-factbook/rankorder/2078rank.html

Customs, General Administration of. (2018). *China customs statistics* Retrieved from http://english.customs.gov.cn/.

Deng, Ping. (2004). Outward investment by chinese mncs: Motivations and implications. *Business Horizons, 47*(3), 8-16. doi: 10.1016/s0007-6813 (04)00023-0

Desvaux, Georges, Wang, Michael, & Xu, David. (2004). Spurring performance in china's state-owned enterprises. *McKinsey Quarterly, 4*, 96-106.

Elliott, Douglas, Kroeber, Arthur, & Qiao, Yu. (2015). Shadow banking in china: A primer. *Brookings Institution, 13*.

Fan, Joseph, Morck, Randall, & Yeung, Bernard. (2011). Capitalizing china: National Bureau of Economic Research.

Farh, Jiing-Lih, Earley, P. Christopher, & Lin, Shu-Chi. (1997). Impetus for action: A cultural analysis of justice and organizational citizenship behavior in chinese society. *Administrative Science Quarterly, 42*(3), 421-444. doi: 10.2307/2393733

Globerman, Steven, & Shapiro, Daniel. (2009). Economic and strategic considerations surrounding chinese fdi in the united states. *Asia Pacific Journal of Management, 26*(1), 163-183. doi: 10.1007/s10490-008-9112-5

Hall, Peter A, & Soskice, David W. (2001). *Varieties of capitalism: The institutional foundations of comparative advantage* (Vol. 8): Wiley Online Library.

Harutyunyan, Artak, Massara, Mr Alexander, Ugazio, Giovanni, Amidzic, Goran, & Walton, Richard. (2015). *Shedding light on shadow banking*: International Monetary Fund.

Johnson, Simon, McMillan, John, & Woodruff, Christopher. (2002). Property rights and finance: National Bureau of Economic Research.

Khanna, Tarun, & Palepu, Krishna. (1997). Why focused strategies may be wrong for emerging markets. *Harvard business review, 75*, 41-54.

Khanna, Tarun, & Palepu, Krishna. (2000). The future of business groups in emerging markets: Long-run evidence from chile. *The Academy of Management Journal, 43*(3), 268-285. doi: 10.2307/1556395

Kuijs, Louis. (2006). *How will china's saving-investment balance evolve?* World Bank, East Asia and Pacific Region, Porverty Reduction and Economic Management Sector Dept.

Lei, Angela Xuying. (2012). *Essays on investment, financing, and institutions in china.* (PhD), The London School of Economics and Political Science.

Li, Hongbin, & Zhou, Li-An. (2005). Political turnover and economic performance: The incentive role of personnel control in china. *Journal of public economics, 89*(9), 1743-1762.

Li, Stan Xiao, Yao, Xiaotao, Sue Chan, Christina, & Xi, Youmin. (2011). Where do social ties come from: Institutional framework and governmental tie distribution among chinese managers. *Management and Organization Review, 7*(1), 97-124.

Li, Tong. (2014). Shadow banking in china: Expanding scale, evolving structure. *Journal of Financial Economic Policy, 6*(3), 198-211.

Liao, Chun. (2008). *The governance structures of chinese firms in the varieties of business systems of contemporary market economies.* Freie Universität Berlin.

Lin, Justin Yifu, Cai, Fang, & Li, Zhou. (2003). *The china miracle: Development strategy and economic reform*: Chinese University Press.

Lin, Nan. (2011). Capitalism in china: A centrally managed capitalism (cmc) and its future. *Management and Organization Review, 7*(1), 63-96. doi: 10.1111/j.1740-8784.2010.00203.x

Lin, Z Jun, & Liu, Ming. (2009). The impact of corporate governance on auditor choice: Evidence from china. *Journal of International Accounting, Auditing and Taxation, 18*(1), 44-59.

Liu, Hong, & Li, Kequan. (2002). Strategic implications of emerging chinese multinationals:: The haier case study. *European Management Journal, 20*(6), 699-706. doi: 10.1016/s0263-2373(02)00119-6

Liu, Yipeng, & Woywode, Michael. (2012). Chinese m&a in germany. In Alon, Ilan, Fetscherin, Marc & Gugler, Philippe (Eds.), *Chinese international investments* (pp. 212).

Lundvall, Bengt-Åke. (2010). *National systems of innovation: Toward a theory of innovation and interactive learning* (Vol. 2): Anthem Press.

Luo, Yadong, Xue, Qiuzhi, & Han, Binjie. (2010). How emerging market governments promote outward fdi: Experience from china. *Journal of World Business, 45*(1), 68-79. doi: 10.1016/j.jwb.2009.04.003

Merryman, John Henry. (2007). *The civil law tradition: An introduction to the legal systems of europe and latin america*: Stanford University Press.

MOFCOM. (2014, September 12, 2014). China's outbound fdi 2013.

Montinola, Gabriella, Qian, Yingyi, & Weingast, Barry R. (1995). Federalism, chinese style: The political basis for economic success in china. *World Politics, 48*(01), 50-81.

Nichols, Theo, & Zhao, Wei. (2010). Disaffection with trade unions in china: Some evidence from soes in the auto industry. *Industrial Relations Journal, 41*(1), 19-33. doi: 10.1111/j.1468-2338.2009.00551.x

Ning, Lutao, & Sutherland, Dylan. (2012). Internationalization of china's private-sector mnes: An analysis of the motivations for foreign affiliate formation. *Thunderbird International Business Review, 54*(2), 169-182. doi: 10.1002/tie.21449

Nolan, P. (2001). *China and the global economy: National champions, industrial policy, and the big business revolution*: Palgrave.

North, Douglass C. (1990). *Institutions, institutional change and economic performance*: Cambridge university press.

OECD. (2009). *Oecd working group on privatisation and corporate governance of state owned assets*. Retrieved from http://www.oecd.org/corporate/ca/corporategovernanceofstate-ownedenterprises/42095493.pdf.

OECD. (2017). Oecd business and finance outlook 2017 highlights

OECD. (2018). Fdi in numbers. Retrieved March 2018 https://data.oecd.org/fdi/fdi-flows.htm#indicator-chart

Oi, Jean C. (1995). The role of the local state in china's transitional economy. *The China Quarterly, 144*, 1132-1149. doi: doi:10.1017/S0305741000004768

PBC. (2015). Annual report 2014. Retrieved October 10, 2015, from http://www.pbc.gov.cn/eportal/fileDir/image_public/UserFiles/english/upload/File/20146.15.pdf

Peerenboom, Randall. (2001). Globalization, path dependency and the limits of law: Administrative law reform and rule of law in the people's republic of china. *Berkeley Journal of International Law, 19*(2), 161.

Peng, Mike W. (2003). Institutional transitions and strategic choices. *Academy of management review, 28*(2), 275-296.

Peng, Mike W., & Heath, Peggy Sue. (1996). The growth of the firm in planned economies in transition: Institutions, organizations, and strategic choice. *Academy of management review, 21*(2), 492-528.

Peng, Mike W., & Luo, Yadong. (2000). Managerial ties and firm performance in a transition economy: The nature of a micro-macro link. *Academy of management journal, 43*(3), 486-501.

Ramamurti, Ravi, & Singh, Jitendra V. (2009). *Emerging multinationals in emerging markets*: Cambridge University Press.

Ravallion, Martin, & Chen, Shaohua. (2007). China's (uneven) progress against poverty. *Journal of development economics, 82*(1), 1-42.

Redding, Gordon, & Witt, Michael A. (2007). *The future of chinese capitalism: Choices and chances*: Oxford University Press.

Ren, Bing, Liang, Hao, & Zheng, Ying. (2012). An institutional perspective and the role of the state for chinese ofdi. In Alon, Ilan, Fetscherin, Marc & Gugler, Philippe (Eds.), *Chinese international investments* (pp. 11-37): Palgrave Macmillan.

Reuters. (2018). China social security fund's 2017 annual returns at more than 9 pct.

Rosen, Daniel H., & Hanemann, Thilo. (2011). An american open door? Maximizing the benefits of chinese foreigner direct investment. Asian Society.

SAFE. (2018). Template on international reserves and foreign currency liquidity.

Schlevogt, Kai-Alexander. (2001). The distinctive structure of Chinese private enterprises: State versus private sector. *Asia Pacific business review, 7*(3), 1-33.

Schüler-Zhou, Yun, Schüller, Margot, & Brod, Magnus. (2011). Push and pull factors for chinese ofdi in europe. In Alon, Ilan, Fetscherin, Marc & Gugler, Philippe (Eds.), *Chinese international investments* (pp. 157).

Scott, W Richard. (2002). The changing world of chinese enterprise: An institutional perspective *The management of enterprises in the people's republic of china* (pp. 59-78): Springer.

Tam, On Kit. (2004). Financing the private sector. *China's third economic transformation: The rise of the private economy*, 118-132.

Teece, David J, Pisano, Gary, & Shuen, Amy. (1997). Dynamic capabilities and strategic management.

The World Bank. (2015). Gdp per capita (current us$). Retrieved February 5th, 2015, 2015, from http://data.worldbank.org/indicator/NY.GDP.PCAP.CD

Thompson, James D. (1967). Organizations in action: Social science bases of administration. *Organizations in action: Social science bases of administration*.

Torres de Oliveira, Rui, & Figueira, Sandra. (2018). The specificities of interviewing in china. *Qualitative Market Research: An International Journal, 21*(1), 118-134.

Torres de Oliveira, Rui, & Rotting, Daniel. (2018). Chinese acquisitions of developed market firms: Home semi-formal institutions and a supportive partnering approach. *Journal of Business Research forthcoming*.

Torres Oliveira, Rui, Menzies, Jane, Borgia, Daniel, & Figueira, Sandra. (2017). Outward foreign direct investment from emerging countries: Theoretical extension and evidence from china. *The International Trade Journal, 31*(5), 402-428.

Transparency International, Corruption Perceptions Index Report. (2014). Corruption perceptions index report. Retrieved July 8, 2015 https://www.transparency.org/cpi2014/results

Walton, Julie. (2008). Managing government affairs. *China Business Review, 35*(5), 46-49.

Whitley, Richard. (1992). *Business systems in east asia: Firms, markets and societies* (Vol. 1): SAGE Publications Limited.

Whitley, Richard. (1999). *Divergent capitalisms: The social structuring and change of business systems*: Oxford University Press, USA.

Williamson, Oliver E. (1979). Transaction-cost economics: The governance of contractual relations. *Journal of law and economics*, 233-261.

Xinhua. (2017). China's sovereign wealth fund hits 900 bln usd.

Yang, Dali L. (2004). *Remaking the chinese leviathan: Market transition and the politics of governance in china*: Stanford University Press.

Zhang, Jianjun, & Keh, Hean Tat. (2010). Interorganizational exchanges in china: Organizational forms and governance mechanisms. *Management and Organization Review, 6*(1), 123-147. doi: 10.1111/j.1740-8784.2009.00148.x

Zhang, Xiaobo. (2006). Fiscal decentralization and political centralization in china: Implications for growth and inequality. *Journal of Comparative Economics, 34*(4), 713-726. doi: http://dx.doi.org/10.1016/j.jce.2006.08.006

Zhou, Kevin Zheng, Poppo, Laura, & Yang, Zhilin. (2008). Relational ties or customized contracts? An examination of alternative governance choices in china. *Journal of International Business Studies, 39*(3), 526-534.

Chapter 3

Impact of Technology on the Chinese Economy and Workforce

By Jorge Diaz-Herrera

Since the dawn of the industrial age, a recurrent fear is that technological change will create mass unemployment. Neoclassical economists, however, predicted this would not happen because people would find other jobs, albeit possibly after a long period of painful adjustment. There is no denying that technological change nowadays has accelerated, potentially leading to deeper and more profound dislocations.

Digital technologies, such as advanced cyberinfrastructure, deep learning, and artificial intelligence (AI), may have both positive and negative effects on a workforce. This process is likely to displace some workers from existing roles, but technology also creates new markets for innovative products and services, increasing demands for workers with digital skills.

China is not immune to these global technological developments, which could increase competitiveness and enable Chinese firms to expand their labor force. Or, because of automation, it might be labor-saving, thereby enabling Chinese firms to produce more output with fewer employees. More than likely, it will be a combination of both. New types of jobs for designing, building, and servicing new manufacturing machines will be created and they will also displace traditional manufacturing jobs.

China has embraced digital technologies, particularly the Internet, in all sectors of the economy. The country's major economic initiatives attest to this observation.

- Internet Plus: China seeks to drive economic growth by integrating Internet technologies with manufacturing and business.
- Made in China 2025: China wants to become a modern, world manufacturing power, adding cyber connectivity and intelligence to manufacturing.
- Belt and Road (B&R): China is promoting an orderly and free flow of economic factors, highly efficient allocation of resources, and deep integration of markets by enhancing physical connectivity of Asia, Europe, and Africa and their adjacent seas.

In this chapter we will cover aspects of these three major initiatives. We begin, however, with a brief summary of the global development of high tech in the last six decades or so, and conclude with a discussion on its impact on the workforce of the future, world-wide and specifically in China.

Industrial Revolutions and the Advent of the Digital Era

The speed of technological change is exponential. See Figure 1.The Neolithic Revolution saw the invention of farming, and it was not until thousands of years later (not shown in the figure) that we saw the next revolution: the First Industrial Revolution. In the 1780s, industrial

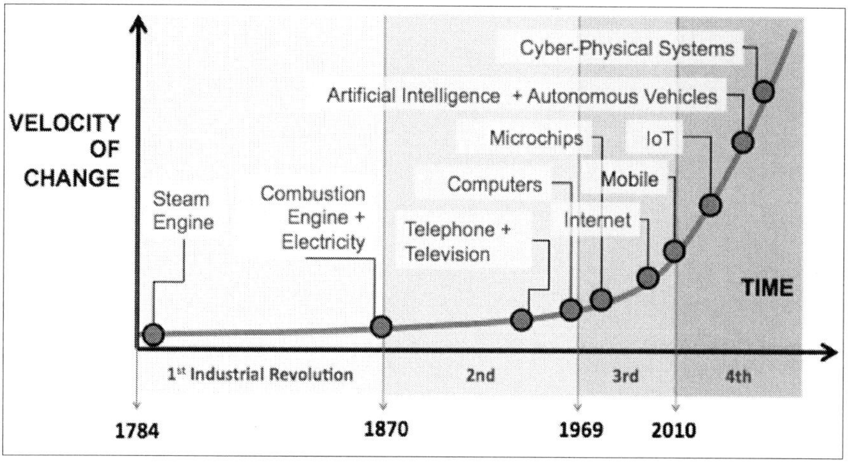

Figure 1: The Exponential Speed of Technological Change (adapted with permission from McGowan, 2018)

manufacturing used water and steam power to mechanize production. The Second Industrial Revolution, 100 years later, used electric power to create mass production and the combustion engine to create mobility. The Third Industrial Revolution, 60 years later, used electronics and communication technology and the first computers to automate the office through information systems, and from the 1990s to the present this progress has accelerated rapidly, leading to the fourth industrial revolution, also known as the Second Machine Age (Brynjolfsson, 2014). The Fourth Industrial Revolution or Industry 4.0, building on the Third, is characterized by a fusion of technologies blurring the lines between physical, digital, and biological spheres into cyber-physical systems.

It took roughly 40 years from the 1940s to the 1980s (see Figure 2) to replace the one-computer-many-users concept of the (1) *central computer* or *mainframe* with the (2) *personal computer*, or one-computer-one-user concept. Fewer than 20 years after that, (3) *smart phones* and cards appeared, followed very quickly by ubiquitous (4) *embedded computers* and (5) *intelligent environments* that allow the

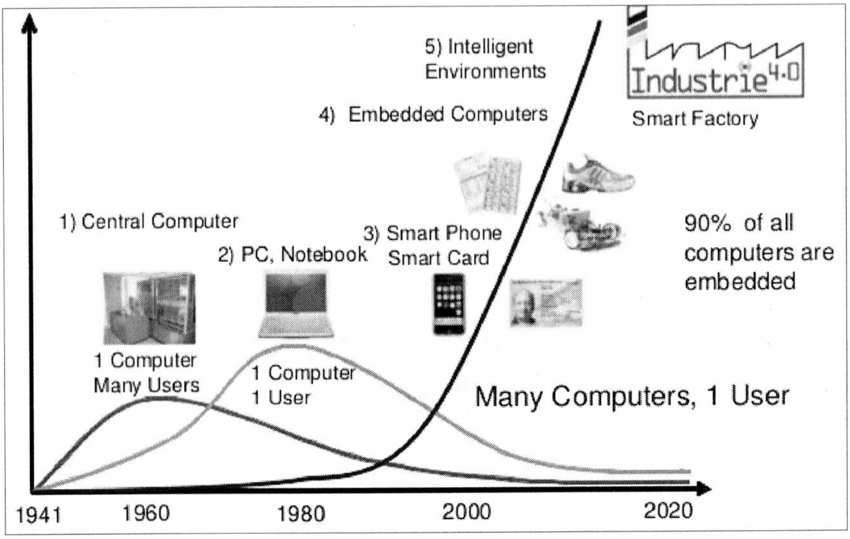

Figure 2: Digital Computer Evolution (based on Abrahart, 2014)

many-computers-one-user paradigm of today.

Computer technology 50 years ago was expensive and very complicated, requiring specialized training for mastering arcane computer logic and programming languages. Since the 1960s, major milestones in the development of computational machinery range from (a) mainframes, mini computers, and personal computers to (b) the Internet, mobile access devices, and the cloud. The last three in combination — Internet and the web, new multi-modal, mobile connecting devices, and the cloud — are having a far greater impact and adoption speed than any of the previous technologies. Computers are constantly improving and doing new tasks.

All of this is being generated at a breakneck pace, faster than anything we have seen before and will continue to accelerate. We will continue to witness an increase in the number, shapes, and sizes of digital devices, as well as an exponential increase in local and global connectivity. This is why this fourth industrial revolution has been termed the hyper-digital, Industry 4.0 revolution.

Industry 4.0 Revolution

Astonishing digital technological progress is transforming everything in the world and all aspects of our daily lives, touching every human endeavor, and drastically changing both the economy and the nature of work. We are witnessing a hyper-digital technological revolution that is fundamentally altering the way we live, work, and relate to one another. This transformation is unlike anything humankind has experienced before. Technological improvements have transformed early large machines into compact devices that enable, mediate, support, and organize our lives. The possibilities of billions of people connected by mobile devices, with unprecedented processing power, storage capacity, and access to knowledge, are unlimited. Already, artificial intelligence is all around us, from self-driving cars and drones to virtual assistants and software that translates or invests.

This hyper-digital revolution has led to unprecedented emergent businesses, and entirely new behavioral and industrial intelligence. The information economy — the *new economy* — brought about by these unprecedented advances in digital revolution, has superseded the industrial economy of the past two-and-a-half centuries. We live in a world in which information and ideas "establish economic value chains and encourage further technological innovation and diffusion of knowledge," (Peters, 2009) causing an unprecedented reallocation of wealth and income. Several industries have been shaken to their core, driving some companies out of business. (Andreessen, 2011) For example, Facebook, with less than 15,000 employees, has 10 times more value than Kodak ever had — in a fraction of the time it took Kodak to become a world economic power — and Facebook has at least 10 billionaires each with 10 times more money than George Eastman, the founder of Kodak and the richest man in the world during his time, ever had. Twitter has less than 4,000 employees world-wide.

If physical infrastructure, such as roads, ports, and airports, is required by an industrial economy, then we can say that *cyberinfrastructure* is that required by an information economy, and it refers to infrastructure based upon distributed computing and information and communication technologies. Industry 4.0 is the move toward a cyberinfrastructure populated with advanced industrial devices, systems, and services, to deliver less costly, more efficient use of assets and increase businesses values. These outcomes are achieved by analyzing data to improve decision-making about the use of resources. Digital solutions are linking the physical world via the Internet of Things (IoT), by the combination of Internet, mobile devices, cloud computing, embedded sensors, and a plethora of other sources delivering data continuously, resulting in a world of cyber-physical systems everywhere but most especially on the shop floor.

Impact on the Labor Force

Like previous industrial revolutions, Industry 4.0 heralds a new stage in industrial manufacturing that will disrupt existing markets and competition and will demand new requirements of businesses' staff. It has the potential to raise global income levels and improve the quality of life for populations around the world. At the same time, as the economists Erik Brynjolfsson and Andrew McAfee have pointed out [*op. cit.*], the revolution could yield greater inequality, particularly in its potential to disrupt labor markets.

The world of work is changing dramatically and people need to be prepared for jobs requiring digital capability. Digital technologies change rapidly, but organizations and people's skills aren't keeping pace. As a result, millions of people are being left behind. It is predicted that in the not too distant future, half of today's jobs will change or disappear altogether.

Back-of-the-envelope calculations suggest that, worldwide, technological change could easily lead to the loss of 5-10 million jobs each year. An Australian agency recently reported that "sixty percent of Australian students are training for jobs that will not exist in the future or will be transformed by automation," indicating that 44 percent of jobs will be automated in the next 10 years.[1] Backing up this statement, a 2013 study by Oxford University predicted that 47 percent of today's jobs will be automated in the next two decades.[2] Davidson projected that 65 percent of U.S. students in K-12 schools today will work in jobs that do not currently exist. (Davidson, 2011) According to research at Gartner one-third of all jobs will be converted into software, robots, and smart machines by as early as 2025.[3] As the advent of cheap smartphones fuels a boom in Internet access, online purchases will likely eliminate a vast number of retail jobs.

These technological advances diminish the demand for previously important types of labor. The effect is increased demand for more skilled labor while decreasing demand for less skilled labor. Non-routine cognitive jobs and non-routine manual jobs (e.g., hair dressing) will be increasing, providing more opportunities for creative and interactive work, with less need for work doing boring, repetitive tasks that can be automated. In the future, people will probably be paid depending on how well they work with robots. Marc Andreessen, the co-creator of the Netscape web browser, likes to say, "In the future there will be two kinds of jobs: those that involve telling computers what to do, and those that involve being told what to do by computers."[4]

In a nutshell, the jobs of the future belong to those who are more than just critical thinkers — they must also be digital thinkers.

Industry 4.0 and China's Response

While the Chinese manufacturing sector has yet to embrace fully

---

1. ABC News on August 23, 2015. http://www.abc.net.au/news/2015-08-24/next-generation-chasing-dying-careers/6720528

2. http://www.oxfordmartin.ox.ac.uk/downloads/academic/The_Future_of_Employment.pdf

3.http://www.gartner.com/binaries/content/assets/events/keywords/symposium/sym25/gartner-sym24-executive-report2.pdf

4. In "What is code?" http://www.economist.com/blogs/economist-explains/2015/09/economist-explains-3

industrial automation, forward-thinking businesses and players are positioning themselves to take advantage of the potential growth of Industry 4.0. Indeed, China is transitioning from the world's factory to a provider of quality information products, and high-end technology and services.

Service industries dealing with IT, software, accounting, finance, marketing, and customer management are expected to grow and absorb a substantial number of professionals. This has led to greater demand for high-skilled labor, which is in short supply in China. For example, data from the Ministry of Human Resources and Social Security shows that skilled workers account for only about 19 percent of the entire workforce, with highly skilled workers constituting only five percent.

China's rise in technology development is no accident. This is well understood: Chinese leaders have seen it as integral to economic growth, and have taken steps to develop China's cyberinfrastructure.

The Internet Plus

Until recently, China's Internet has been largely consumer-focused, but that is about to change with the central government emphasis on the Internet penetrating across many sectors of the economy. Successive Chinese plans are quite focused on technology development. In the twelfth five-year plan (2011-15), China listed the promotion of scientific and technological progress and innovation as a major tool for supporting strategic economic restructuring. The plan targeted the intelligent manufacturing equipment industry. Technology development and innovation also figure prominently in the current thirteenth five-year plan (2016-20). The 13th plan has set a target of establishing a complete system and industry chain for intelligent manufacturing equipment with a total market value of more than RMB 300 billion. (Veugelers, 2017)

On March 5, 2015, Premier Li Keqiang unveiled the *Internet Plus* plan "to integrate mobile Internet, cloud computing big data, and the

Internet of Things with modern manufacturing, to encourage the healthy development of e-commerce, industrial networks, and Internet banking, and to get Internet-based companies to increase their presence in the international market to boost a decelerating economy through advanced digitalization."[5] Premier Li also mentioned the policy goals of network convergence, accelerating fiber optic network construction, improving broadband speed, and promoting information consumption. To this "guidance," a package of US $4.4 billion is added to invest in startups and technologies.

Cyberinfrastructure Development

The effort involves adding connectivity and intelligence to manufacturing equipment and factories, to improve overall flexibility and efficiency. Inspired by Germany's automation initiative launched in 2011 and by similar efforts to promote more advanced manufacturing in the USA, China is in the midst of a digital revolution, making steady progress in the "Internet economy."

In 2016, China overtook the U.S. in the latest Top 500 ranking of supercomputers by a margin of 202 to 143 (six months earlier, the U.S. led with 169 systems to China's 160), representing the largest number of Chinese systems on the list and the lowest number of U.S. systems in 25 years. China's Sunway TaihuLight and Tianhe-2 were ranked first and second on the list as the fastest supercomputers in the world.

As of June 2017, there were 3.89 billion Internet users around the world, of which 751 million were in China, the most of any country worldwide. Some five billion daily searches are made through Baidu, and hundreds of millions communicate via WeChat, Tencent's mobile messaging app. The U.S. may lead the world in tech research, but China has managed to build better wireless infrastructure that gives people Internet access in more places. Chinese telecommunications companies

5. The State Council, the People's Republic of China. http://english.gov.cn/2016special/internetplus/

have an easier time building cellular towers. To build towers in the U.S., companies need approval from multiple government agencies. China's government, in contrast, allows companies to build cell towers quickly, providing the country with 10 times as many towers than in the U.S. (Vanjan, 2017)

In 2013, China experienced US $300 billion in e-tailing (online retailing) sales. In 2010, China's Internet economy stood at 3.3 percent of its GDP, lagging behind most advanced economies. By 2013, its iGDP had reached 4.4 percent, moving China into the ranks of the global leaders (overtaking the U.S., Germany, and France, only behind the UK, Korea, and Japan). China's digital economy reached 22.58 trillion yuan ($3.4 trillion) in 2016, ranking second globally and accounting for 30.3 percent of the national GDP.[6]

The Internet of Things has the capability of reducing supply-chain costs helping increase manufacturing.

As we can see, the Internet is already generating enormous economic value in China. As the country transitions from sustained to sustainable economic growth, China's Internet has given rise to a dynamic technology sector, thriving social networks, and the world's largest e-tailing market. But the Web is just beginning to penetrate many Chinese businesses — and the most sweeping changes are yet to come.

The Internet will not only be a source of much-needed momentum for China in the years ahead, but it will also change the very nature of growth. The aim is to promote innovation-driven development and upgrade China from being a "big industrial country" to a "powerful industrial country."

The Internet is fueling the ongoing process of moving China's industry from less productive to more innovative and technologically advanced business models. Indeed, much of the Internet's impact will likely come in the form of productivity gains. As individual companies

---

6. China's digital economy accounts for 30% of 2016 GDP: Report. *China Daily*, December 5, 2017.

step up their adoption of Web technologies, they will streamline their operations, from product development and supply chain management to sales, marketing, and customer interactions.

The economy's shift toward the Internet will entail some risks and disruptions, but it can ultimately support China's goal of creating a more sustainable model for economic growth (Woetzel, 2014): The Internet's contribution to China's productivity growth could be up to 22% by 2025. The potential savings in healthcare expenditures can reach RMB 610 billion by 2025. The expected annual GDP would be RMB 10 trillion (equivalent in size to Australia's 2014 GDP), based on productivity, innovation, and consumption through the Internet.

The Internet creates information transparency that improves investment decisions so that capital can be better allocated. The Internet can spur skill upgrades within the workforce and create consumer surplus by lowering prices, making information more widely available, and enabling a multitude of new conveniences. The Internet provides a platform for millions of daily online transactions and communications that make a significant contribution to individual economies. The Internet intensifies competition allowing the most efficient enterprises to win out more quickly. For example, farmers can use their mobile phones to sell their products online, and small businesses can achieve similar "success in the world" by embracing technology.

Alibaba's long-term e-commerce goal is to create 100 million jobs across the world by 2036. Over the same time period, it is expected that it will become a true global brand with a user base to quintuple to a staggering two billion users.

Recently, one buzzword that has dominated China's tech scene is *xin ling shou,* which translates into "New Retail," blending offline to online (O2O) by digitizing and automating e-commerce. (Ambler, 2017) Many think that New Retail is "online going offline." The world's e-commerce giants, Amazon and Alibaba, have both been making aggressive purchases of offline supermarkets like Whole Foods, in the

U.S., and Intime, a Chinese mall operator.[7] Amazon is also experimenting with an unmanned convenience store Amazon's Go, and Alibaba has been developing its own futuristic offline supermarket, Hema, showing how online and offline shopping are merged into a seamless "New Retail" experience.[8] This is certainly one aspect of New Retail: using technology to digitize and automate offline stores, where the vast majority of commercial activities still take place (e-commerce only takes up around 8% of all commercial transaction volume in the US and 15% in China). Online sales of physical goods, one of China's major new business patterns, rose 28.6 percent to 2.37 trillion yuan (about $350 billion), accounting for 13.8 percent of the country's total retail sales.[9]

Made in China 2025

A more comprehensive effort to upgrade China's manufacturing base is already underway, under a new program announced in May 2015 that aims to make China an innovative and green "world manufacturing power" by 2025. (Kennedy, 2015) The plan has a 10-year goal that emphasizes innovation. Looking ahead to 2049, coinciding with the 100th anniversary of the communist revolution, the Chinese Government's long term plan is to transform China into a leading manufacturing power to rival Germany, Japan, and the USA. The aim of the plan is to turn the country into a global leader in manufacturing of high-tech industries such as automotive, aviation, robotics, medical devices, and information technology. Ultimately, this would lead to technological catch-up and import substitution in sectors crucial for long-term growth.

---

7. https://techcrunch.com/2017/01/10/alibaba-intime-2-6-billion/
8. http://www.alizila.com/video/take-tour-hema-supermarket-experience-new-retail/
9. China Daily: 07-18-2017

The Made in China 2025 strategy and the national scientific and technological innovation plan are aimed at strengthening the country's innovation capabilities. China is seeding innovation and entrepreneurship by piling cash into the *new economy*. A structural move from traditional manufacturing to modern drivers of growth in consumer, service-led technology, and the breaking up of state-owned-enterprises to boost private sector competitiveness. The central government has handpicked areas such as artificial intelligence, robotics, and clean energy, among others, as priorities of the initiative.

The high-tech and equipment manufacturing sectors are leading China's industrial growth, with year-over-year output increases of 13.1 percent and 11.5 percent in the first half, respectively, compared with a 6.9 percent rise in overall output. In the first six months of 2017, up to 45.6 percent of the total industrial investment went into technological improvement, paving way for future industrial upgrades.

Belt and Road

The third major economic initiative, introduced by President Xi Jinping in 2013, is the Belt and Road (B&R). A more conventional trade effort, this initiative covers the "*New*" *Silk Road* connecting China overland and the "*Maritime*" *Silk Road* that links it to countries by sea. Thus:

- Linking China to Europe through Central Asia and Russia
- Connecting China with the Middle East through Central Asia
- Bringing together China and Southeast Asia, South Asia and the Indian Ocean.

Focusing on the above routes, the project takes advantage of international transport routes as well as core cities and key ports by building six international economic cooperation corridors. These have been identified as the New Eurasia Land Bridge, China-Mongolia-

Russia, China-Central Asia-West Asia, China-Indochina Peninsula, China-Pakistan, and Bangladesh-China-India-Myanmar.

India remains sensitive about the manner in which China's B&R initiative is being pursued in its neighborhood, which includes Kashmir. (Kantha, 2017) China is redeveloping the port of Gwadar in Pakistan, a $57 billion project that connects Pakistan to western China and includes highway upgrades, new railways and rail stations, and a major fiber optics link. India is responding with cyberinfrastructure, banking on its Global Cloud Xchange by building a submarine fibre-optic cable system spanning 16,650 km from Hong Kong to Italy.[10]

All these initiatives have major consequences for the Chinese labor market and the development for tomorrow's workforce. It will decrease the need for low-skill manufacturing workers while requiring higher levels of education.

Impact on the Chinese Workforce

The Internet is already reshaping China's labor market, and its impact is likely to grow over time. Robotics is also having an impact in the manufacturing sector of China, and it is estimated that China will account for more than one-third of all industrial robots installed worldwide by 2018.[11] Companies will need fewer workers to perform routine activities that can be replaced by technology. Some jobs will be lost while others will change and new ones created.

The challenge is that labor costs are rising, supply and demand of labor is dangerously skewed, and vocational training is unable to fill the breach fast enough. This has resulted in increased skills mismatches in the Chinese labor market, facing an acute skills shortfall along with the

---

10. http://globalcloudxchange.com/media-center/releases/2018/01/rcoms-global-cloud-xchange-unveils-strategic-plan-for-2018-with-cloud-fiber-initiative-at-the-core/

11. International Federation of Robotics. https://ifr.org/

challenges of an aging population and a shrinking labor force — more accurately the quality of labor and the speed of training.

> *Aging labor workforce:* In the past, China's workforce has been a main driver of the country's economic success, but China is currently facing a fast-dwindling working-age population. The labor force peaked at 925 million in 2011 and has been in decline ever since. By 2050, the working-age population is expected to shrink by 20 percent from the 2011 peak, to just 700 million.

> *Rapidly rising labor costs:* Dramatic increases in labor costs is pressuring many manufacturers to move operations to lower-cost countries (e.g., Vietnam) or look at ways in which they can reduce their dependency on manual labor. At the same time, Chinese manufacturers are under pressure to increase labor productivity to stay competitive.

The workforce is the engine that needs to be re-tuned to ensure that China's growth does not grind to a halt. Chinese factory managers are already looking for opportunities to replace employees with robots. China intends to fully implement automation in production processes — to shift the manufacturing focus toward technology-intensive industries by promoting the use of robotics. As manufacturers look for different solutions to continue to improve labor productivity, the advantages offered by industrial robotics will be on their radar. Companies embracing Web, cloud, and mobile technologies become more efficient thus increasing productivity.

To meet the need of Internet Plus development and other strategic economic directions, China will need to train new kind of workers, and should make a better use of foreign talent.

Nevertheless, penetration rates of industrial automation in China currently lag behind other developed markets, but probably not for long.

The number of robots per worker in China is far lower than in many industrially advanced countries, such as compared to Korea, Japan, Germany, and the United States. However, this is an indication of a huge potential for growth. China will soon become not only an important market for more advanced robotics technology, but possibly a producer of more advanced robot systems itself.

Tianran Wang, a member of the Chinese Academy of Engineering and an expert on industrial automation, writing about China's manufacturing industry indicated that it lagged behind those of other nations and would need a major technological overhaul. (Wang, 2010) Mr. Wang emphasizes that the challenge will be figuring out which tasks can be automated most effectively, and how machines and humans can share the workload. "Not all labor-intensive industry can be automated, we need Hybrid automation." (We talk about this augmented, symbiotic relationship man-machine later in this chapter.) A priority is to develop more flexible systems with advanced sensing and finding better ways for robots to toil effectively and safely alongside with humans. But a fact remains that digital machines keep getting better at performing cognitive tasks.

From 2014 to 2015, sales of industrial robots worldwide rose by 12 percent, fielding 250,000 units. (Pooler, 2016) The scale and importance of China's robot ambitions were made clear when Vice President Li Yuanchao appeared at the country's first major robotics conference in Beijing in 2015. Li delivered a message from President Xi Jinping congratulating the organizers for the effort. In China, "co-bots" — machines that can work in factories safely alongside human beings — are upending its manufacturing sector, becoming more productive with fewer workers.

Looking ahead, it is the combination of connected machines and big data analytics with skilled humans that will cut manufacturing and service costs. By 2020, it is predicted that Internet-connected (smart) objects will grow to 50 billion. (Evans, 2011; Caterpillar, 2015) The greatest benefits delivered by the IoT will be applications that capture and analyze the vast amount of data generated by automated systems. For those players wanting to take advantage of the opportunities from a rapidly automating Chinese manufacturing sector, *an effective IoT strategy is crucial*,[12] and this requires advanced training and education. Although computers are becoming exponentially smarter each day, we must also focus on areas where people will outperform the most advanced "intelligent" machines, i.e., creative work.

Worldwide, some increase in unemployment as a result of more rapid technological change is certainly likely, especially in places like Europe, where a plethora of rigidities inhibit smooth adjustment, and in China, due to high numbers of unskilled workers.

As China's economy transitions and evolves toward a more service-driven model, the country's education system needs to ensure that it keeps pace with this change and equips its workforce with the skills required by the market. Despite tremendous reforms, the country's skills mismatch continues to challenge the vitality of the workforce and the success of its new innovation-driven growth model. The skills of college graduates — including those returning from overseas — typically do not match market demand. These graduates have unrealistic career expectations with resultant low job satisfaction, while job-training opportunities are lacking.

A fundamental problem is that school programs, courses and enrollments are determined by higher educational institutions without a proper consideration of market demand.

This happened in previous generations and people turned to education to maneuver the requirements of a *new economy* brought about by technology advancements. As in any nation, better education is critical to creating a more productive workforce. Historically, education has played a role in elevating people to the next level of economic development. In the U.S., college-educated workers earn

12. https://www.brinc.io/

considerably more than individuals with just a high school diploma; in other words, the difference between obtaining a middle-income job vs. a lower income job is determined by the individual's educational level. Since 1980, the number of U.S. jobs that require more than high school education has grown by 68 percent. This dynamic is even more prevalent in today, the age of intelligent machines, and the "learning curve" is getting steeper. In fact, advanced degrees command the most value in the workplace today.

At first blush, China may seem to be in an enviable position. It is churning out science, technology, engineering and math talent at a rate far surpassing that of Europe and the United States. A recent Accenture study of analytics talent revealed that China will produce a surplus of key people with skills in statistical and quantitative analysis.[13]

But China suffers from its own *talent mismatch*. Too many Chinese graduate from universities with only theoretical knowledge, and too few have the vocational skills that appeal to employers. The consequences are illustrated by the ratio of job vacancies to applicants, which increased from 0.7 to 1.1 between 2006 and 2011. In other words, by 2011, there were more jobs available than people with the skills to fill them.

Experiential learning, a tradition in many colleges and Universities in the U.S., Germany, and other European countries, is a model that integrates what is learned in the classroom with real-world experiences. Typically, in mainly technical institutions, students engage in internships, co-ops, work-study jobs, global experiences, undergraduate industry-led research. Keuka College, a liberal arts institution, introduced experiential learning formally in its curriculum in 1942 with their trade-marked, Field Period®. The College was given the opportunity to introduce this model in China 2002, through partnerships with Yunnan University of Finance and Economics, Tianjin University

---

13. https://www.accenture.com/au-en/insight-outlook-beyond-capital-and-labor-china-productivity-frontier

of Science and Technology, and Jemei University, and under the leadership of Dr. Michael Hwang and his writings in career management. (Hwang, 2007)

To sum up, the labor supply in China suffers from two serious structural problems: *low-skilled workers not ready for automation and 'intelligent' production while the skills of 'high-skill' workers are not what firms really need.* With the development of information technology, production processes are changing together with the level of skills required. Well-educated university graduates and overseas returnees do not, in general, meet the needs of the market.

Simply put, structural unemployment and worker groups vulnerable to unemployment are the result of the skills supply-and-demand gap. Analyses show that the three groups with the greatest risk of unemployment are migrant workers aged 16–29, college graduates aged 22–24, and the middle-aged and elderly aged 45-60. (Morgan, 2016) Enhancing the skill levels of these three groups is the key to reducing their unemployment risk and keeping China's unemployment rate low. Policy makers and business leaders will need to consider whether displaced workers have avenues for retraining and whether the education system is producing enough high-tech and specialized talent to meet the economy's future needs. Here are some recommendations:

> Grant universities greater autonomy, promote interaction between universities and enterprises, and encourage universities and industry to cultivate high-skill workers together, so that the educational institutions can better respond and adapt to market needs.
>
> Increase workers' access to vocational training and assist migrant workers in upgrading skills through government subsidy. As suggested by Premier Li Keqiang, "To enhance employment quality and the well-being of migrant workers and their families, migrant workers should be motivated to obtain

employment in sunrise economic sectors, sunrise industries, and sunrise business models through information consultation and skills training."

Establish a vocational education system with greater participation by businesses.

The emergence of a hyper-digital economy means that talent, culture, and organizational forms will have to be rethought. Our skills, organizations and institutions are lagging while technological advances keep moving ahead faster and faster.

In addition to being a key economic concern, inequality represents the greatest societal concern associated with the Fourth Industrial Revolution. The largest beneficiaries of innovation tend to be the providers of intellectual and physical capital — the innovators, shareholders, and investors — which explains the rising gap in wealth between those dependent on capital versus labor.

On the whole, there are three main effects that Industry 4.0, the Fourth Industrial Revolution, has on the economy: on customer expectations and product enhancement, on collaborative innovation, and on organizational forms. There is also an important impact on employment and workforce development.

Expectations and Product Enhancement

Although the computer revolution has brought substantial changes to the way we live, the population at large does not completely understand, for the most part, the real impact of this revolution, and what's more, it cannot begin to imagine the possibilities and what is yet to come. Indeed, a large portion of the world's population uses computers for everyday tasks, but most fail to benefit from the power of computation. They are limited to being passive consumers because they don't understand computers' technical underpinnings: *a universal problem for every citizen of this century is know how to get access to information and how to acquire skills to articulate and organize that information to solve today's problems effectively in the course of their professions*. This is because people can no longer thrive in a digitized world with a constant stream "big data," connectivity, and instant information flow.

Physical products and services can now be enhanced with digital capabilities that increase their value. New technologies make assets more durable and resilient, while data and analytics are transforming how they are maintained. The rapidly evolving 3D printing technology allows entrepreneurs to quickly produce prototypes and even test preferences of the market.

In the information economy, human creativity is the ultimate economic resource, where more than ever high-value soft skills, those so uniquely human, such as working productively in teams, critically thinking, and communicating to solve complex problems are in great demand.[14]

Expectations are changing about how learning experiences and formats should evolve to incorporate new behaviors and expectations from our digital lives. Changes in the labor economy have driven the rising expectation that individuals must keep themselves "up-skilled" to stay employed.

Collaborative Innovation

Anyone who is motivated to participate in innovation in this emerging Industry 4.0 era can do so without any formal technical training. Increases in access to digital tools by anyone is opening up innovation to all who, with a good education and a good idea, can use technology to solve the problem that needs to be solved. It's worth

---

14. Great Jobs Great Lives, the 2014 Gallup-Purdue Index Report. http://www.purdue.edu/newsroom/gallup/docs/GPI_overview.pdf

noticing that the evolution of technology and its rapidly declining cost have made possible the progress we are witnessing, at least in the U.S., of building commercially viable enterprises by individuals not versed on rocket science or technology. It is no longer the case that computers are so mysterious that only technical experts can understand their capabilities. A technical degree is not required anymore to thrive in many areas of today's information economy.

Entrepreneurship is always risky, but with new digital tools readily accessible, the possibilities of vanguard innovation is truly without limits. Given the plasticity of these tools, constrained only by our imagination, truly the sky is the limit. The advent of technology services, such as software as a service and platform as a service, which led to the cloud, together with prefabricated components, both hardware and software, are greatly reducing time to market and increasing innovation.

People anywhere in the world can take advantage of these developments. Truly, anyone can and will participate in the digital economy, and combine digital tools and services, many of which are totally free of charge and easily accessible through the Web, in new ways pioneering new and increased innovation.

Technology continues to improve, and there no is doubt that it will continue this path at greater pace. As this process continues, we can envision that innovation throughout the world will continue to increase, especially if one understands the basics of digital technology. Technical skills are important, but a technical education on its own will not automatically ensure employment in the Industry 4.0 economy. The emphasis should not be on teaching these skills exclusively.

The Role of a Liberal Arts Education

As technology offers ever more accessible toolbox, the 21st-century professional's differentiation is the very thing liberal arts programs instill. Skills gained through a liberal arts-based education will make graduates more agile and employable in today's and tomorrow's economy; although gaining fluency in tech tools is important within this context. We believe that the combination of liberal arts skills — such as working productively in teams, critically thinking, and effectively communicating to solve complex problems — with digital skills — such as analytics, systems thinking and coding — provides graduates with a more expansive skill set. These liberal arts skills have become *essential skills*, while digital skills are the *new literacy*.

Michael Staton (Staton, 2012) captured this idea well: "Many liberal arts colleges require a foreign language — not because they believe their history majors will land jobs in France or Mexico, and not because they are being trained as translators, but because they believe the skills learned in a new language create global citizens who are open to and comfortable with interacting in a multicultural, multilingual world. It's the same with the above digital skills. They need to be understood not as a way to turn philosophy majors into geeks, but as a way to tell the world that a philosophy major can be open to and comfortable with, daresay even take advantage of and thrive in, a technologically changing world."

A liberal arts-based education brings many skills that are not only valuable to the business world but are in fact vital for innovation. Today's most exciting innovations are happening in the merging of liberals arts thinkers with digital experts. Similarly, as factory workers in the early 1900s understood basic mechanics and the inner workings of engines, today workers need to understand the basics underneath digital devices. This empowers us to deploy software and hardware to their fullest potential, greatly increasing our capabilities to create. *Because coding is the lingua franca in the digital world, everyone should understand its foundations*, not necessarily the syntax of a popular, but complex, programming language, but the underpinnings of logic and algorithmic thinking, and the conceptual elements required to write computer programs.

In his recent book, Scott Hartley (2017), a leading venture

capitalist offering surprising revelations on who will drive innovation in the years to come, beautifully and convincingly makes the case for the liberal arts in the digital world. "Our technology ought to augment rather than replace, and ought to provide us with great hope rather than fear. Finding solutions to our greatest problems requires an understanding of human context as well as of code; it requires both ethics and data, both deep thinking people and Deep Learning AI, both human and machine; it requires us to question implicit biases in our algorithms and inquire deeply into not just how we build, but why we build and what we seek to improve. Fuzzies [students of the humanities and social sciences] and techies [students of engineering and hard sciences] must come together and the true value of the liberal arts must be embraced as we continue to pioneer our new technological tools."

Organizational Forms and Workforce Development

The current, accelerated rate of technological innovation will lead to even more severe job displacement than in previous industrial revolutions. Job displacement by machines is commonly referred as "technological unemployment." Machines now are not only able to perform manual routine tasks, but they are also increasingly automating cognitive routine tasks as AI is mimicking human intelligence. Everything that can be turned into a process is going to disappear. Any routine job, following instructions, is on its way out. When machines come for our jobs, we will need skills in communication, creativity, collaboration, and complex thinking to compete. As technology does more routine work, humans must tackle non-routine, complex tasks requiring team-work, task trading, and consequently social skills. (Katz, 2015)

Economists say the United States has lost about five million manufacturing jobs since 2000. Meanwhile, the economy has added tens of millions of service jobs, which require higher levels of education.

(Carlson, 2017) The *new economy* will need more workers with digital skills.

Machines have been replacing human labor since prehistoric times. The history of workforce development is as old as the history of work, and, "as technologies increase our capacity for labor, the nature of labor changes." (Aoun, 2017) The rapid evolution of technological capacities in today's information economy is unlike anything we have seen before. As advanced cyberinfrastructure continues to leap forward, "and attains high levels of cognition," it will replace "thinkers," professionals that work with information, something that "intelligent" machines can do much better and incredibly much faster. The software industry is what economists call "non- rival" economics: It is not consumed after use. Software is also incredibly cheap to reproduce, thus any digital advances can instantly be replicated and shared widely throughout the world at basically no cost.

Can China continue to grow rapidly?

With new approaches to the most important components of economic growth and a willingness to open up the economy to the benefits (and risks) of competition, China can transform itself from the world's manufacturing to the world's service: banks, technology, etc. The Internet will spur growth, but how much of this potential China will actually capture depends on the government's ability to create a supportive policy environment, the willingness of companies to go digital, and the adaptability of workers.

A very interesting situation is unfolding in China: *national leaders in their five-year plans, are embracing the automation revolution.* Chinese leaders had launched major programs of mass automation with large investments (billion of renminbi) across its industrial sector. Over the next few years it will integrate thousands of advanced robotics into factories currently heavily staffed by human workers. Many of the jobs that moved to China were low skill jobs that are themselves ripe for automation, and thus likely to disappear. Can the digital economy replace these lost jobs?

In less than four decades, China has traversed a path that took other countries of the developed world a couple of centuries to travel. Now China is entering a new stage accelerated by automation and digitization of the economy. The Internet is not just a tool for automation — it is also a force that rapidly expands markets and it is significantly changing the structure of employment. If the government and industry take the right steps to facilitate its development, the Internet could lead to the introduction of entirely new products and services, while allocating capital more efficiently and boosting demand. AI and robotics will further dramatically structure the labor markets. As the cost of assimilating these technologies continue to decrease, there will eventually be a threshold crossed where it makes more economic sense to replace human labor by machines, even in China where labor has been much cheaper.

Companies will face increasing talent shortages, particularly for highly specialized roles using big data and advanced analytics. This has resulted in increased skills mismatches in China. The largest developing country in the world faces an acute skills shortfall along with the challenges of an aging population and a shrinking labor force. Labor costs are rising, supply and demand is dangerously skewed, and vocational training is unable to fill the breach fast enough. Business and policy leaders must shift from thinking about workers as "labor" to developing people as "talent." In the future, talent, more than capital, will represent the critical factor of production. This is giving rise to a job market increasingly segregated into "low-skill/low-pay" and "high-skill/high-pay" segments, which in turn will lead to an increase in social tensions.

Despite China's investments in education and research being at an all-time high, the gap is increasingly widening. The government can ease this dislocation by collaborating with industry to ensure that training programs are available to help workers continually refresh their skills. China can also adapt school curricula to cultivate greater digital literacy and create a true education-to-employment pipeline. In fact, new digital education tools could accelerate China's ability to improve the quality of education across all regions at low cost. Companies may also need to develop their own talent pipelines through training for existing employees, industry collaboration, partnerships with education providers, or public-private efforts to design external training programs.

What's the role of technology on the world of 21st-century professional?

In 1945 there were a handful of programmable digital electronic computers and virtually few of the 2.5 billion human beings in our planet touched one. One such machine helped the allied forces win the war by breaking the enigma code. (IWM, 2018) Up until very recently, the Oxford English Dictionary lacked an entry for "mobile phone," "microchip," and similar technical terms. The world of 70 years ago seem very apart from today, but there are important similarities. Technology transformed the way people lived and worked then and now; fears of its potential negative impact as well as praises as society salvation both existed then and now.

Looking at these factors, the inescapable conclusion is that the benefits of digital technology depend on what we make of it: *It is up to us to leverage digital technologies in the best possible way*. Unless individuals can transcend technology within their professional context, they will be replaced by it. Technological literacy gives students a grounding on the fundamentals, so they know how their machines tick. This is an important point with enormous implications for higher education. Higher education must adapt to this acceleration.

The idea is to forge professionals who can "connect people, information, and technology in effective and innovative ways in order to address the critical and complex issues and problems facing our fast-paced, global, and increasingly digital society … people who want to develop or use information and technology in ways that help to make the world a better place for individuals, groups, schools, businesses, governments, and society as a whole." (Lawson, 2010)

It is clear today, that the 21st century professional needs to understand today's society in a digitally connected world where the effective design, implementation, and the ability to bend digital technology to one's personal or professional needs are driving career opportunities. This requires all professionals knowing something about digital technologies, especially within the context of their discipline, by adding digital fluency interwoven throughout the entirety of the educational experience.

The idea is to augment the professional preparedness with a sound understanding of the fundamental underpinnings of information and the technologies that manipulate it — as well as their limitations. The key here is augmentation. Augmentation makes the combination of humans and computers effective. This partnership is better than either one working alone. Humans and machines work best together, as Albert Einstein once said, "Computers are incredibly fast, accurate and stupid; humans are incredibly slow, inaccurate and brilliant; together they are powerful beyond imagination."

While specialists in computing will always be needed and although it is not difficult to learn to code, particularly if you have a logical turn of mind, the goal here is not for everyone to become a professional programmer. Everyone needs greater digital fluency; it is essential that everyone understand the intellectual and human meaning of what digital technology is all about. Everyone should develop a base digital acumen so as to make sure technology is doing the best it can for them. "Nothing tends so much to the advancement of knowledge as the application of a new instrument."[15]

Most crucially, users often have to perform repetitive actions manually because they are not able to use the uniquely powerful features of digital devices: *programming*. People can work 10 times faster by writing computer programs to automate tedious tasks that they would otherwise need to do by hand, for example using relatively simple macro

---

15. Sir Humphrey Davy in the 1830s.

languages available for many computer applications. If you know how to program, computer-related tasks that used to take you a week to finish will now take only a few hours. Programming allows you to discover more creative solutions than your colleagues who don't know how to program. By doing so, you're more likely to make a creative innovation that your colleagues wouldn't even think of exploring due to lack of programming skill.

No one can predict what jobs will be created in the near future (not even five years out). What we know is that the core of skills of a liberal arts education — critical thinking, problem solving, teamwork, oral and written communication, creativity, flexibility, and understanding of today's word and diversity — prepares graduates who can adapt to changing economic factors and build successful careers. What matters in the digital age is an ability to ask questions, to think critically, as well as the capability to utilize the tools of the time, digital tools, to solve problems.

Considering those born by the 2020s, it is expected that they will be working well into the 2080s! What will their skill needs be? We cannot not know this now, but we can safely say that they will require technological literacy and fluency beyond creativity and other soft skills. Will this technical literacy be on digital technology?

Alan Perlis argued in the 1960s that computer science should be part of a liberal education. He argued that all students should learn to program because computer science is the study of processes, the automated execution of processes including how we think about things we already know. (Perlis, 1962) He argued that everyone should know about programming "to have a powerful new tool to think with."

Alan Kay, the inventor of the mouse, sees the computer as humanity's first metamedium: "A medium that can represent all other media. To have full expressive power with the most powerful and creative medium humans have ever invented. Programming as an important new medium."

Jeannette Wing, who popularized the phrase computational

thinking (Papert, 1996, Wing, 2006, Barr, 2014), observes that everyone must learn computation "to make difficult problems more tractable and, because it's necessary to participate in and understand the modern world."

We are at an inflection point in history. The hyper-digital transformation is too big and important to our future success not to understand it. There is no turning back! Data is not going away and we are not going to regress to a computer-less society. Quite the contrary, there will be more digital devices, tools, and services at an exponential rate into the future.

Math is linked to physics. Statistics is linked to the social sciences. My idea is to link computation to every discipline in a similar way. We need to add digital fluency to reading, writing, and arithmetic — the three "Rs" that have been the foundations of learning for thousands of years. "Instead of educating college students for jobs that are about to disappear under the rising tide of technology, twenty-first-century universities should liberate them from outdated career models and give them ownership of their own futures. They should equip them with literacy and skills they need to thrive in this *new economy* defined by technology." (Aoun, 2017)

Educating professionals with no technical proficiency other than point, click, and drag through a suite of office productivity programs is no longer sufficient. Digital competency involves how to synchronize professional work with digital tools and systems. It is more than being able to work with computers; it's the ability to understand and utilize technology power to our advantage. Adding the digital tools and computing cognitive skills "super charges" the fundamentals of other disciplines. Imagine the possibilities when combined with powerful computational tools seamlessly integrated in a digital infrastructure that the *user community can easily exploit — because they have the technological sophistication to do so* (i.e., the ability to bend digital technology to one's personal or professional needs). And therein lies the rub and the proposed solution.

The greatest threat is NOT technology, it is our prioritization of technology against human capabilities. How do humans and AI can work together? As computing devices leap forward to higher levels of cognition, would they replace professionals? Can they replace thinkers?

Human-machine symbiosis is leading most effective, and most humane, innovations. "Given the pace of technology's advances, we can predict that computers, robots, and artificial intelligence will be even more intricately intertwined into the fabric of our personal and professional lives." (Aoun, 2017) Higher education must, therefore, change to keep abreast of developments and master these technological advancements.

Professional work is getting much more complex, requiring people to function beside intelligent machines. Although specific bodies of knowledge are needed to be effective in the workplace, knowledge by itself is necessary but not sufficient for the economy of the 21st century. Professions must demonstrate higher-level thinking. Digitization is disrupting many industries and driving up the value of technological skills. Together, the liberal arts and digital "literacies" and our very human cognitive capacities must integrate to help graduates to rise above the ever increasing computing power by *engendering human creativity.*

References

Abrahart, R. J. (Ed.) (2014). GeoComputation, Second Edition.CRC Press, Taylor & Francis Group. Boca Raton, FL.

Ambler, P. (2017). "China's 'New Economy' Agenda Doesn't Match Investor Ambitions -- Here's Why." *Forbes Magazine*, October 13, 2017

Andreessen, Marc. (2011). Why Software Is Eating The World." *The Wall Street Journal.* August 20, 2011. http://www.wsj.com/articles/SB10001424053111903480904576512250915629460

Aoun, J. (2017). Robot-proof: Higher Education in the Age of Artificial Intelligence. The MIT Press, Cambridge MA.

Barr, V (2014). "Computational Thinking." In Computing Handbook Third Edition: CS&SE volume. T. Gonzalez and J.L. Díaz-Herrera (Eds.) CRC Press, April 2014.

Brynjolfsson, E. and A. McAfee (2014). *The Second Machine Age: Work, Progress, and Prosperity in a Time of Brilliant Technologies*. New York : W.W. Norton & Company, 2014.

Carlson, S. (2017). "How Real-World Learning Could Help People Compete With Machines" *The Chronicle of Higher Education*, November 20, 2017. https://www.chronicle.com/article/How-Real-World-Learning-Could/241811

Caterpillar (2015). *Caterpillar and the Internet of Things*. Caterpillar, October 15, 2015. https://www.caterpillar.com/en/news/caterpillarNews/innovation/caterpillar-disrupted.html

Davidson, C. N. (2011). *Now You See It: How Technology and Brain Science Will Transform Schools and Business for the 21st Century*. Penguin Books, New York:2011.

Evans, D. (2011). *The Internet of Things: How the Next Generation of the Internet is Changing everything*. Cisco Internet Business Solutions, Group, April 2011.

Hartley, S. (2017). *The Fuzzy and the Techie: Why the Liberal Arts will Rule the Digital World*. Houghton Mifflin Harcourt. Boston.

Hwang, M. T. C. (2007). *Career Management – Theory and Practicum* (College Edition) Higher Education Press, Beijing. Editor: Gao Ting. ISBN 978-7-04-020018-8

IWM (2018). *How Alan Turing Cracked the Enigma Code.* Imperial War Museums, January 5, 2018. https://www.iwm.org.uk/history/how-alan-turing-cracked-the-enigma-code

Kantha, A. K. (2017). "Why India is Cool Towards China's Belt and Road." http://www.scmp.com/week-asia/opinion/article/2094167/why-india-cool-towards-chinas-belt-and-road. May 14, 2017.

Katz, L.(2015). "Get a liberal arts B.A., not a business B.A., for the coming artisan economy." PBS Newshour, July 15, 2015. https://www.pbs.org/newshour/nation/get-a-liberal-arts-b-a-not-a-business-b-a-for-the-coming-artisan-economy

Kennedy, S. (2015). "Made in China 2025." Center for Strategic and International Studies. June 1, 2015 https://www.csis.org/analysis/made-china-2025

Lawson, K. and Kowatch (2010). The New Information Professional: Your Guide to Careers in the Digital Age.. Neal-Schuman Publishers, New York.

McGowan, H. (2018). "Work to Lear." https://cra.org/wp-content/uploads/2018/01/10-McGowan-Presentation.pdf. January 10, 2018.

Morgan, J. P. (2016). Skills Shortages in the Chinese Labor Market. October 2016.

Papert, S. (1996). "An Exploration in the Space of Mathematics Educations." International Journal of Computers for Mathematical Learning 1, 1996

Perlis, A. (1962). "The computer in the university." In M. Greenberger, Ed., Computers and the World of the Future, MIT Press, Cambridge, MA, 1962:180–219

Peters, M. A. et. al. (2009). "Academic Entrepreneurship and the Creative economy." In Creativity and the Global Knowledge Economy, New York, NY: Peter Lang Publishing Inc.

Pooler, M. (2016). "Industrial Robot Sales Hit Record," Financial Times, June 22, 2016. https://www.ft.com/content/d8d80f32-3874-11e6-a780-b48ed7b6126f

Staton, M. (2012). "The New Liberal Arts," Inside Higher Ed., October 16, 2012.

Vanjan, J. (2017). "4 Ways China Is Influencing the U.S. Tech Industry." Fortune, September 14, 2017. http://fortune.com/2017/09/13/china-united-states-wireless-technology/

Veugelers, R. (2017). "The Challenge of China's Rise as a Science and Technology Powerhouse." Bruegel Policy Contribution, Issue no. 19, July 2017.

Wang, T., Zhang, Y., Yu, H., Wang F.-Y.[Eds]. (2010). Advanced Manufacturing Technology in China: A Roadmap to 2050. Chinese Academy of Sciences, Springer. Beijing.

Wing, J. (2006). "Computational Thinking." Communications of The ACM, March 2006/Vol. 49, No. 3, pp 33-35.

Woetzel, J. et al. (2014). China's digital transformation: The Internet's impact on productivity and growth. McKinsey Global Institute, July 2014.

Chapter 4

China's Mandate and Readiness for Social Development

By Lichia Saner-Yiu and Raymond Saner

The impressive economic growth of the past 40 years in China has altered not only the perception of China but also its role and place in the global economic system. This chapter reviews the *second revolution* that China is currently committed to achieve — social development, including eradication of extreme poverty — through the launch of the 13th Five-Year Plan that set China's policy priorities and development strategy for 2016-2020.

The 2030 Development Agenda

Social Development is about enhancing equality of social opportunities and reducing or eliminating discriminatory practices (Sen, 2000). In order to achieve social development, it is essential to enhance individual capabilities through investment in education, health and social welfare. Social development is about improving the well-being of every individual in society, so that they can reach their full potential and reap the benefits from the opportunities offered by the communities and society.

According to the World Bank, social development needs to "put people first" in the development processes. Poverty is more than simply being stuck with low income — it is also about vulnerability, exclusion, unaccountable institutions, powerlessness, and exposure to violence. Thus, "social development is about promoting social inclusion of the poor and vulnerable by empowering people, building cohesive and resilient societies, and by making institutions accessible and accountable to citizens" (World Bank Group, 2017).

The 2030 Agenda for Sustainable Development seeks to strengthen the social, economic and environmental dimensions of the society. It requires a more holistic, coherent and integrated approach at the national, regional and global levels. Within social sectors, the following goals have been adopted: poverty eradication strategies, policies to promote employment and decent work and social inclusion, policies to enhance access to quality education, basic healthcare, safe drinking water, sanitation, group-specific policies — youth, older persons, persons with disabilities, and indigenous peoples. Existing institutions and institutional mechanisms that are designated to foster social development will have to adjust or expand the scope of work so as to accommodate the new mandates arising from implementing the Social Development Goals (SDGs) (UNESC, 2016).

Most SDG Goals have a social dimension related to equitable access to different services that could enhance human development (Appendix 1 lists all 17 SDGs). In September 2015, Xi Jinping, President of China, attended the United Nations Sustainable Development Summit and joined other leaders in endorsing the 2030 Agenda for Sustainable Development, providing guidance for the national development of member states and offering international development cooperation over the next 15 years (UNDESA, 2016). In China's 2017 Progress Report on Implementation of the 2030 Agenda for Sustainable Development, the following statements were made: "The

Chinese government attaches great importance to implementing the 2030 Agenda, integrating it into the 13th Five-Year Plan for Economic and Social Development (hereinafter referred to as the 13th Five-Year Plan) and other mid- and long-term development strategies. At the 2015 Global Poverty Reduction and Development Forum held in October 2015, President Xi Jinping announced that in the five years to come, China would lift all the 70 million-plus people living under its current poverty line out of poverty. This marked an important step in China's efforts to implement the 2030 Agenda" (Ministry of Foreign Affairs of the People's Republic of China, 2017).

Landscape of Social Development Issues

Poverty and education are consequential for social inclusion and well-being.

Poverty

The goal of the Chinese government is to achieve a moderately prosperous society in all respects by 2020, focusing on improving social welfare of its population in addition to achieving quality growth. Some of the essential ingredients of achieving social inclusion and equity are a further reduction in economic inequality, improvement of minimum social protection and equal access to quality education.

China has so far managed to continuously reduce the number of individuals living in poverty (measured by living at or under US $1.00 per day). The World Bank attributes this reduction in poverty to the continuous economic growth, above 6%, annually since 2010. This growth is illustrated in Figure 1. The Gini Coefficient for rural and urban income inequality has also declined. From 2008 to 2015, the Gini Coefficient decreased from 0.491 to 0.462 (World Bank, 2017). Nonetheless, the problem of income inequality is still a significant issue.

Both local and national factors affect poverty. For example,

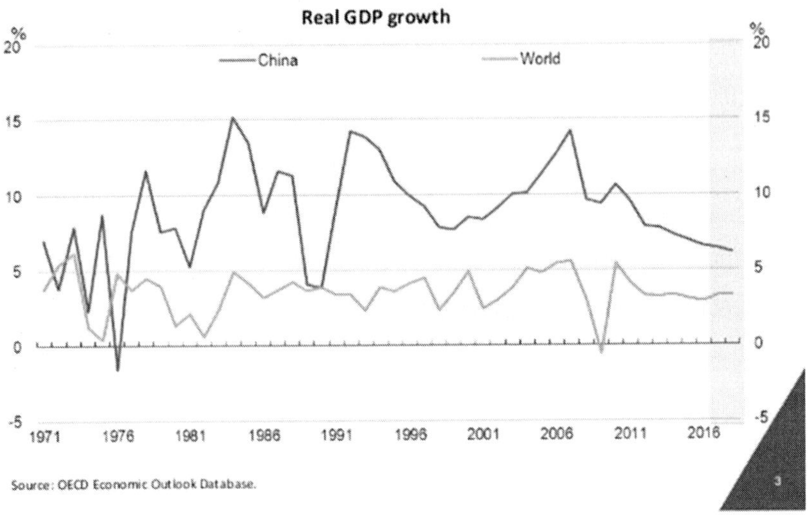

Figure 1. Economic Growth of China from 1971-2016
(Source: OECD Economic Outlook Database)

remoteness and low population density make it challenging for individuals living in impoverished areas to access the services and infrastructure they need. The economic gap between coastal and inland parts of China is just as important — if not more so — than the urban/rural divide. Key factors which help achieve moderate prosperity for all and invigorate rural economy are better jobs and local entrepreneurial engagements. These are some of the measures that the Chinese government is pursuing in its 13th Five-Year Plan.

Figures 2 and 3 illustrate income disparity and GDP by province, revealing a stark contrast between the metropolitan areas and regions — essentially indicating a two-tier society. During the post-1978 reform period, China dramatically reduced large-scale poverty through specific government reform policies and rapid economic growth. Figure 4 illustrates the significant difference between major metropolitan areas like Shanghai and Beijing and more rural regions such as Xizang and Gansa.

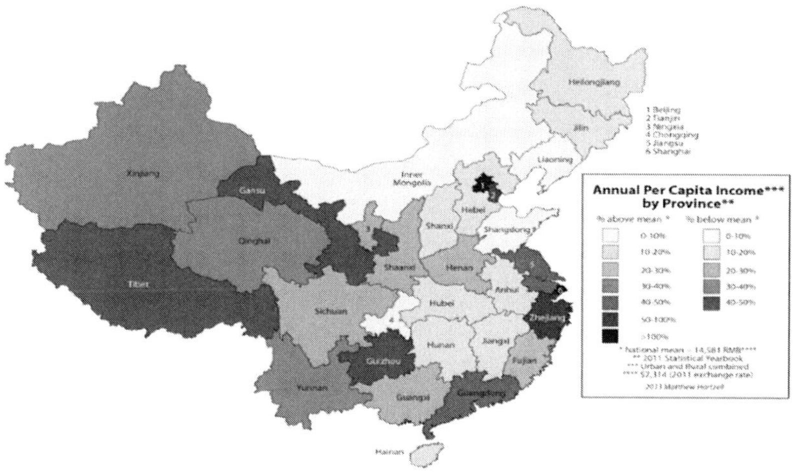

Figure 2. Income Distribution of China by Provinces in 2011 (Note: Most of the Provinces on the east coast have above average income, while those in the middle and far west are below average; Source: Mapping China's Income Inequality: M. Schiavenz, *The Atlantic*, 2013)

During the last few decades, China has managed to reduce poverty by more than fifty-percent, thus contributing to the attainment of the Millennium Development Goals of reducing half of the poverty rate. Using the World Bank's $1 per day income measure, the number of poor is estimated to have dropped from about 490 million to 88 million over the same period, a decline from 49 percent in 1981 to 6.9 percent in 2002. China's large-scale poverty reduction has been achieved mainly through rapid economic growth. The success of its poverty reduction strategy is particularly exemplary in rural China, where poverty rate has dropped from 98% of the rural population to about 8% in 2015, according to the National Bureau of Statistics, China (see Figure 5).

Despite this impressive achievement, the poverty affected populations in rural areas continue to fall further behind, exasperating the rich-poor disparity effect. Therefore, any effort in reducing poverty needs to address the rural poverty ever more urgently because economic opportunities and public services in rural areas are also lagging. The

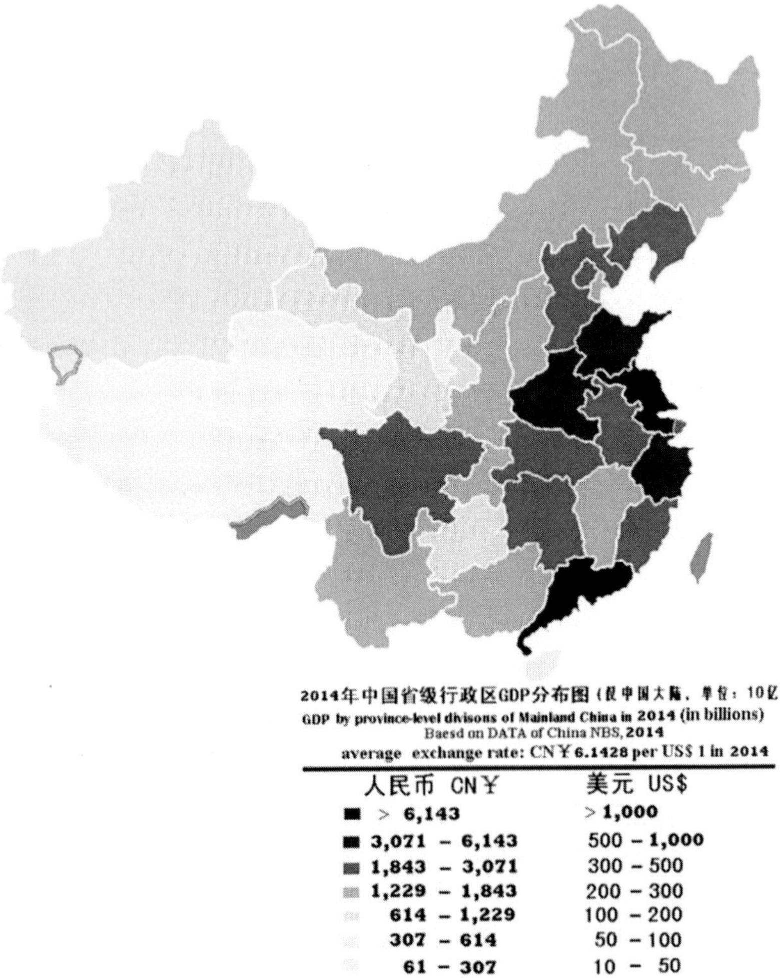

Figure 3. GDP Distribution in China (Note: The darker the area, the higher the GDP; Source: Byzh: User: CNS Wikipedia-based on China National Bureau of Statistics figures)

urban and rural dichotomy has also directly led to a continued migration flows and a worsening of social conditions in the rural areas. A root cause of this deterioration is the lack of proper education that would support entrepreneurial spirit, innovation and greater employability in

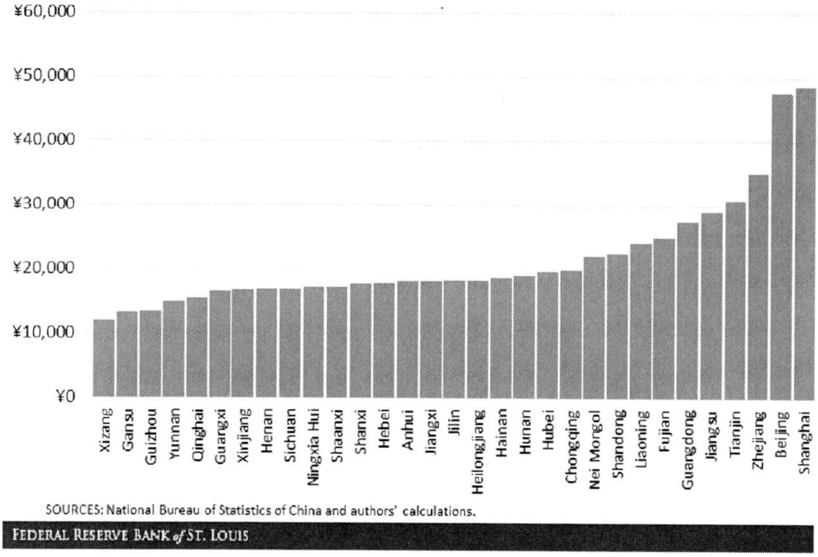

Figure 4. China's Household Disposable Income, Real 2015 Per Capita Yuan

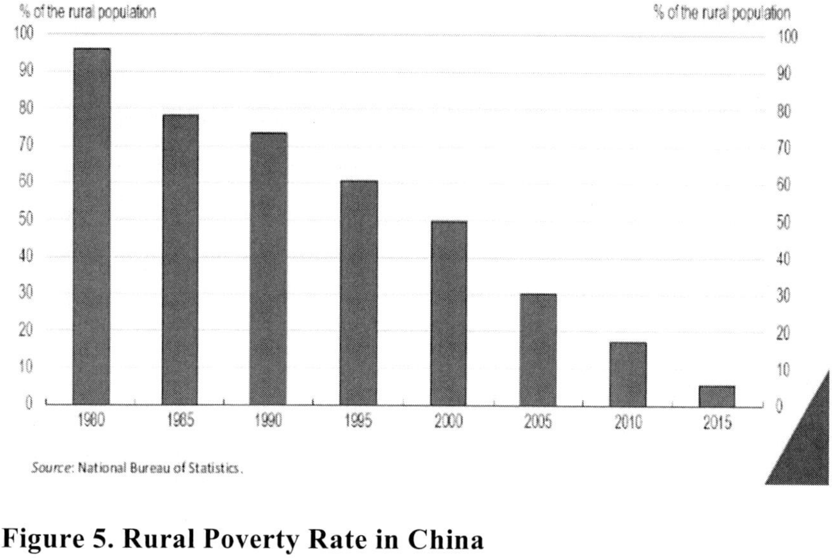

Figure 5. Rural Poverty Rate in China

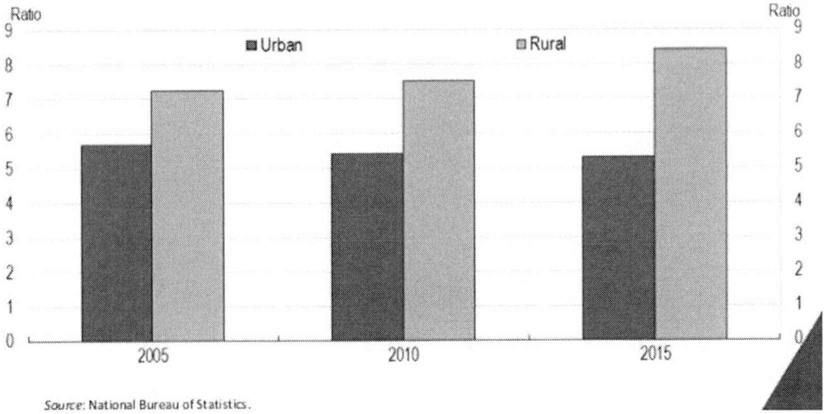

Figure 6. Disposable Income of the Top 20% Over the Bottom 20% of the Income Distribution

a modern economy. That disparity in access to education directly impacts disposable income and the gap has worsened (see Figure 6).

Education

Poverty has two dimensions: income poverty and human poverty (Zhang, 1993). In 2011, the China Development Research Foundation, a major policy think tank based in Beijing, advocated a new phase for poverty eradication in China. The Foundation proposed an alternative strategy by eradicating poverty starting from the roots which emphasized the inadequate enabling environment in mostly rural and remote regions, including malnutrition of the infants and young child. This strategic recommendation included a human capital strategy that directs poverty alleviation efforts toward human capital investment, particularly in education and improvement of health in rural populations with infants and young children as development targets. This strategy was meant to mitigate the severe imbalance of the human development that affected the productivity of various backward regions in China.

高等教育学校（机构）学生数
Number of Students in Higher Education Institutions

	毕(结)业生数 Graduates	位
研究生 Postgraduates	563938	
博 士 Doctor's Degrees	55011	
硕 士 Master's Degrees	508927	
普通本专科 Undergraduates in Regular HEIs	7041800	
本 科 Normal Courses	3743680	
专 科 Short-cycle Courses	3298120	
成人本专科 Undergraduates in Adult HEIs	2444650	
本 科 Normal Courses	1021846	
专 科 Short-cycle Courses	1422804	
网络本专科生 Web-based Undergraduates	1874787	
本 科 Normal Courses	700906	
专 科 Short-cycle Courses	1173881	
在职人员攻读硕士学位 Master's Degree Programs for On-the-job Personnel		
自考助学班 Class run by Non-government HEIs for Students Preparing for Self-directed State-administered Examinations	81890	
普通预科生 College-preparatory Class		
研究生课程进修班 Postgraduate Courses	20009	
进修及培训 In-service Training	8526875	
留学生 Foreign Students	109894	

Figure 7. Number of Students in Higher Education Institutions in China in 2016 (Source: Ministry of Education, China)

Since the start of the reform in 1979, the Chinese government continued to increase its national budget for education provision. However, due to the low start of the educational stock in terms of physical infrastructure, qualified teachers, teaching materials and tested curricula, China experienced an on-going strategic tension in its policy choices of human capital investment. On one hand, it needed to eliminate illiteracy of the population in hundreds of millions as soon as possible. On the other hand, China needed to reorient and educate generations of future managers and public administrators to meet the transformative objectives of the reform.

For this purpose, innovative delivery modalities were used to reduce illiteracy quickly by applying distance learning through the use of radio and TV (so-called Broadcasting University) and structured program learning through individual self-study on a mass scale. This national effort achieved spectacular results by 2015, as the adult literacy rate increased from 65.51% in 1982 to 96.36% in 2015, out of a population of more than 1.4 billion. Graduates of tertiary education institutions also grew to 11,925,169 in 2017, which represents more than 35% of the age cohorts according to the statistics of the Ministry of Education. Enrollment rate at the pre-primary level also reached 83.7% in 2016, 100.85% in primary education, 95.03% in secondary education and 48.44% in tertiary education (UNESCO, 2018). Figure 7 illustrates the formidable number of enrollees in higher education.

The dramatic increase in literacy in China directly relates to the efficacy of numerous political, economic and educational policies. In 1982, compulsory education was written into the Chinese constitution, which requires a nine-year compulsory education funded by the government. As shown in Figure 8, there was a large gender gap in literacy rate in China as of 1982. Though this gap still existed in 2010, it was narrowed down to 5.7 percent, starting from 28 percent in 1982. Since 1990, the national education policy has been focused on females, especially from poor and/or minority families. Over the past years, China has achieved gender parity in primary schooling.

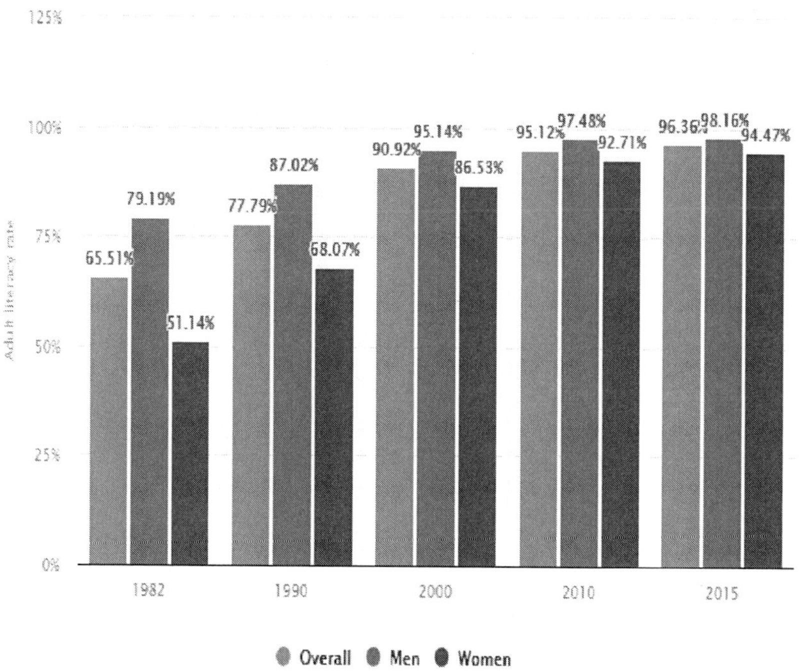

Figure 8. Adult Literacy Rate in China (Source: Statista, 2018)

While quantitative objectives are achieved, qualitative aspects of educational development still remain problematic. Regional literacy disparities in China should not be overlooked. Regions with a strong economic background tend to display illiteracy rates below national average. In contrast, economically underdeveloped regions have a higher population percentage of people who cannot read or write. Tibet for instance, a region where 92 percent of the population belongs to an ethnic minority, showed the highest illiteracy rate nationwide, with 41.12 percent in 2016 (Statista, 2016).

Advances in educational attainment were not only achieved in the

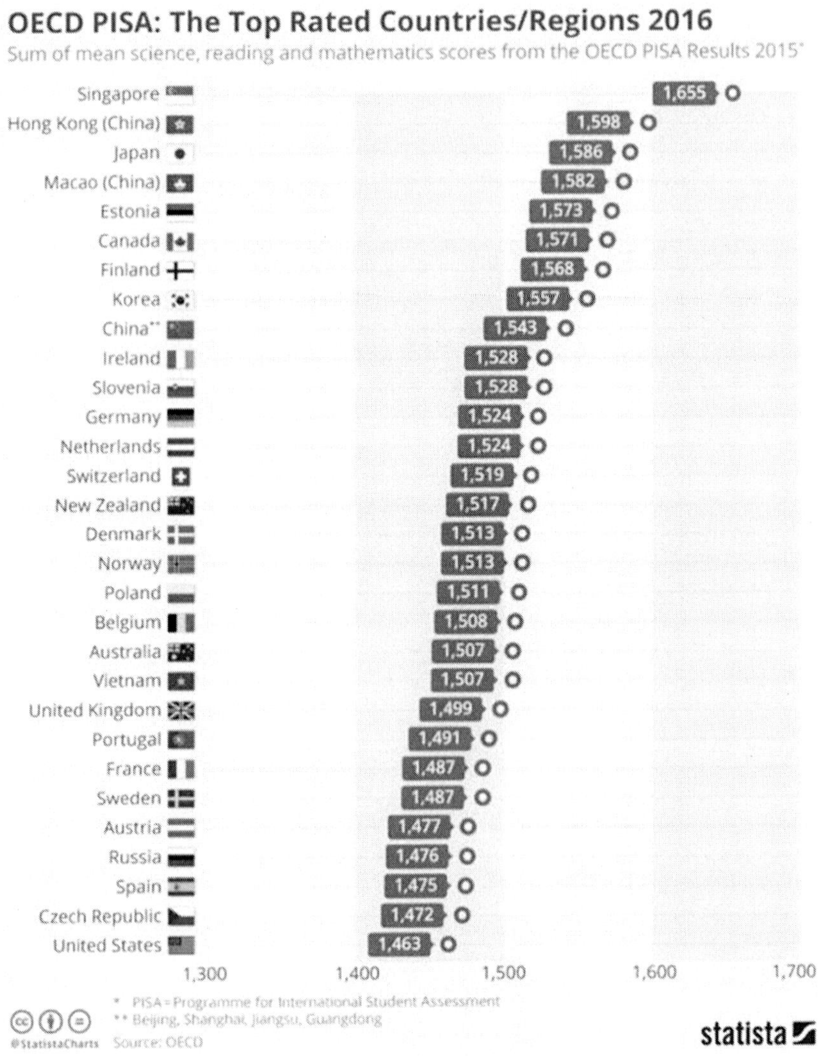

Figure 9. Mean Science, Reading and Math Scores, 2015

number of students enrolled but also in terms of schooling outcomes; however, social disparity persists. Students from the affluent coastal cities and provinces, such as Beijing, Shanghai, Jiangsu and Guandong, are high performers in the global PISA (Programme for International Student Assessment) ranking and even ahead of countries like Germany,

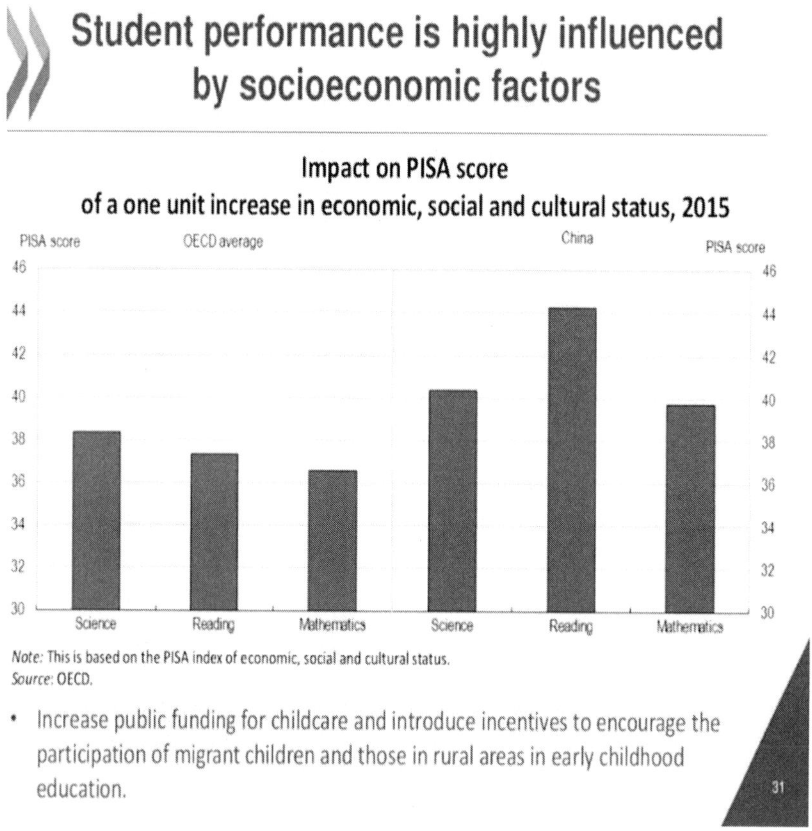

Figure 10. Student Performance as a Consequence of Socioeconomic Factors (Source: OECD, PISA, 2015)

Switzerland, and USA. Figure 9 illustrates worldwide rankings by nation.

No comparative data is publicly available to compare the educational achievements of other regions of the country. However, existing indirect data show that an increase of public funding for childcare and introduction of incentives to encourage participation of migrant children and those in rural areas in early childhood education had a significant positive learning impact. In other words, the socioeconomic factors of students that affect access to early childcare and pre-schooling have a determining effect on the children's ability to read, write, count and perform well in science. Figure 10 illustrates the impact even a slight improvement on economic, social and cultural status can make. These educational resources are not necessarily guaranteed nor available in most of the rural areas of China, where regular schooling with sustainable, acceptable quality is not always available.

Teachers at primary schools remain in short supply, especially in the rural and remote regions of China where students are dispersed. This makes it impossible to have a full class at different levels. Often these students are grouped together and taught by supplementary or voluntary teachers who might not possess a full teaching qualification. The turnover rate of teachers is generally high in these places, despite government policies to incentivise the teachers to stay. After earning enough credits for a placement in the cities, qualified teachers often return to them, thus resulting in a chronic shortage of competent teachers in the countryside. Families with financial means migrate to the townships, small cities or larger cities for schooling and access to quality education purposes. These families will pay extra fees to enroll their children. Most often the mother will accompany the child to the towns and cities; grandparents are left behind in the villages to tend to farming and taking care of family homes. This schooling-related migration has social and health implications for the elderly in the rural areas as well. The Chinese government has built caring facilities (also known as Jin Lao Yuan) in the cities and rural areas to provide shelter and long-term care to the vulnerable old age group. Yet, there are many cases shown in a recent survey by the authors that many of the elderly refuse to move into these social institutions, particularly when the parents have migrant children working in the cities.

There are other issues that affect schooling of children of rural origin. Distance and disparity of households necessitate boarding from the Grade 3 onward. Although the government provides subsidies to help alleviate the financial burden, many of the small towns do not have

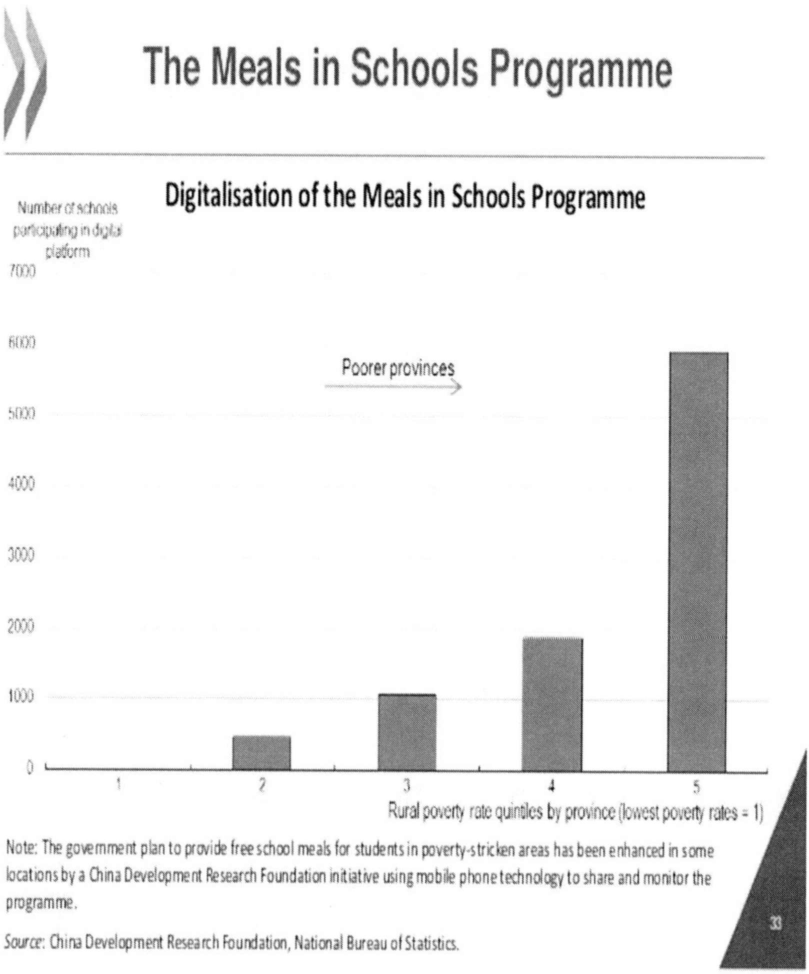

Figure 11. Number of Students Participating in Digital Meals Platform

the necessary infrastructure to provide a school lunch or a cafeteria. Young students will bring rice to school that will be cooked at the school facility and eat dry or preserved dishes brought back from home over the weekend. While efforts are made to provide universal school meals for students, the China Development Research Foundation initiated a mobile platform to monitor school meal programmes of the poorest regions.

Figure 11 illustrates the severity of this challenge.

The 13th Five-Year Plan and Its Poverty Eradication Mandate

China has reached a historical juncture because it re-directed its development trajectory to a path that leads to social equity and moderate prosperity through inclusive and green growth. This political ambition was reaffirmed during the 19th Communist Party Congress that was held in March 2018. This vision of "achieving moderate prosperity" is not only highlighted in the speech given by President Xi, it has already been outlined in China's 13th Five-Year Plan as well (2016-2020).

Concretely, China's 13th 5-year plan outlined the steps of building a moderately prosperous society and adapting to an ever-changing world. As an integral part of the 13th plan, Part XIII, "The Fight against Poverty," set out poverty reduction strategies requiring targeted individual household measures to ensure attainment of this development objective by 2020. The goal is to ensure that the rural poor can meet their basic needs, achieve self-sufficiency and have the opportunity of social-economic mobility. This plan is intended to lift approximately 70 million of the registered poor out of poverty (Chow, 2018). Many measures of this plan will provide impoverished individuals with targeted tools to move upwards in society.

Part XIII of the 13th Five-Year Plan states that China will "develop businesses based on local strengths, find alternative employment, relocate, claim subsidies for ecosystem conservation, and gain access to educational and training programs, medical insurance, and assistance for medical treatment" as basis for poverty eradication (Central Committee of the Communist Party, 2013). This program plans on ensuring the attainment of wealth creation for all by formulating strict and well-defined procedures as well as implementing transparent standards and procedures. Some of the current goals of the five-year plan are:

- Strengthening the ability of poor areas to tap into their developmental potential.
- Ensure per-capita disposable incomes of farmers will increase at a higher rate than the national average.
- Upgrading power grids in poor rural areas.
- Creating transportation to help the poor connect to other areas.
- Improving water conservancy facilities in poor areas.
- Implementing broadband internet in up to 90% of rural impoverished areas.
- Investing in replacing direct relief and aid with work instead.
- Supporting construction of small and medium public benefit infrastructure.

President Xi Jinping has set an ambitious development agenda to launch his second term in office and ensuring the years that follow according to the newly adopted Chinese Constitution. His recent speeches at the 19th Party Congress (18 October 2017) and then in March 2018 at the 13th National Political Consultative, reaffirmed his commitment and political objective in eradicating poverty by 2020. He urged party cadres to redouble their effort in precisely targeted intervention in order to lift the millions of poor people out of poverty. A total number of 800,000 strong are currently executing this historical task.

Private Sector Initiatives

Corporations can be at the forefront of poverty eradication by implementing strategies in the developing world that could aid the countries' efforts to achieve the Sustainable Development Goals. According to the United Nations Industrial Development Organization (UNIDO, 2018), Corporate Social Responsibility (CSR) provides an opportunity for companies to achieve the *Triple-Bottom-Line*, economic, environmental and social imperatives.

Many MNCs and other corporations have embarked on a journey to fulfil their CSR (UNIDO, 2018). Companies like Twinning, PWC and Alibaba Group have established programs that align themselves with the Chinese government goal of poverty eradication. Senior Director for Poverty and Equity GP of the World Bank Carolina Sanchez points out that "growth is important, but it must be inclusive. The benefits of overall growth simply cannot be captured by a privileged few if we expect to see progress and prosperity in the world.

To fuel that growth and build a healthy, educated, engaged society, countries must invest in quality education, in health, in good infrastructure, sanitation, and water for everyone. Without these things, the potential of millions is left on the sidelines, permanently curbed due to preventable barriers. . .progress is not the responsibility of the government alone- private sector partners, citizens, and local communities have an important role to play in developing solutions and spurring action on poverty reduction and equal opportunity" (Sanchez, 2017).

Path 1: Corporate Social Responsibility

CSR in China today has undergone decades of change since it was first introduced. After Deng Xiaoping announced the Open Door Policy in 1978, MNCs began to perceive China as the new factory of the world due to its favorable government policies, the abundance of cheap labor, and lack of stringent environmental standards. In the 1990s, MNCs brought along their CSR practices with them, mostly focusing on supply chain management and labor conditions. In response to these new influences, the Chinese government enacted several laws that put CSR on course for further popularization, such as the Environmental Protection Law (1989), Trade Union Law (1992), Consumer Protection Law (1993) and Labour Law (1994) (Bu et al, 2013).

The year 2000 marks when China joined the WTO and international standards began to be applied to companies operating in

China. MNCs, as well as Chinese-owned companies, started to face increasing pressure to conduct CSR. The public called for a movement toward more open and transparent reporting practices by enterprises. Based on a 2006 survey by AC Nielsen, more than half of Chinese consumers prefer to purchase goods and services from companies that actively engage in charitable activities (Tian, 2016).

The pressure to pursue CSR came from both within and outside of China. Externally, Chinese companies with global ambitions sought legitimacy by incorporating improved sustainability practices, largely at the request of western-based MNCs and foreign governments. Internally, formerly state-owned enterprises needed to build their social legitimacy by more transparent reporting on various activities. In response to these demands, various foreign MNCs in China have publicly declared their commitment to CSR. In 2007, more than 1,400 foreign MNCs in China published "A Written Proposal for Fulfilling Social Responsibilities."

China has increasingly exerted pressure on foreign MNCs to conduct CSR activities, with the goal of developing stronger, more institutionalized, and regular CSR practices. Many enterprises operating in China are required by SASAC to issue a CSR Report. Likewise, the Shenzhen Stock Exchange and the Shanghai Stock Exchange require about two-thirds of listed companies to disclose social responsibility (Interview with Liu, Baocheng, 2013). To further entrench CSR practices in China, many CSR awards were also established to incentivize businesses.

Comparatively, the advantage of foreign MNCs gradually faded away. Some leading brands, including KFC, Shell, Walmart and Unilever, were blamed for applying lower standards to customer service in China. Furthermore, along with the ascendant trend of exposed negative environmental and labor incidents related to foreign MNCs, suspicions and mistrust arose over their double standards in China and other countries with regard to all CSR issues.

More recently, some foreign MNCs have paid greater attention to environment, health and safety (EHS) issues, making improvements through their supply chains and improved CSR training. For instance, GE is working together with other companies which include Walmart, Honeywell, Citibank and SABIC Innovative Plastics to support a new EHS Academy in China's Guangdong province.

Furthermore, some foreign MNCs have established philanthropic programs involving environmental protection, community improvement, education enhancement and agricultural development. Others are imposing SA 8000 Standard on their suppliers in China. SA8000 is used to certify working conditions and social compliance in factories and organizations in line with labor provisions contained within the universal Declaration of Human Rights and the ILO Conventions (ILO, 1998). The ILO Tripartite Declaration of Principles concerning Multinational Enterprises and Social Policy (2017) is the latest iteration of such effort in promoting higher labor standards practiced by the MNCs.

Besides providing CSR training to their staff, foreign MNEs also set up philanthropic programs to support education, health and other worthwhile activities. Table 1 summarizes some of the philanthropic activities conducted by the foreign MNCs in China.

Examples of business partnering can also be found. Twining has facilitated business development that may eventually lead to the goal of eradicating poverty by 2020. It is creating opportunities for individuals living in the rural area to work directly with its supply chain. Twining provides training and education programs that show the links between nature, tea production, economy and society (Lu & Tong, 2016). PWC partnered with several charity foundations and initiatives to fund programs for underprivileged children and ethnic minorities. They established programs such as the "Log-off, Restart and Recycle" to minimize their e-waste by donating computers to underprivileged children in rural China (PWC CSR report, 2017).

Challenges for Foreign MNCs Doing CSR in China

Some of the challenges include:

Table 1. Examples of the MNCs Philanthropic Activities in China

Community Improvement	The residents in the Mt. Everest area suffer from inhospitable climate and geographic conditions. DuPont China provides them with a group of innovative energy-saving buildings.
Poverty Alleviation	Amway has been sponsoring the 'New Year Charity Concert' during the spring festival since 2004, aimed at raising funds for poor and handicapped children and other vulnerable groups.
Environment Protection	Walmart launched a series of science popularization activities in 2010.
Education Enhancement	In June 2010, Mercedes Benz and China Youth Development Foundation jointly established the Future Star Fund with initial funding of 30 million RMB, for the purpose of fostering musical education for students in the Hope School system.
Post-Disaster Reconstruction	To improve the nutrition and health conditions of children in the earthquake-stricken areas of western China after May 2008, the China Foundation for Poverty Alleviation, the World Food Program and Yum (China) initiated a "One Yuan to show you care" program. Over 15,000 children in Sichuan and over 22,200 children in Yunnan benefited from nutritious meals.

- *Differences in CSR standards applied by the Chinese subsidiary compared to those in developed countries of the same foreign MNCs.* Some MNCs including KFC, Shell, Walmart and Unilever, have been widely denounced for using a lower customer service standard in China. Consumers have also pointed out inconsistencies in environmental and labor conditions of MNCs, which tarnish the reputation of these international brands.

- *Many MNCs in China lack a strategic, long-term and value-based system of CSR.* Professor Liu Baocheng observed that "the majority of CSR behaviors are impulsive, or subject to major events (such as disaster relief), or the implementation of executive will, in short, they lack strategic planning."
- *Lack of transparency and capability in conducting CSR activities.* Professor Liu also observed that CSR reports tend to lack credibility because they are not written by unbiased third parties. They also lack sufficient monitoring of CSR activities.

CSR Trends

CSR will continue to be in the spotlight in China and foreign MNCs doing businesses in China should be mindful of the importance of these practices. According to a study conducted jointly by the Embassy of Sweden in Beijing and CSR Asia, the major cities (Beijing, Shanghai and Guangzhou) and the Eastern and Southern China regions are the areas where CSR is the most developed in terms of knowledge and performance among companies.

According to the same study, environmental protection and labor conditions are viewed as the most pressing and urgent CSR issues in China for the next decade, followed by transparency, anti-corruption and ethical behavior of businesses. Evolving business context in this regard will definitely increase the transactional costs as happened in the advanced economy decades ago. The allure of China originates from its substantial and affluent middle class. When more Chinese persons move up the economic ladder, MNCs and investors can forego China in pursuit of other low labor costs countries without being penalized by not directly participating in the Chinese economy.

Path 2: PPPs (Public Private Partnerships)

The value of PPPs for social development has long been recognized in China, especially after the year 2014, when the

Communist Party of China declared its support for PPPs through publishing circulars, regulations, declarations and debates (Thieriot & Dominquez, 2015).

According to General Secretary Xi Jinping, "The Chinese nation is inclusive and tolerant to diversity, keeps learning good things of others in the long history and transforms such good things into things of our own, thereby forming national features of our own. Since the 1980s, Britain, Canada, Australia and other developed countries have been applying PPP into public utility fields such as infrastructures, so PPP has become mature in such countries; PPP has expanded from initial economic infrastructures to social and government fields. In developed countries, PPP has played an active role in the government increasing, improving and optimizing the supply of public products and services, enhancing the efficiency of financial funds, facilitating market access, pushing forwarding market unification and so on. It is very important to scientifically, regularly and efficiently boost the PPP work in China, and learn and use for reference of the mature experience of developed countries" (China Public Private Partnership Center, 2015).

As a result of government support, PPPs flourished in China. Most of them are in the energy, water and transportation sectors (IISD, 2015). The Shajiao B power plant in Shenzhen, which came into operation in 1988, is a build-operate-transfer project that is usually considered to be the first PPP (Wu, 2013).

PPPs have been developing in China since the late 1980s. The Third Plenum of the 18th Communist Party of China in 2013 emphasized the decisive role that market forces should play in the Chinese economy (Davis, 2013, and Huang, 2013). The Party's actions in 2014 confirmed this direction, particularly as it relates to PPPs, resulting in many associated circulars, regulations, declarations and debates. Figure 12 represents major legislation concerning PPPs in China.

Currently, there is no centralized monitoring of PPP projects in China. However, the World Bank does provide the Private Participation

DATE	ISSUING BODY AND TITLE	REF.
Ma'' 18, 2014	National Development and Reform Commission (NDRC), *Notice to encourage private capital to invest in first infrastructure projects*	NDRC, 2014c
September 21, 2014	State Council, *Opinions of the State Council on strengthening the management of local government debt*	State Council, 2014c
September 23, 2014	MOF, *Notice on questions relating to expanding the use of PPPs*	MOF, 2014c
November 16, 2014	State Council, *Guiding opinions on the innovative investment mechanism and encouraging social investment in key sectors*	State Council, 2014a
November 29, 2014	MOF, *Guide on operation of public-private partnership projects (interim)*	MOF, 2014a
December 2, 2014	NDRC, *Guidelines on development of public-private partnership projects*	NDRC, 2014a
2015?	NDRC, State Council: infrastructure and public project franchise law	

Figure 12. Major PPP Legislation and Regulations in China (Source: International Institute for Sustainable Development, 2015, p. 3)

in Infrastructure Databases, documenting any projects where public and private companies partner up, but records are limited to Infrastructural projects (World Bank, 2017).

Figure 13 illustrates the major projects; Figure 14 the number and total investments in China. Participation in PPP deals in China might not

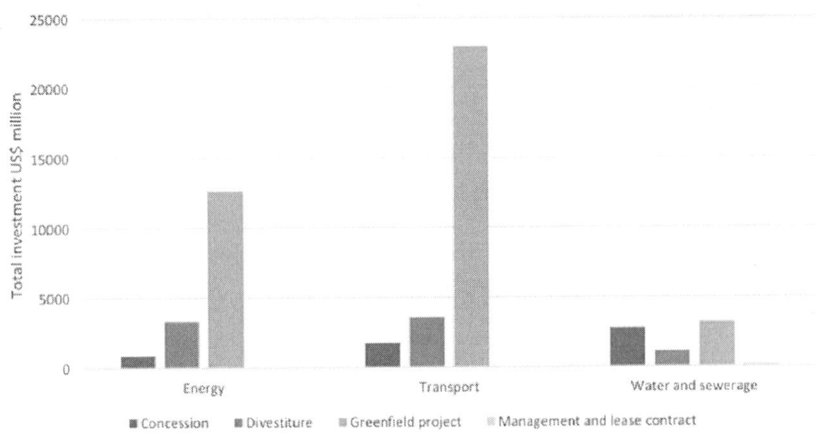

Figure 13. Type of PPPs in Different Sectors, 2004-2013 (Source: World Bank, 2014, in IISD, 2015)

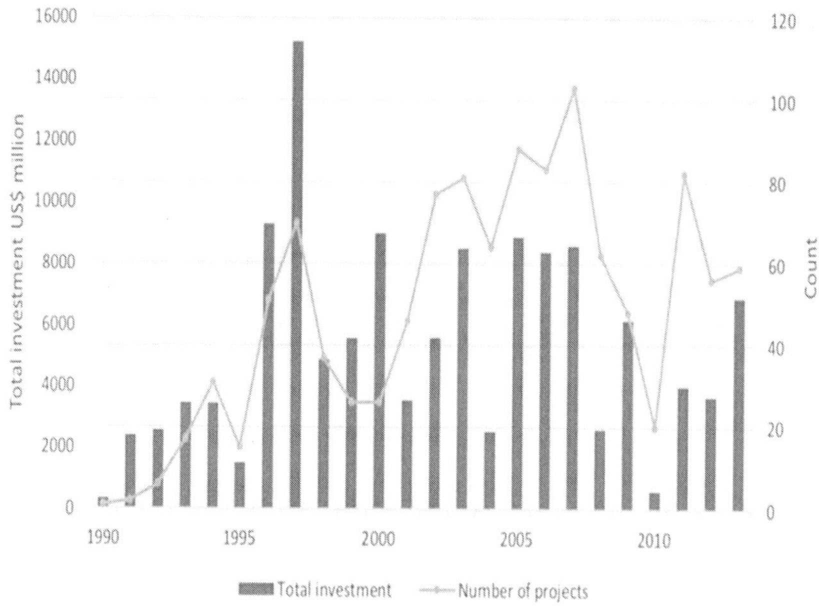

Figure 14. Number of Projects and Total Investment in China (Source: World Bank, 2014, in IISD, 2015)

be as straightforward as one might expect. According to analysts at Fitch Ratings Ltd., Bank of America Corp. and Oxford Economics Ltd., the majority of partners in PPP projects have turned out to be state-owned enterprises (Bloomburg, 2017). The upshot of this arrangement is that while debt pressure will be relieved for local governments, it will just end up on the books of another arm of the state. For a foreign MNC entering such investment scheme, one might need to consider the following:

> Political Risks: Policy risk was considered as the biggest risk for foreign enterprises wanting to invest in China whether in PPP or other modes. Li (2004) argued that many private companies experience an implementation lag caused by the lack of coordination between the central and the local governments.

Protectionism: Most PPPs in China are undertaken by Chinese-owned companies, including state-owned companies. The government could impose barriers to foreign companies to protect local businesses.

Conclusion and Recommendations

In the context of China's declared goal of reaching moderate prosperity by 2049, there is an expectation that enterprises engage in social activities or deliver positive social impact. This public expectation holds true for both Chinese and foreign MNCs. The private sector is expected to share their business acumen, financial resources and technological know-how to assist rural China and the poor to step out of poverty.

Active participation in philanthropic endeavors or corporate social responsibility programs would be useful in promoting the brand of a foreign MNC. Yet, active partnering to form or create upward supply chains by linking farming or rural communities and cooperatives with higher value-added tasks would be very much appreciated. Such partnerships would also strengthen the business integration and corporate citizenship of the foreign investor in China.

Expanding the business mandate to include social and environmental considerations would mean interfacing with multiple non-traditional stakeholders and business partners. It is recommended for foreign MNCs to develop novel corporate competencies and function — Business Diplomacy — to deal with this new operational context in China. Business diplomacy supports foreign MNCs in moving from "business as usual" to "business with ethics" (Saner & Yiu, 2016). Through the interaction with non-business stakeholders, business diplomats also identify creative ways of complying with the wishes of local hosts for social engagement, but also in spotting opportunities and needs for socioeconomic innovations and in creating both tangible and intangible long-term values for the foreign MNCs.

Appendix 1. A table of UN Sustainable Development Goals (SDGs) 2030

1. End poverty in all its forms everywhere;
2. End hunger, achieve food security and improved nutrition and promote sustainable agriculture;
3. Ensure healthy lives and promote well-being for all at all ages;
4. Ensure inclusive and equitable quality education and promote lifelong learning opportunities for all;
5. Achieve gender equality and empower all women and girls;
6. Ensure availability and sustainable management of water and sanitation for all;
7. Ensure access to affordable, reliable, sustainable and modern energy for all;
8. Promote sustained, inclusive and sustainable economic growth, full and productive employment and decent work for all;
9. Build resilient infrastructure, promote inclusive and sustainable industrialization and foster innovation;
10. Reduce inequality within and among countries;
11. Make cities and human settlements inclusive, safe, resilient and sustainable;
12. Ensure sustainable consumption and production patterns;
13. Take urgent action to combat climate change and its impacts;
14. Conserve and sustainably use the oceans, seas and marine resources for sustainable development;
15. Protect, restore and promote sustainable use of terrestrial ecosystems, sustainably manage forests, combat decertification, and halt and reverse land degradation and halt biodiversity loss;
16. Promote peaceful and inclusive societies for sustainable development, provide access to justice for all and build effective, accountable and inclusive institutions at all levels;
17. Strengthen the means of implementation and revitalize the global partnership for sustainable development.

Appendix 2. Number of School, Educational Personnel and Full-time Teachers by Type and Levels (Source: Ministry of Education, 2018, authors' compilation)

	Schools	Educational Personnel	Full-time Teachers
Pre-school Education Institutions	239,812	3,817,830	223,2067
Regular Primary Schools	177,633	5,537,298	5,789,145
Adult Primary Schools	11,802	23,249	12,399
Regular Junior Secondary Schools	36,471	2,770,381	2,514,419
Vocational Junior Secondary Schools	16	492	461
Adult Junior Secondary Schools	569	2,779	2198
Secondary Vocational Education	10,893	1,086,100	839,589
Senior Secondary Schools	13,818	2,595,259	1,735,980

References

Bloomberg L.P. (2017, February 27). In China, Public-Private Partnerships Are Really Public-Public. Retrieved fromhttps://www.bloomberg.com/news/%20articles/2017-02-27/in-china-public-private-partnerships-are-really-public-public

Bu, L., Bloomfield, M., & An, J. (2013). *CSR Guide for Multinational Corporations in China: Prosperity with Integrity*. Harmony Foundation.

Central Committee of the Communist Party (2013). The 13th Five Year Plan for Economic and Social Development of the People's Republic of China. Retrieved from http://www.en.ndre.gov.cn/newsrelease/201612/po2016

China Public Private Partnerships Center. (2015, April 3). *Selections of Foreign PPP Cases*. Retrieved from http://www.cpppc.org/en/DomesticKnowledge/3967.html

Chow, E. K. (2018, January 08). China's war on poverty could hurt the poor most. Retrieved from http://foreignpolicy.com/2018/01/08/chinas-war-on-poverty-could-hurt-the-poor-most/

Davis, B. (2013). Beijing Endorses Market Role in Economy. Retrieved from www.wsj.com/articles/china-pledges-greater-role-for-market-in-economy

Huang, C. (2013). Party's third plenum pledges 'decisive role' for markets in China's economy. November 13. Retrieved from http://www.scmp.com/news/china/article/1354411/chinas-leadership-approves-key-reform-package-close-third-plenum

IISD (2015). Public Private Partnerships in China: On 2014 as a landmark year with past and future challenges. Retrieved from www.iisd.org/sites/default/files/publications/public-private-partnerships-china.pdf

ILO. (1998). *ILO declaration on fundamental principles and rights at work and its follow-up*. Retrieved from http://www.ilo.org/declaration/thedeclaration/textdeclaration/lang--en/index.htm

Li, S. (2004). Statement from the Chairman of the Bank of China. Retrived from www.h2o.china.com.news

Lu, J., & Tong, Z. (2016). Social responsibility: Chinese and MNCs are leading the way., May 17. Retrieved from http://www.chinadaily.com.cn/business/2016-05/17/content_25324074.htm

Ministry of Education of the People's Republic of China. (2015). Number of students higher education institutions. Retrieved from http://en.moe.gov.cn/Resources/Statistics/edu_stat_2016/2016_en01/201708/t20170822_311603.html

Ministry of Foreign Affairs of the People's Republic of China. (2017). China's Progress Report on Implementation of the 2030 Agenda for Sustainable Development, August. Retrieved from http://www.fmprc.gov.cn/web/ziliao_674904/zt_674979/dnzt_674981/qtzt/2030kcxfzyc_686343/P020170824650025885740.pdf

OECD. (2017). An immediate Chinese challenge: Further addressing vast income inequality. March 21. Retrieved from https://oecdecoscope.wordpress.com/2017/03/21/an-immediate-chinese-challenge-further-addressing-vast-income-inequality/

PwC. (2017). *Making a difference PwC China and Hong Kong's FY17 corporate responsibility report*. Retrieved from https://www.pwchk.com/en/corporate-responsibility/cr-fy17-full.pdf

Sanchez, C. (2017). From local to global: China's role in global poverty reduction and the future of development. December 7. Retrieved from http://www.worldbank.org/en/news/speech/2017/12/07/from-local-to-global-china-role-global-poverty-reduction-future-of-development

Saner, R., & Yiu, L. (2016). Looking on the Bright Side. *EFMD Global Focus*. Vol. 10 (2): 52-57.

Schiavenza, M. (2013). Mapping China's income inequality. September 13. Retrieved from https://www.theatlantic.com/china/archive/2013/09/mapping-chinas-income-inequality/279637/

Sen, A. (2000). Social exclusion: Concept application and security. Social Development Papers no. 1, Office of Environment and Social Development. Asian Development Bank, 1-54.

Sin, K. Y. (2013). Prof. Liu Baocheng was interviewed about CSR in China. April 28. Retrieved from http://www.cibe.org.cn/en/page/Default.asp?ID=918

Statista. (2018). China: Adult literacy 2015: Statistic. Retrieved from https://www.statista.com/statistics/271336/literacy-in-china/

Statista. (2018). China: Illiteracy rate by region 2016: Statistic. Retrieved from https://www.statista.com/statistics/278568/illiteracy-rate-in-china-by-region/2016

Thieriot,H., & Dominguez, C. (2015). *Public-Private partnerships in China: On 2014 as a landmark year, with past and future challenges.* International Institute for Sustainable Development, Canada. Retrieved from https://www.iisd.org/sites/default/files/publications/public-private-partnerships-china.pdf

Tian, X. (2016). *Managing international business in China* (2nd ed.). Cambridge: Cambridge University Press.

UNDESA (2016). Executive Summary of China's Actions on the Implementation of the 2030 Agenda for Sustainable Development, Voluntary National Review 2016. Retrieved from https://sustainabledevelopment.un.org

UNESCO (2018). China Education Report. Retrieved from www.uis.unesco.org/country/cn

UNIDO. (2018). What is CSR? Retrieved from https://www.unido.org/our-focus/advancing-economic-competitiveness/competitive-trade-capacities-and-corporate-responsibility/corporate-social-responsibility-market-integration/what-csr

United Nations, Economic and Social Council. (2016). *Commission for Social Development: Report on the fifty-third session* (E/2015/26). Retrieved from: https://undocs.org/E/2015/26

World Bank. (2017). Country snapshots: Private participation in infrastructure database. Retrieved from http://ppi.worldbank.org/snapshots/country/China

World Bank. (2017). *Country Poverty Brief: East Asian and Pacific China.* October. Retrieved from http://databank.worldbank.org/data/download/poverty/

World Bank. (2017). Social development overview. September 21. Retrieved from http://www.worldbank.org/en/topic/socialdevelopment/overview

Wu, D. D. (2013). *Modeling Risk Management in Sustainable Construction*. Berlin: Springer Berlin.

Zhang, A. (1993). Poverty alleviation in China: Commitment, policies and expenditures. United Nations Development Programme Reports. Retrieved from http://hdr.undp.org/sites/default/files/amei_zhang_0.pdf

Chapter 5

China's Worldwide Influence as a Disruptive Economy

By Arthur Rubens, Daniel Borgia and Roland Bardy

China's forty-year record of continuous growth and development is unmatched in recorded history. No other economy has grown so fast and has so dramatically altered the economies of the rest of the world. With its enormous working-age population, relatively low wages, pervasive government support for key industries, and availability of cheap currency, China is in a category of its own.

In recent years, China has emerged as the second largest economy in the world at $10 trillion. While the US economy remains the world's largest at $17 trillion, China's rate of annual GDP growth has long outpaced that of the US as well as most other nations of the world. At its current GDP growth rate, which has averaged about 7 percent in recent years, the size of China's economy is likely to surpass the United States within the next twenty years (Patton, 2016).

According to the World Bank, more than a half a billion Chinese have emerged from poverty during the last forty years (World Bank, 2017). In a study by the consulting firm McKinsey & Company, 76 percent of China's urban population will be considered middle class within the next five to six years. In contrast, just 4 percent of the urban population was considered middle class in the year 2000 (Iskyan, 2016).

Not only is the middle class growing in China — so, too, is the extreme wealthy. The Hurun Report states that China now has 568 billionaires, outpacing the United States with 535. Based on this same report, real estate, manufacturing and technology represent the leading industries producing these new billionaires class.

The resulting explosion of the middle class unleashed China's culture of business and entrepreneurship that served as the foundation for growth and development. As the economy has modernized, private enterprise has blossomed and state enterprises have steadily contracted.

The first three decades of China's opening to the outside world could be characterized as a period of catching up. It is marked by relatively unconstrained and unregulated growth and development. The last decade has been more strategic, controlled, and centralized, particularly since the ascension of President Xi Jinping.

Despite this more centralized approach, doing business in China still moves at a more rapid pace than it does in many other parts of the world. China's business environment is one that rewards quick decisions — the agility to seize opportunities before the competition gets there first. Companies are constantly revisiting their business plans and projections. Priorities change as frequently as schedules, and change seems to be the only constant (Ngai, 2018). The overriding strategy is growth, and this phenomenon is seen everywhere. You can find China's footprint in economies throughout the world, not only in the USA, but in many other economies in Western Europe, Asia, Africa, South America, and more recently Central and Eastern Europe.

China's Economic Growth

The brief story that follows illustrates the economic impact that trade with China can have on an industry and the economy. For many years, North Carolina was widely-recognized as the furniture capital of the world. When competition from inexpensive Japanese and Taiwanese imports decimated the U.S. steel and automobile industries in the 1980s and 1990s, furniture makers in North Carolina felt little impact and continued building beds, tables and chairs for consumers throughout the world. After the North American Trade Agreement (NAFTA) was passed, U.S. companies flocked to Mexico to establish Maquiladora (factories) to manufacture inexpensive duty free and trade free products for the U.S. and global markets. Again, the furniture industry of North Carolina continued to prosper, thrive and grow.

Then China happened.

Beginning around 2000, firms in the North Carolina furniture industry began to trade with China to take advantage of the cost advantages. Not long after those early investments, North Carolina's furniture manufacturers began to contract. Within a decade, long established furniture makers were driven out of business, thousands of jobs were lost, and unemployment in the region grew beyond 15%. In 2016, total U.S. imports of furniture and fixtures from China reached $20.4 billion (up from $4.4 billion in 2000). Today, the U.S. imports almost three quarters of all the furniture it consumes — much of it from China (Davis and Hilsenrath, 2016).

One of the authors of this chapter experienced first hand the rapidity of change in the Chinese economic environment. In the fall of 2002, when he settled into his apartment at Nanjing University at the beginning of a year-long sabbatical as a China Fulbright Scholar, he began working on a lecture that would be presented to audiences at several universities throughout China during the coming year. The objective in developing the presentation was to create a visual narrative that would be both compelling and easily understandable to his largely Chinese audiences. Using the World Bank's World Development Indicators (World Bank), he created a series of charts that compared the United States with China across a wide range of economic indicators, including labor and employment, financial market development, energy consumption, carbon emissions, trade, and economic growth.

Based on then current nominal GDP levels and 10-year average historical GDP growth rates for each country, he estimated that China would surpass the United States in economic output (GDP) in about 38 years, which at the time would have been around the year 2040. The comparison of the United States and China GDP carries enormous national and international political significance. Since the fall of the Soviet Union, the United States has been widely regarded as the world's only superpower. Over time, however, America's political, economic and military superiority over China has continued to narrow. Moreover, under Chinese President Xi Jinping, China's global power across all dimensions has arguably accelerated relative to the United States, particularly under President Donald Trump's America First policy, which has been characterized by United States withdrawal from global leadership.

Because of the drastic changes that have taken place in both China and the United States during the more than fifteen years since that original Fulbright presentation, there was a need to update the forecast. To accommodate the uncertainty inherent in forecasting future economic conditions, he developed new formulas based on two different sets of assumptions for China and the United States: (a) using the most recent 10-year average historical GDP growth rates in both countries and (b) using the most recent 5-year average historical growth rates. The results are shown in Figure 1. As many China observers know, although China's growth is still high by global standards, its GDP growth has slowed significantly in recent years. For example, using current World Bank World Development Indicators data, United States nominal GDP growth has increased from an average of about 2.8% during the 10-year period from 2007 through 2016 to more than 3.5% during the more recent 5-year period. In contrast, Chinese nominal GDP growth has slowed from an average of more than 13.5% during the last 10-years to just under 7% during the most recent 5-year period.

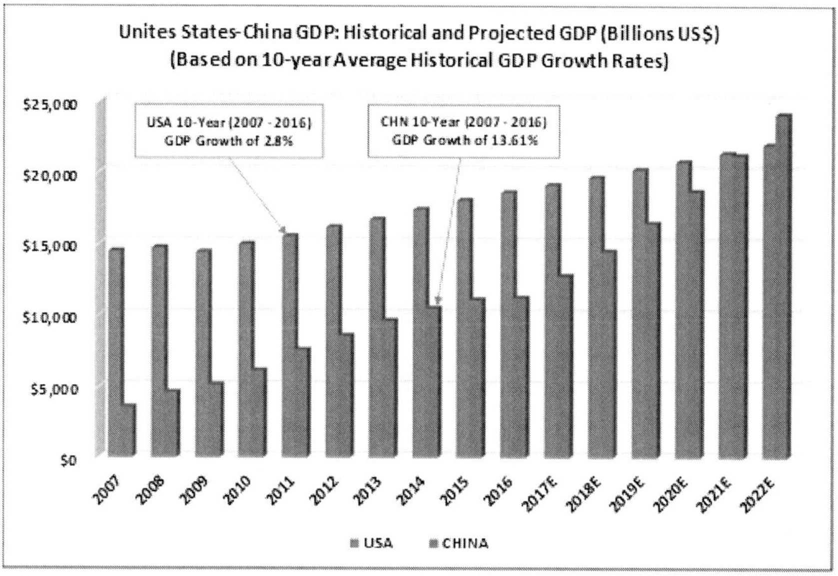

Figure 1

As a result, the length of time it takes for the Chinese economy to match the size of the U.S. economy depends on the rate of growth that prevails for each economy during the next 5- to 15-year period as shown in the accompanying charts. If the average 10-year growth rates for each country prevail, China will surpass the United States by 2022 (see Figure 1). If each country's 5-year growth rates prevail, China won't match the United States in size until about ten years later (see Figure 2).

Message to the West: China is Exceptional

Many readers may be familiar with the adage that when the United States sneezes, the world gets a cold. While that is still certainly true, judging by the global impact of the United States financial crisis a decade ago, or the recent gyrations of global stock markets in response to United States market volatility in February 2018, China is poised to become a significant viral agent as it continues to modernize its

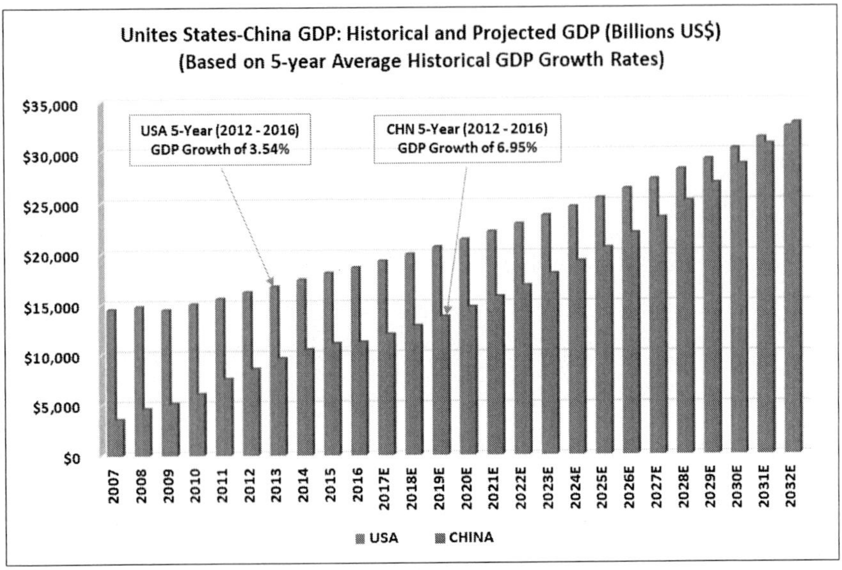

Figure 2

economy and advance its agenda of economic dominance.

In a recent article, a U.S. trade representative said: "China is an unprecedented threat that cannot be tamed by existing trade rules" *(The Economist* a, 2017). Despite the fact that the EU and other countries continue to draft stricter rules on foreign investment to constrain China, its influence abroad continues to grow. For example, while the 2008-2009 Financial Crisis had an impact on virtually all economies worldwide, its effects on countries such as Australia were somewhat muted, most probably because of its close economic ties with China, which has been less influenced by global events due to its strict control over its currency exchange rate and capital flows.

China's influence is likely to grow under President Donald Trump's inward-looking America First strategy. For example, in 2017 the United States, under the direction of the Trump administration, pulled out of the proposed Trans Pacific Partnership (TPP), which brought together 12 nations (many in Asia) and which represented a substantial portion of the world's GDP. Sensing an opening, China quickly stepped in to form its own trade agreement, the Regional Comprehensive Economic Partnership or RCEP. While the TPP imposed restrictions (such as protecting health and safety of workers) that most would argue work in favor of the United States, the RCEP is far less restrictive allowing China to set the rules in its favor. John Brinkley of *Forbes Magazine* (2017), called the U.S. abandoning the TPP as a "gift to China."

Consumption within economies of the west (United States, Europe, etc.) is often said to be driven by a planned and perceived obsolescence of products. Although China, like its western counterparts, is driven by similar desires to have more (idea of perceived obsolescences), China's Communist Party has an implicit message that, in order to be a good communist, one needs to be a good consumer. Some may remember, after the United States was attacked on September 11, 2001, George Bush, made the appeal to the people to "go shopping." Similarly, an appeal of spending money is being put forward by the central government in Beijing. This new mantra to shop has led to a burgeoning middle class in China, which is traveling and consuming products around the globe.

Among certain groups of Americans, the election of Donald Trump has revived a sense of American exceptionalism and a mentality that the United States is better than other nations. This sense of national exceptionalism has also reemerged in China. Historically, China has always viewed itself as the center of the world. In fact, the name of China in Chinese is *Zhong Guo*, which literally translates to "Middle Kingdom." China has worked hard and patiently during the past 40 years to assume its place at the center of global affairs.

According to President Xi and others, China has a 100-year strategy. The strategy, geopolitical in nature, has been termed the *China Dream*, which fundamentally says that China will be the economic, cultural and military superpower of the world by the year 2049 — exactly one century after the founding of the People's Republic of China during the Chinese Communist Revolution. China sees its role as an ancient and unique civilization that is destined and entitled to this position among nations of the world (Miller, 2016). President Xi and other party members are focused and determined to make the *China Dream* a reality (the term *China Dream* was taken from the title of the book with the same name by Col. Liu Mingfu, People Liberation Army).

Several years ago, after returning from a teaching assignment in China, one of the authors related to a group of American colleagues that he thought that China and the United States are similar. This resulted in a look of puzzlement among his United States associates. Many people in the United States feel that their country is the best in the world and that everything is better when compared to other countries. So, too, do many people in China, especially those that have greatly benefited from economic reform.

In 1976 *The New Yorker* magazine had a cover page that showed NYC and everything beyond it was the rest of the world (NYC was the center of the world). A few years ago (May 21, 2009), *The Economist* had a similar cover page for its story, however, this time it was Beijing in the center and the world surrounded it (see Figure 3).

How to Profit from China's Disruption

In business strategy research, academic researchers often study and write about innovations that possess a potentially disruptive impact upon an economy. Examples of disruptive innovations include the automobile at the turn of the century, the personal computer in the 1980s, the Internet in the 1990s, and the smart phone in the 2000s (Christensen, Raynor, and McDonald, 2015). While disruptive innovations are beneficial for the innovators and those who recognize their significance early, they are (of course) disruptive for many other economic participants.

Because of its strategic focus, its growth and its enormous size and population, China could be viewed as a disruptive force in its own right.

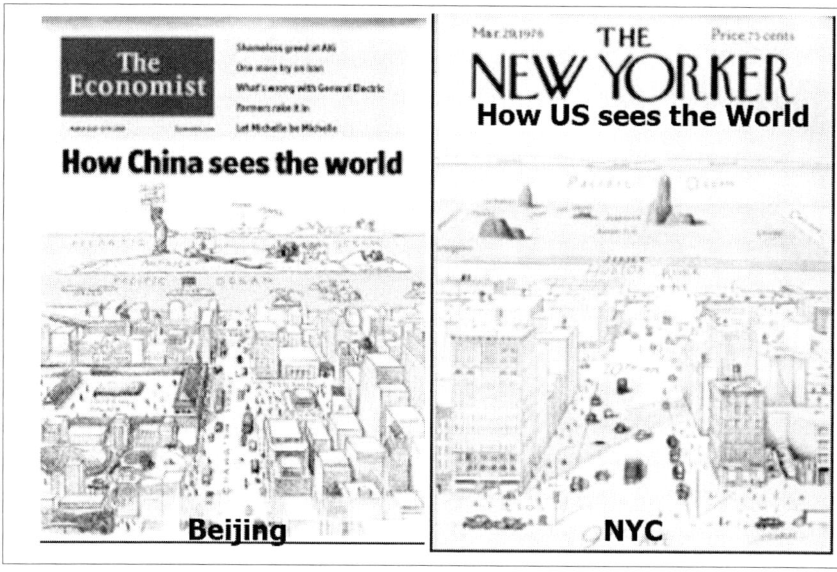

Figure 3

Rather than taking a wait-and-see approach, it is far better to anticipate implications of China's disruption and develop strategies to profit from it. To understand China and the position an investor must assume requires an understanding of key factors.

First, the growth of China as a leading economic power is different than the world has ever seen. This goes beyond the global nature of our world and market, but stems from how it developed into this formidable force. For example, the rise of economic powers in the past usually has been seen as accidental and due to a variety of circumstances out of the control of any one individual or nation. Examples of accidental growth include the United States in the 20th century and the United Kingdom in the 19th Century, as well as other countries in Western Europe in the 18th and 17th centuries. Conversely, China's rise in the late 1990s and this millennium is anything but accidental. When Deng opened the markets of China in 1979, his decision to be a dominant, economic force was calculated, planned, and strategic.

Second, those with limited exposure to China may not realize that it already has one of the world's largest concentration of consumers. Because of its growth and growing middle and upper class, China will soon be the largest global consuming nation. This growing middle class is fueling migration to urban centers. China now has more urban centers than most Western nations (Stalk and Michael, 2011).

Third, and most importantly, potential investors must understand that any private foreign investment in China is still going to be controlled by the local and central government. Although the late President Deng Xiaoping, and others since him, spoke of opening China's doors to the West, potential foreign investors should understand that the Chinese government is fully in control. In fact, control over foreign direct investment is mandated under Chinese law (See Foreign Investment regulations).

The Good, the Bad, and the Ugly

The Good

China is an incredibly exciting place to live and work. It has been developing at break-neck speed for the last 40 years beginning with China's great opening led by the late Deng Xiaoping who assumed power after the death of Mao. The emergence of China's global political and military stature coupled with the rapid development of China's infrastructure, advances in technology, and evolution of business from low-tech industry to high-tech manufacturing and services makes China one of the most attractive countries to invest, work and do business in today.

As it continues to modernize, China is increasingly focused on attracting foreign investment and is also actively looking for opportunities to invest abroad. This combination of factors will create opportunities for businesses and investors around the globe.

The Bad

The Chinese business system is complex and can only be fully understood through years of experience. To be successful, you must approach China through a Chinese lens, which requires identifying an in-country and native associate or intermediary who represents your business interests. A good first step is partnering with, or employing a person that you trust who can represent your business interests. Ideally, this associate or partner must not only be proficient in the nuisances of China's business culture, but must also be familiar with China's legal and regulatory system. Importantly, your partner or associate should have an excellent relationship with the Communist Party, as well as other important government officials. It is essential that you are able to trust this person because you will rely on him or her for almost every important relationship you develop and every strategic decision you make.

Chinese consumers havc very different tastes than Western consumers, and enjoy the status that buying foreign products brings. For example, many Chinese love McDonald's and Kentucky Fried Chicken (KFC), both because of the prestige, as well as for a menu that caters specifically to Chinese tastes. Thus, when dining at a Chinese KFC, a Chinese customer might have the option of a side of seasonal vegetables such as bamboo shoots in spring and lotus roots in summer rather than the American tradition of coleslaw. In addition, KFC in China offers a traditional breakfast menu featuring congee (rice porridge) which can be served with fried crullers or sesame flatbread for dipping. Although the Chinese love McDonald's hamburgers, the world's largest fast food chain has also made a few changes to its menu to cater to the Chinese palate: the Big N' Beefy comes with cucumbers rather than pickles and is also served with a spicier sauce. You can also order a corn cup if you don't want fries and get pineapples or taro root pies for dessert. McDonald's in China also delivers (on their electric moped) and is often open 24 hours a day.

Chinese consumers also have varying perceptions and attitudes toward other products and services. As an investor, you might conduct a survey or focus group to better understand the Chinese preference for a specific product or service you wish to provide. However, in doing so, you need to keep several things in mind as you interpret your findings. If you are using a numerical rating system from 1-7 to assess your product, the Chinese will generally move to the middle with their ratings — say 3 or 4 for example. Where we see things as opposite, the Chinese often don't, and something for them can be both good and bad. Also, for the Chinese, extremes can be undesirable, and they want to be polite. Keep in mind that the Chinese, although collective, want to distinguish themselves — this can be done through consumption, thus they might buy your luxury product to set themselves apart from others. However, in marketing your product, you might do better to steer the message of the marketing away from an emphasis on the individual to an emphasis on family or relationships.

While a signed contract signifies the consummation of a deal in the West, for a Chinese business person, the contract is often viewed as a snapshot of an agreement at a point in time to be renegotiated later. And when you find out that your Chinese counterpart intends to renegotiate a contract you thought was a done deal, you will usually be given very little time to think or react. Don't be fooled into thinking that unexpected changes or demands in terms are a sign of confusion or incompetence. Rather, these are strategies that your Chinese counterpart uses to maximize his or her returns.[1] In addition, many Chinese contracts include a buy-back option which is intended to provide the Chinese partner in a Sino-foreign venture with the ability to buy-out a foreign counterpart completely and on usually very favorable terms. In contracts with Chinese partners, be prepared to give a lot to get a little.

---

1. For additional discussion, see "The Wild, Wild East: Lessons for Success in Contemporary Capitalist China," Alan Refkin and Daniel Borgia, iUniverse, 2011. https://www.iuniverse.com/bookstore/bookdetail.aspx?bookid=SKU-000473150

When doing business in China, it is generally necessary to establish relationships with the government at some level. In many cases, it will be necessary to work with the local, regional, or provincial government where your business is located. However, you might also find it necessary to work with the central government depending on your product or service and the scope or scale of your business. In general, not only are these relationships necessary, but they are fundamentally important to your long-term success and must be maintained throughout the time you are engaged in business in China. These relationships extend beyond the concept of *guanxi*.

The Chinese place tremendous value on harmonious relationships. Whereas Americans value personal goals and accomplishments, the Chinese, as a collective society, value group goals and accomplishments. And when we speak of groups, this includes, not only the individual(s) and his/her place in the organization or political party, but also the family. Furthermore, age and rank are highly respected and acknowledged. When meeting, although shaking hands is becoming increasingly more accepted, an older person or person of different rank may nod or bow. Remember, senior persons begin greetings. Greet the oldest most senior person before others, and during group introductions, line up according to seniority with the senior person at the head of the line. Also, address the person by their rank or title. A good recommendation before you go is to obtain a book on Chinese business etiquette.

Before investing in China, foreign business people must realize that your Chinese counterpart is in control and has most of the power in your relationship. Hence, the power to negotiate and succeed lies in your ability to sell yourself to your Chinese counterpart by convincing them how they will benefit and profit. To a government official, the benefit could be things such as greater employment in their districts, better living conditions for their people, or greater tax revenues. To be successful in business in China it is important to not only understand Chinese culture and the Chinese way of doing business but also to accept and assimilate the Chinese culture and customs and way of doing business. Always remember that you are the guest in China. The more quickly and effectively that you begin to think like a Chinese, the greater your chances of success. Similarly, be sure you don't get involved in Chinese political, legal or social issues, or local affairs. A friend who spent many years in China said that when the do-gooder, or the well-intended spoke up and made judgments about someone or something that was clearly a Chinese issue the officials appeared to listen and showed respect (don't confuse this with agreeing with you); however, the very next day or at the next meeting, they informed everyone that this person was not welcomed back.

You need to know when to stay and when to go. Key to successful business negotiation in China is knowing when to stay (in the meeting), and most important, knowing when to go. For example, a friend who ran a business successfully for many years in China explained that when he was involved in negotiations to discuss his business with his Chinese counterparts, that at a certain point in the meeting and negotiations (often after the broader terms were agreed upon) he would realize that it was best that he leave the meeting, and allowed his intermediary (the local contact that he worked with and trusted) to continue the discussion on his behalf to work out the detail and nuance to implement the business decision. He often said that knowing when to leave was one of the keys to his success in doing business in China over the many years that he lived and worked there.

While Chinese business culture values patience, bluster, socializing, and face (giving and receiving), it is important to always remember that your Chinese counterpart will always be focused on cash. And everything about the deal making or negotiation process will be structured around maximizing cash flow. To maximize cash flow, Chinese businesspeople use a variety of techniques. For example, as noted earlier, while a signed contract signifies the consummation of a deal in the West, for a Chinese business person, the contract is often viewed as a point in time to be renegotiated later. In addition, Chinese business people are often vague, evasive, and indirect. Chinese business people will rarely say "no" even if the answer is no. Again, don't confuse these characteristics as weaknesses. Instead, understand them as strategies that your Chinese counterpart is using to gain the upper hand in the negotiations.

Finally, it is important to understand that some lines of business are off limits to foreign investors in China. In 1995, China's Ministry of Commerce (MOFCOM) published the *Foreign Investment Catalogue*. The Catalogue has been updated and modified occasionally since then and is divided into three sections:

> <u>Encouraged Industries</u>: Industries where the Chinese government is seeking foreign investments. Sometimes tax incentives, cheaper land costs and simplified approval procedures are granted to investors in these industries.
>
> <u>Restricted Industries</u>: Industries where the government has imposed restrictions such as foreign shareholding ratio's, special approvals requirements and limits on the operation of the company.
>
> <u>Prohibited Industries</u>: Companies operating in these industries are not allowed to have foreign investments.

However, the one thing you should already draw from the readings of this chapter and other chapters of this book is that there is a general lack of willingness on the part of China to offer a level playing field for foreign businesses and investors. For example, in both the encouraged and restricted categories of the FIC, certain industries require joint ventures and/or requirements that a company be controlled by Chinese nationals. For example, in the oil and natural gas exploration and development industry, foreign investment is required to take the form of equity joint ventures and cooperative joint ventures. In the accounting and auditing sectors, the Chief Partner of a firm must be a Chinese national.

Similarly in some sectors, the foreign shareholder's proportion of the investment is restricted and may not exceed a certain percentage. For example, foreign equity ownership is limited to: 50 percent in value-added telecom services (except in e-commerce); 49 percent in basic telecom enterprises; 50 percent in life insurance firms; and 49 percent in security investment fund management companies. Also, mandatory joint venture structures and equity caps give Chinese partner firms significant control, often allowing them to benefit from technology transfer. In addition, the relative opacity of the approval process and the broad discretion granted to authorities foster an environment where the Chinese government can impose deal-specific conditions beyond written legal requirements, often with the intent to force technology transfer as a condition of market access or to support industrial policies and the interests of local competitors (export.gov, 2018). Prior to investing in China, you are encouraged to understand the regulatory guidelines of the market or industry in which you are investing. Sources such as the United States Chambers of Commerce's can provide this information.

The Ugly

The bottom line for any American or other foreign entity that is thinking about making a significant investment in China is that while the opportunities available in this vast and rapidly expanding market are significant, succeeding in China is immensely challenging and you have to realize going in that you are ultimately not in control and have to be willing to give up a great deal to operate.

The Chinese have a plan and that plan is all about China. Although this might sound cynical, in the viewpoint of the authors as well as others, foreigners who have invested in China are tolerated only as long as they advance Chinese objectives.

China's Impact on the World Economy

China has turned decisively outward as part of its global economic strategy and few corners of the world have been untouched by China's influence including East Asia, the new center of its focus. America's status as the linchpin of the global economy is clearly under threat. All indicators are that China is gradually replacing the United States in this role. For example, in 2016, for the first time, China overtook the United States in outbound mergers and acquisitions (Yu, 2016). In the first nine months of 2016, the total value of mergers and acquisitions by Chinese companies jumped 68 percent with 601 proposals with a total dollar value of $173.9 billion. Although there was a slight drop in Chinese outbound deals (572) in 2017, the value of these transactions was over $97.7 billion in the first three quarters. As a result, the United States is seeing some of its classic holdings being acquired by China: New York City's Waldorf Astoria Hotel, the Starwood Hotel chain, Smithfield Foods, GE Appliances, and Motorola Mobility to name a few.

As part of this outward investment strategy, the New Development Bank was created in June 2015 by the BRICS (Brazil, Russia, India, China and South Africa) countries under the leadership of China with the objective of financing infrastructure and sustainable development projects in developing and emerging economies throughout the world. Similarly, the Asian Infrastructure Investment Bank was established in January 2016 as an initiative by the Chinese government in partnership with 37 regional and 20 non-regional nations. While officially partnering with the World Bank, both institutions should be viewed as financial institutions that consolidate China's financial power to further Chinese national interests.

Chinese firms possess multiple advantages when investing abroad relative to their Western counterparts. First, Chinese private and state-owned enterprises are not as focused on short-term outcomes. In fact, Chinese enterprises are often willing to accept short-term losses to secure long-term market dominance. Second, Chinese firms benefit from the support and expansion politics of its government. Third, and most importantly, United States and European investors must compete with Chinese firms that enjoy both home and foreign country advantages in many markets. For example, when a Western firm wishes to expand into Africa or Asia, they not only need to compete with Chinese investors, but also restrictions imposed by their home country (and sometimes the host country as well). For many Chinese firms, such restrictions either do not exist or have been addressed through negotiation or other means (*The Economist* 2017 a, b; Johnson 2017).

To consider some of the advantages held by China, let's consider the approach to investment in Africa in which foreign aid is intertwined with Chinese economic policy. Chinese aid (or "Official Development Assistance) totaled roughly $5 billion in 2016 (IMF). Fully half of that goes to Africa (China-Africa Research Initiative 2018). While U.S. development assistance 2000 to 2014 was $366 billion as opposed to $81 billion spent by China, other finance flows from China were $273 billion vs. $28 billion from the U.S. (Griffiths 2017). You might ask, why would an investor have to worry whether Chinese financing falls under the category of development assistance or not? The reason is that when the U.S. or any other Western donor dispenses aid money, it is about supporting structural and political reforms like improvement of governmental institutions. Donor assistance is tagged to those reforms, and both the Western donors and the recipients look at assistance to be conditional. China, as per the above statistics, only tags a small amount of money to such conditions. So finance flows from China are considered more attractive than Western aid by recipient countries. They only have a few or no political strings attached as they are given unconditionally, which ultimately tends to undermine the effectiveness of Western aid.

Chinese assistance includes grants for commercial purposes: aid intended to promote exports, subsidies to the private sector, and funds in support of private development (Dreher et al., 2015, p. 22). In contrast, firms in Europe and the United States are generally not directly engaged with their country foreign aid programs and strategies. Still, aggregate Chinese direct investment in Africa compared to total African foreign direct investment is relatively modest. China, over the span of the 20th century, certainly is a latecomer to Africa. However, it is now surpassing its competitors from the West and its pattern of investment is different from that of all other countries: The world as a whole has six times as much direct investment in the U.S. as in Africa, reflecting the fact that most of it goes to advanced economies. While Chinese foreign direct investment in Africa accounted for only about 6% of total foreign direct investment of $728 billion in 2016(UNCTAD 2017), Chinese foreign direct investment in Africa ($36 billion in 2016) now exceeds that of the U.S. (Kazeem 2017).

In addition to traditional brick and mortar business, communications enterprises and media initiatives play a central role in China's Africa strategies. The privately owned Huawei and the state-owned ZTE (Zhong Xing Telecommunication Equipment Company Limited) are omnipresent in Africa. Both companies have training centers in several African countries, and Huawei estimates that its initiatives provide job opportunities for more than 10,000 Africans (Rønning 2014). In addition, StarTimes, a private Chinese media enterprise with no Western counterpart, expanded into Africa just ten years after it was founded in 1988 and has since established subsidiaries in 30 of the 54 African countries (Jiang et al. 2016).

Overall trade between Africa and China grew at a compound annual rate of 24.7% from 1995 to 2015. Chinese commodity exports to Africa grew by 22.7% on average, increasing from $2.5 billion in 1995 to $92.7 billion in 2015. China is the single largest trading partner of Africa, accounting for about 15 percent of the continent's total trade. Africa accounts for only about 5 percent of Chinese trade. In 2014, trade between Africa and China was worth $221.5 billion (up from $ 114 billion in 2010). Imports from China and exports to China accounted for $106 billion and $116 billion respectively (UN Comtrade, 2015).

Given China's deliberative strategy for dominating investment in many developing and emerging nations, how can foreign investors from other countries hope to compete? One alternative would be for Western firms to partner with their home and/or developing country governments on strategic investments and projects. This approach would be supported by the targets set out by the United Nations 2030 Development agenda (e.g. in the targets group of goal 9 regarding sustainable industry and of goal 17 on partnerships). Partnering with non-industry partners has been a successful arrangement in the past. For example, when the communist regime finally was defeated in Angola, Chevron entered into partnerships (Kolk and Lenfant 2013) with the new government. A similar approach was used by Unilever which sought partnerships with local government authorities and civil society organizations like UNICEF, the WWF and the World Conservation Union for almost all of their African operations (van Lakerveld and van Tulder, 2017).

Beyond these partnering strategies are there other ways for the Western investor to circumvent the dominance of China? One other approach to compete with China is to take advantage of the negative reputation China has earned in quite a few markets. Several nations have viewed the intervention of China in their countries with much reserve.

For example, some of China's immediate neighbors have become irritated over expanding power across their border. Take the case of Vietnam, Malaysia and Myanmar and other places in ASEAN (Association of Southeast Asian Nations) area. "Vietnam has become a rich environment in terms of mergers and acquisitions and capital market activity … as is Myanmar … and Malaysia could emerge as a dark horse as well …" City Bank's ASEAN corporate investment head is quoted in a January 2, 2018, interview in the *Singapore Straits Times* (Luo 2018). The values of mergers and acquisitions in South East Asia in the first three quarters of 2017 hit $53.5 billion, up 23% from the year before (Zhu 2017).

One main issue is logistics, and United States and/or European firms would have the chance to partner with local enterprises from

ASEAN. However, the Western investor must be prepared to meet a completely different competitor in this region. Southeast Asia has become what is called a pivot of current Russian foreign policy and strategic thinking, with the opening up of bilateral ties and multilateral trade and investment mechanisms (Tsvetov 2016). As experienced observers are noting, there is still a chance for the U.S. to enter the regional calculus, building on the new and emerging security partnerships with Indonesia, Vietnam and Myanmar (Huang 2017). It is hoped that U.S. politicians and business people will deploy joint forces in that direction.

Perhaps the most promising way for Western firms to effectively compete with Chinese operations in developing and emerging markets is to increase multilateral cooperation. In this respect, the United Kingdom's government and firms within that country have learned lessons from their colonial past and are now building a framework for a trilateral UK-China-Africa cooperation. In terms of strategy, special attention is being given to projects involving infrastructure, agriculture and trade facilitation, with trial engagements in Kenya and South Africa (Gu et al. 2017).

One benefit of a multilateral approach is that it could contribute to building trust and a positive perception of Western investors. The investor will benefit from policy-makers and operatives on the ground in fostering sufficient levels of cognitive-based political trust with their African counterparts (Barton 2016).

Trust has at all times been the basis for getting along with other parties. But mutual trust is not what Africans see in their relations to the Chinese: When China went into Africa to undercut the U.S. and other Western nations, it received some goodwill (and a lot of resources) for her money. However, it has not purchased the hearts and minds of the Africans. The stance of Africans on relations contradicts Chinese ideology and culture cold-war style (Alozie and Thomas, 2016, p. 18).

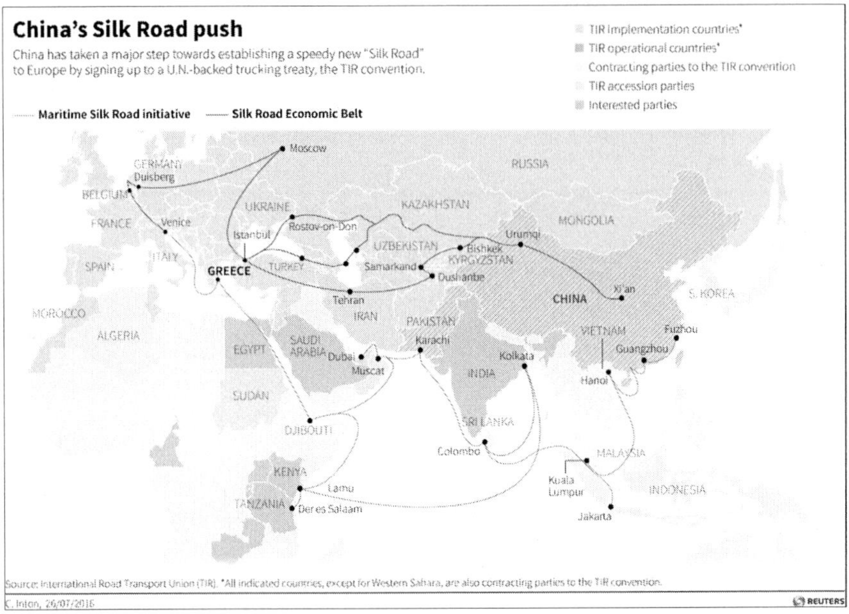

Figure 4

Xi Jinping's Belt and Road Initiative (BRI)

Under the leadership of President Xi Jinping, China initiated in 2013 its well-known Belt and Road Initiative (BRI). This ambitious strategy places China in the driver's seat for far-reaching improvements in the infrastructure of European and Asian land and sea routes that places China at the center of regional and global trade and capital flows. When the strategy is fully implemented, BRI will connect nearly 70 countries across Asia, Africa and Europe in order to facilitate the distribution of goods and services to consumers in both established developed economies and rapidly growing emerging economies (see Figure 4) (Dollar, 2017).

China's BRI initiative has implications for firms wishing to do business both inside and outside of China. Opportunities will be available not only for countries and firms located in member countries along these land and sea routes but also for companies and investors across the globe as China and the member countries continue to develop and grow, creating an enormous number of new middle-class consumers who will increasingly demand goods and services.

During its first three years, the BRI initiative has been focused largely on raw material, basic industries, and infrastructure investment including iron and steel, the power grid, real estate and construction, automobiles, railways and highways (Freedom House, 2018). This has created opportunities for U.S. and European investors. For example, the Silk Road's dry port installations in the newly built town of Nurkent in Kazakhstan will be operated through DP World of Dubai (Higgins 2017), a firm that is partnering with U.S. Customs and Border Patrol in the Customs-Trade Partnership Against Terrorism initiative (WorldTribune.com 2008). If a firm is eligible for this partnership, it could potentially use this as justification for expanding the deal to include U.S.-Dubai-Kazakh cooperation. For example, a U.S. firm such as the United Technologies Corporation (UTC) subsidiary in Dubai (UTC Building & Industrial Systems) could become involved (Dawley 2014). By comparison: Why would a construction equipment engineering firm from the relatively small country of Austria (Palfinger) establish a regional headquarter in Singapore and enter into a partnership with a local offshore outfitter (Wong-Fong), and there is no comparable U.S. venture? (Wong Fong Engineering 2017).

One reason for the current lack of joint U.S.-Chinese operations might be that there is not enough history of handling cross-border consortia in the civil engineering and construction (Ngowi et al. 2005). However, globalization has transformed the engineering industry in a way that civil engineers need to be prepared to address in the increasingly diverse field of multi-national projects that span across countries and cultures. Firms that sponsor professional practice that meets these requirements will be able to expand in areas currently occupied by their Chinese counterparts (Jesiek et al. 2014).

According to McKinsey & Company, beginning in 2018, China will begin to shift focus from infrastructure and basic industries and material to technology-related industries such as finance, medicine, education, and artificial intelligence (McKinsey, 2018). The West is still ahead with technologies in these fields, and if a Western firm can effectively secure the technology transfer, a broad array of opportunities will open up.

Aside from the BRI initiative, potential investors should increasingly look to China as a destination for expanding production, distribution, and services. China's government continues to invest in and expand the size and number of its free trade zones (FTZs) to attract increasing amounts of foreign direct investment. According to a September 2017 report by the China Briefing, China currently has eleven FTZs (with seven more are either planned or under development) with each providing incentives for investments focused on a specific industry (Dezan Shira & Associates, 2017).

Beyond some of the planned initiatives of BRI there are a number of sectors that provide opportunities for investors. Sectors such as: technology-oriented businesses, especially artificial intelligence, high value sectors like aviation and automotive, and service sectors such as wealth management, education and healthcare might all be desirable for outbound investment. It's also worth noting that if the political headwinds in the U.S. look bad for Chinese investment, particularly with the uncertainty generated by the Trump administration, China is likely to take its money elsewhere where it is more likely to be welcomed with open arms. Examples of this might be elsewhere in Asia and part of Europe, including the Central and Eastern countries.

In regard to inbound investment, China is likely to target inbound investment in sectors such as:

> *Electric Cars and other new-energy vehicles, including batteries and power cells.* China plans to dominate the global electric-vehicle (EV) during the next decade and electric

vehicles are already pervasive and easy to rent, buy and service (one of the authors is currently leasing a small electric car in China).

Health care and pharmaceuticals. China is focused on modernizing its entire health care industry including medicine and pharmaceuticals, hospitals and surgical capabilities, med-tech startups and other health-related businesses.

Financial Services. Another industry that is poised to attract a lot of foreign investment in the financial services industry including banking, insurance, investment banking, mutual funds and asset and wealth management.

In pursuing these sectors of possible opportunities in China, savvy investors might need to look beyond the major cities of Beijing, Guangzhou or Shanghai to locate their businesses. Opportunities in these sectors might be found in what some have called the third China: cities like Xi'an, Nanjing, or Wuhan. Also, investors might look beyond the urban centers. As China's middle class grows and many flock to the cities, new opportunities might develop in current or previous rural communities.

In March 2018, the Chinese government's new Five-Year Plan was presented. The plan focuses on three overriding concepts: the BRI policy, a supply-side reform (closing down inefficient industries), and the more recent *Made in China 2025* strategy, an industrial policy that aims to increase indigenous innovation and self-reliance (Letts 2017). Whatever the outcome of President Xi Jinping's announcements on the new Five-Year plan, the challenges on the political side for the European Union and the United States will remain high.

Summary

China is in the midst of a shift from an investment-driven economy to a productivity-and-consumption-driven economy. Increasingly, China's massive and growing middle class is showing signs of saving less and spending more. In fact, the McKinsey Global Institute (MGI) reported that China's working-age population will account for 12 percent of global spending by 2030 and will increasingly gravitate toward consumption of premium quality products and brands, presenting enormous opportunities for manufacturers of products and services worldwide (MGI, 2016). According to the China Internet Network Information Center (CNNIC), which is the administrative agency responsible for Internet affairs under China's Ministry of Information Industry, by early 2017, China had more than 730 million internet users or more than 52 percent of the population online. Moreover, more than 95 percent of those online had mobile internet access (Statistical Report on Internet Development in China, 2017).

Since the beginning of China's reform period forty years ago, a number of foreign companies have found success in China. Brands like Coca Cola, McDonald's, Walmart, KFC, General Motors, Volkswagen, Boeing, and many others have been doing business and selling products in China for decades. As successful as these firms have been, for a variety of reasons, many other companies have chosen not to do business in China or have been prohibited from doing so, include Google, Twitter, Facebook, the *New York Times*, and YouTube.

For example, China has very strict regulations on Internet access and VPNs to prevent consumers from circumventing the Great Firewall. As a result, firms operating in China have experienced a variety of challenges with Internet access and networking: Examples include networks that are frequently down or blocked and the inability for companies to link with their partner companies or corporate offices. Apple recently received orders from China's Ministry of Industry and

Information Technology (MIIT) to remove all VPN apps from their App Store in China. Other VPN providers in China have also been subject to this same requirement, according to Mayo (2017). More recently Marriott International was ordered by the Shanghai Cyberspace Administration to shut down its Chinese websites and apps for a week after Marriott conducted an e-mail survey in which it categorized Hong Kong, Macau, Taiwan and Tibet as separate countries. Shanghai officials said Marriott survey had "violated Chinese law" and "hurt the feelings of Chinese people" (Sun, 2018). A recent study by Freedom House (2018) placed China at the end of its list of countries in regard to internet access. For most firms, good, fast, reliable Internet is essential for doing business in our global world. As a result, continued or increased restrictions on Internet access may cause many Western businesses to rethink their China strategy or to leave China permanently if Internet access to the outside world is curtailed or further restricted.

Western investors should also carefully consider China's recent economic slowing. While China became the world's leader in international trade in 2014 (accounting for 10% of global trade), the growth in trade has recently slowed. For example, Chinese imports increased only 4.5 percent, year-on-year, to $177.10 billion in December of 2017, much slower than expectations of 13 percent. This was the weakest increase in inbound shipments since December 2016 (Trading Economics 2018). This slowing may have an impact on African countries that are dependent on trade with China and could spill over to countries that are not highly dependent on trade with China. Morever, economists are increasingly concerned that China's economy is largely built on credit and government-driven investment. The long-awaited transition to a consumption-based economy driven by Chinese consumers has not yet begun. If the Chinese economy falters unexpectedly, its slowing could lead to a global recession. If China sneezes, the world may catch a cold.

Before concluding this chapter, we leave you with a few words of caution. As mentioned earlier in the chapter, while China's growth

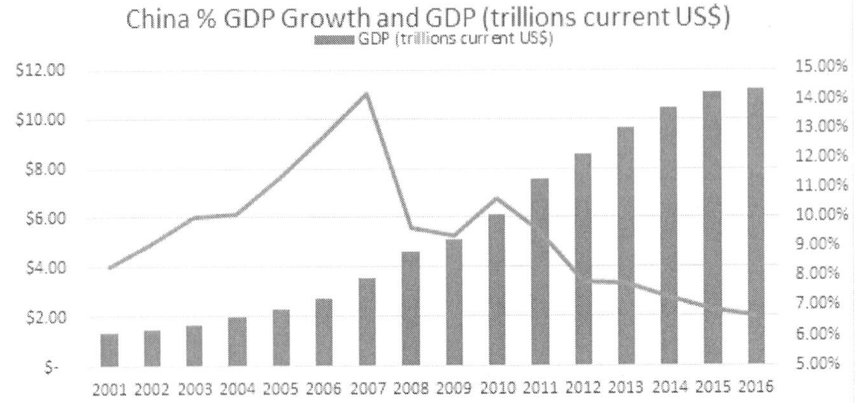

Figure 5. *(Source: World Bank, World Development Indicators)*

during the past 40 years has been fast and impressive, there has been a marked slowing beginning with the onset of the financial crisis in 2007. As Figure 5 shows, China's annual GDP growth rate of around 7% in 2016 is about half that at its peak of around 14% in 2007. Many economists and China observers expect that its lower GDP growth is here to stay. In fact, some predict it will continue to decline in the years ahead even in the absence of a shock such as a recession, which China hasn't experienced for more than forty years, or a financial crisis, which could be looming on the horizon.

China's debt as a percentage of GDP surpassed 300% in late 2017 and is expected to continue to soar in the years to come, according to the Institute for International Finance. Many financial experts are alarmed, and some are even predicting a U.S.-styled financial crisis leading to a global recession. So, while the promise of China is great, so are its risks, and potential investors should carefully weigh the potential against the risks before making a significant commitment.

In closing, our advice to those interested in doing business is one of cautious optimism. While the challenges and barriers to engaging successfully in business in China are great, so, too, are the opportunities. We hope you agree that this chapter provides useful guidance doing business in China. Whether you decide to invest or not, the reality is that China will have an impact on you and your business no matter where you are in the World.

In a recent article, Diongding Chen (2017) wrote that "China has a new grand strategy and the West should be ready." In a speech just before his second term as the party's general secretary, Chinese President Xi Jinping claimed that there were more takers internationally for Chinese values. China, he said, offers "a new option for other countries and nations who want to speed up their development while preserving their independence." With China rapidly taking its place alongside the United States as an equal in global affairs, the most important question for the West and the international order is: "How will China define herself and the relationship between China and the world? The answer to this question will have huge implications for future international cooperation and conflict, and even peace and war" (Chen, 2017).

References

Alozie, N. O., and Thomas, K. (2016). United States vs. China in Africa: The Policy Battle for Hearts and Minds and the Difference it Makes. *Journal of Public Management & Social Policy*, Vol. 22 (3), Article 5, pp. 1 - 26.

Barton, B. R. (2016). *Trust and the politics of security risk management : the European Union's engagement of China in Africa*. PhD Thesis. University of Hong Kong, Pokfulam, Hong Kong.

Brinkley, J. (2017). Trump hands China a gift in dumping Trans Pacific-Partnership. Forbes, 24, January 2017. Retrieved Oct 25, 2017 from: https://www.forbes.com/sites/johnbrinkley/2017/01/24/trump-dumps-trans-pacific-partnership-sad/#1e1ee73475dc

China-Africa Research Initiative (2018). *Chinese foreign aid data.* China Africa Research Initiative *at* Johns Hopkins University's School of Advanced International Studies. Baltimore, MD. http://www.sais-cari.org/data-chinese-foreign-aid-to-africa

Christensen, C., Raynor, M. & McDonald, R. (2015). What is disruptive Innovation. *Harvard Business Review.* Jan-Feb.

Davis, B. & Hilsenrath, J. (2015). The Great Unraveling: How the China Shock, Deep and Swift, Spurred the Rise of Trump. Retrieved October 24, 2017 from: http://www.wsj.com/articles/how-the-china-shock-deep-and-swift-spurred-the-rise-of-trump-1470929543?mod=djem_jiewr_MG_domainid

Dawley, S. (2014). Creating new paths? Offshore wind, policy activism, and peripheral region development. *Economic Geography*, Vol. 90 (1), pp. 91-112.

Dezan Shira & Associates (2017). "Investing in China's Free Trade Zones." China Briefing: Business Intelligence from Dezan Shira & Associates. September 21, 2017. Retrieved January 26, 2018, from: http://www.china-briefing.com/news/2017/09/21/investing-in-chinas-free-trade-zones.html

Dollar, D. (2017). Order from Chaos. Foreign Policy in a Troubled World: A how-to guide for managing the end of the post-Cold War era. *Brooking Institution's Blog.* Retrieved January 26, 2018 from: https://www.brookings.edu/blog/order-from-chaos/2017/05/08/yes-china-is-investing-globally-but-not-so-much-in-its-belt-and-road-initiative/)

Dreher, A., Fuchs, A., Hodler, R., Parks, B., Raschky, P., and Tierney, M. (2015). Aid on demand: African leaders and the geography of China's foreign assistance. Cesifo Working Papers 5439, CESi6 Group, Munich.

The Economist (2017 a*)*. How China is battling ever more intensely in world markets. But does it play fair? Sept. 23. https://www.economist.com/news/leaders/21729430-does-it-play-fair-how-china-battling-ever-more-intensely-world-markets

The Economist (2017 b). What to do about China's "sharp power" China is manipulating decision-makers in Western democracies. The best defence is transparency. Dec. 14. ttps://www.economist.com/news/leaders/21732524-china-manipulating-decision-makers-western-democracies-best-defence

Export.Gov. Openness-to-Restrictions-Upon-Foreign-Investment (2018). Retrieved Jan 15, 2018 from: https://www.export.gov/article?id=China-1-Openness-to-Restrictions-Upon-Foreign-Investment

Frank, R. (2016). China has more billionaires than US: Report. CBS.com, Febuary 24, 2016. Retrieved January 1, 2018, from: https://www.cnbc.com/2016/02/24/china-has-more-billionaires-than-us-report.html

Freedom House (2018). Retrieved Feb 5, 2018; https://freedomhouse.org/regions/asia-pacificLi General Office of Leading Group of Advancing the Building of the Belt and Road Initiative (2016). "Belt and Road in Big Data 2016". Beijing: the Commercial Press.

Griffiths, J. (2017). *Report exposes size of China's secretive aid budget.* CNN, updated October 11, 2017. http://edition.cnn.com/2017/10/11/asia/china-overseas-aid/index.html

Gu, J., Holmes, P., Rollo, J., Snell, S., Mendez-Parra, M., and Procopio, M. (2017). *China–UK–Africa Trilateral Cooperation on Trade and Investment: Prospects and Challenges for Partnership for Africa's Development.* IDS Evidence Report No. 218. IDS (Institute of Development Studies), University of Sussex. Brighton, UK.

Higgins, A., (2017): New Port for China: Landlocked Kazakhstan. NY Times, Dec. 30., p. 1.

Huang, X. (2016). Is China Building Africa? *European Financial Review*, Vol. 7, pp. 7 -13.

Huang, C. H. (2017). Book review on David BH Denoon „China, the United States and the Future of Southeast Asia". *Contemporary Southeast Asia: A Journal of International and Strategic Affairs*, Vol. 39 (3), p. 587 – 589.

IMF (International Monetary Fund; 2016). *External Debt Statistics: Guide for Compilers and Users – Appendix III, Glossary.* IMF, Washington, DC.

Iskyan, K (2016). China's Middle Class is Exploding. *Business Insider.* Retrieved Jan 12, 2018, from: http://www.businessinsider.com/chinas-middle-class-is-exploding-2016-8

Jesiek, B.K., Zhu, Q., Woo, S.E., Thompson, J., and Mazzurco, A., (2014). Global engineering competency in context: Situations and behaviors. *Online Journal for Global Engineering Education*, Vol. 8 (1), pp. 1-14. http://digitalcommons.uri.edu/ojgee/vol8/iss1/1

Jiang, F., Li, S., Rønning, H., and Tjønneland, E. (2016*).* The voice of China in Africa: media, communication technologies and image-building. *Chinese Journal of Communication,* Vol. 9 (1), pp. 1- 7.

Johnson, I. (2017): Xi Jinping and China's New Era of Glory. *New York Times*, Oct. 13.

Kazeem, Y. (2017) China doubled its investment spend in Africa in 2016 as US and UK fell. *Quartz africa*, May 09.

Kolk, A., and Lenfant, F. (2013). Multinationals, CSR and partnerships in Central African conflict countries. *Corporate Social Responsibility and Environmental Management,* Vol. 20 (1), pp. 43-54.

Letts, S. (2017). China's next five-year plan on the way and it is a big deal for Australia. *ABC News Australia, Oct. 15.*

Luo, S. (2018). Eye on Vietnam as Asian Confidence Rises. Singapore Straits Times, Jan. 02.

Mayo, S. (2017). Apple Removes VPN Apps from App Store in China to comply with local laws. *9To5MAC.* Retrieved Feb 7, 2018, from: https://9to5mac.com/2017/07/29/apple-removes-vpn-apps-from-app-store-in-china-to-comply-with-local-laws/

McKinsey Global Institutes (MGI). (2016). "Urban world: The global consumers to watch," March 2016. Richard Dobbs, James Manyika, Jonathan Woetzel, Jaana Remes, Jesko Perrey, Greg Kelly, Kanaka Pattabiraman, and Hemant Sharma. Retrieved January 26, 2018, from: https://www.mckinsey.com/global-themes/urbanization/urban-world-the-global-consumers-to-watch

Miller, A. (2016). China's 100 Year Strategy: Beijing has a documented plan to be the premier global superpower by 2049. It's hallway there. *Trumpet.* Retrieved January 21, 2018 from: https://www.thetrumpet.com/14006-chinas-hundred-year-strategy

MOFCOM (Ministry of Commerce of China; 2012). *Statistical Bulletin of China's Outward Foreign Direct Investment*. Beijing: China Statistics Press.

Ngai, J. (2018). What you need to know about working for a Chinese company? McKinsey & Company Retrieved January 3, 2018, from: . https://www.mckinsey.com/global-themes/china/what-you-need-to-know-about-working-for-a-chinese-company

Ngowi A. B., Pienaar, E., Talukhaba, A. and Mbachu, J. (2005). The globalisation of the construction industry—a review." *Building and Environment* Vol. 40 (1), pp. 135-141.

Patton, M. (2016). China's Economy will overtake Americas in 2018. Forbes (29, April 2016). Retrieved Oct 25, 2017 from: https://www.forbes.com/sites/mikepatton/2016/04/29/global-economic-news-china-will-surpass-the-u-s-in-2018/#782747f6224a

Refkin, A. and Borgia, D. (2011). The wild wild east: Lessons for success in contemporary capitalist China. iUniverse. Available at: https://www.iuniverse.com/bookstore/bookdetail.aspx?bookidesku-000473150.

Rønning, H. (2014). *How much 'Soft Power' does China have in Africa?* Paper presented at the international conference "China and Africa Media,

Communications and Public Diplomacy". Christian Michelsen Institute: Bergen, Norway.

Stalk, G., and Michael, D. (2011). What the West Doesn't Get About China. *Harvard Business Review*, June, pp. 25 – 27.

Statistical Report on Internet Development in China (January 2017), China Internet Network Information Center (CNNIC). Retrieved January 26, 2018, from: https://cnnic.com.cn/IDR/ReportDownloads/201706/P020170608523740585924.pdf

Sun, N. (2018). China orders Marriott to shut down website for a week. *Nikkei Asian Review*. Retrieved Jan 7, 2018 from: https://asia.nikkei.com/Politics-Economy/International-Relations/China-orders-Marriott-to-shut-down-websites-for-a-week?utm_source=taboola&utm_medium=%7Bsite%7D&utm_campaign=BA%20JP&utm_term=%7Bcampaign_id%7D&utm_content=Evergreen%20content

Trading Economics (2018). *China Imports 1983-2018*. Retrieved from https://tradingeconomics.com/china/imports

Tsvetov, A. (2016). After Crimea: Southeast Asia in Russia's foreign policy narrative. *Contemporary Southeast Asia: A Journal of International and Strategic Affairs*, Vol. 38 (1), pp. 55-80.

Yu, X. (2016). China is now buying more companies than the US. *South China Morning Post* (October 5, 2016). Retrieved January 28, 2018 from: http://www.businessinsider.com/china-buying-more-companies-than-us-2016-10

UN Comtrade (2015). *United Nations commodity trade statistics database.* United Nations Statistics Division: New York.

UNCTAD (United Nations Conference on Trade and Development; (2017). World Investment Report 2017. United Nations, Geneva.

van Lakerveld, A., and van Tulder, R. (2017). Managing the transition to sustainable supply chain management practices: Evidence from Dutch leader firms in Sub-Saharan Africa. *Review of Social Economy*, Vol. 75 (3), pp. 255-279.

Wong Fong Engineering (2017). *Our joint venture with global group Palfinger.* Wong Fong Media: Singapore. http://www.wongfong.com/news_bulletin/our-joint-venture-with-global-group-palfinger-palfinger-marine-singapore

World Bank (2017). The World Bank in China. Retrieved December 20, 1017, from: http://www.worldbank.org/en/country/china/overview#3

WorldTribune.com (2008): Gulf firm is first international port operator to be certified for security by U.S. World Tribune, June 23. http://www.worldtribune.com/worldtribune/WTARC/2008/me_gulf0246_06_16.asp

Zhu, M. (2017). GLP & Grab among highest contributors to Southeast Asia M&A deals in 3Q. *The Edge: Business and Investment Weekly*. Singapore, Oct. 24.

Chapter 6

China's Environmental Awareness and Potential for Leadership

By Attilio Mucelli, Francesca Spigarelli and Jonathan Marano

After the opening reforms, launched by Deng Xiaoping, China embraced a transition process that led to epochal institutional, legal, economic and social transformations. The centrally planned system was gradually dismantled with the rise of a dynamic private economy system accompanied by the equalization of State Owned Enterprises. The result was a four-decade unceasing growth that lead the country to the status of second world economic power in early 2010s. At the same time, environmental deterioration and social imbalances emerged. Industrialization was pursued with little attention to social and environmental negative externalities, which in turn started undermining the country's economic and political stability.

Indeed, the global economic crisis had an extensive impact on China's path to modernization. The government acknowledged that the double-digit economic growth obtained by the so-called world factory model, and characterized by the developmental strategy after the reform, was not suitable anymore. The adoption of a new model emerged in order to avoid the risk of falling into a middle-income trap and to address social and economic issues of growth.

The awareness took the name of New Normal in the public narrative — that is, a new phase of reform where quality replaced growth "by any means." Within this framework a major attention on environmental protection, green growth and social stability has been promoted along with capital-intensive and more value-added industries, advanced services and a new public welfare.

One of the main pillars of the New Normal phase is the so-called Green Revolution, which is making China one of the most active players and contributors to the 21st century environmental protection global challenge. Massive investments in green technologies and environmental restoration are ensured and supported by a deep re-visitation of the related policies, legal frameworks and institutional patterns.

While China is becoming the world's largest investor in environmental protection, the quest for high-end technologies is turning into a big opportunity for western companies, which can leverage their higher capability in this sector. The increased attention to the quality of life for a wide portion of Chinese citizens and the re-shaping of the country's industrial landscape have created business opportunities for foreign firms, even in the agriculture and food sector. Foreign firms can leverage their advanced know-how and technologies with a decisive competitive advantage.

Legal and institutional reforms also present challenges and barriers, for both authorities and foreign firms. Lack of financial and technical capability, along with institutional imperfections and imbalances, often undermine enforcement of regulations and policies at the local level.

Air, Soil, Water: A Comprehensive Disaster

To better understand the reforms, it is useful to look to the main areas of environmental degradation in China. (Kan, 2009)

The first area is outdoor air pollution. In Chinese cities this is the biggest challenge for public health, considering the exorbitant level reached by the annual average concentrations of inhalable particles. Effects on health include increase in respiratory symptoms, hospitalization, and premature mortality. (Chen et al. 2004)

At the beginning of the last decade, the World Health Organization (WHO) and some Chinese scientists estimated that outdoor air pollution caused around 300,000 premature deaths per year in China. (Cohen et al. 2005; Zhang et al. 2008) Another study (Zheng, 2017) estimates that outdoor PM2.5 exposure contributed to approximately 1.22 million deaths in China in 2013. Far from the cities, the situation is not better, considering the use of coal and biomass fuels. Health effects include lung cancer, acute respiratory infection, and chronic obstructive pulmonary disease. (Zhang and Smith 2007) Based on early WHO estimates, solid fuels used in Chinese households cause around 420,000 premature deaths every year. (Smith et al. 2004)

Huge efforts by the government to tackle the air quality problems are yielding some results. Based on a recent study from Tsinghua University, Beijing, "promoting end-of-pipe control measures, limiting coal use in small combustion devices and retiring old vehicles" so far has led "to a 21 per cent reduction of population-weighted mean PM2.5 concentration in just two years," while "the premature mortality related to PM2.5 pollution has been reduced by nine per cent as the consequence of air quality improvement." (Zheng, 2017)

Another source of severe health danger is related to water pollution, especially in rural areas. Kan (2009) reports that "in 2008, among 200 major rivers in China, water quality in 20.8% of 409 monitored sections was below grade V, the worst grade in the Chinese National Standard for Water Quality" (Ministry of Environmental Protection of China 2009). Consider that water of this extent is virtually of no use, even for agricultural irrigation.

Based on data from the 2003 National Health Services Survey (Ministry of Health of China 2004), two-thirds of the rural population in

China did not have access to piped water. The use of contaminated drinking water might have caused the surge of digestive cancers and infectious diseases, including hepatitis and cholera. (Wu et al. 1999)

A huge impact on human health and the environment is also linked to the fact that about 70% of the electronic waste generated worldwide is processed in China. (Ni and Zeng, 2009) The same is true for pollution linked to heavy metals (lead, mercury, chromium, cadmium, and arsenic). (He et al. 2009)

The severity of environmental pollution is having a huge impact not only at the domestic level, but in the world at large. China became the world's largest emitter of greenhouse gases in 2007, surpassing the United States. In 2014 the country was responsible for 27 percent of global emissions. China also became the world's largest coal producer, accounting for around half of global consumption. Those trends contributed to put pressure on China from other nations around the world to address environmental concerns. As a result, China has been cooperating at the international level to show its commitment toward a greener model of growth. (Spigarelli et al., 2016)

In 2014, U.S. President Barack Obama and Xi Jinping[1] "underpinned the consensus reached by the international community in late 2015 at the UN-led climate summit in Paris." Recently, the country moved forward, taking the lead at global level to preserve the COP21 agreement reached in Paris.

Later in 2017, when President Donald Trump announced the withdrawal from the agreement, China started to play a key role in the climate diplomacy, with internal efforts to adopt a greener and sustainable growth model.

---

1. The White House, Office of the Press Secretary, "US-–China Joint Announcement on Climate Change", Beijing, China, 12 November 2014, https://obamawhitehouse.archives.gov/the-press-office/2014/11/11/us-china-joint-announcement-climate-change.

Sustainable Growth and Environment Protection

Indeed, the environmental pressure described above contributed to the shift of policies and development strategies in China. As already mentioned, the Chinese government introduced the narration of the New Normal, which can be considered as the acknowledgment that the double-digit growth age has come to its end and that the country's development model needed to evolve to embrace the concept of sustainability. The first time that the idea of a New Normal had been publicly mentioned was in the occasion of the PRC President Xi Jinping's visit to Henan Province on May 2014. At the core of the New Normal development model there is the shift to a quality approach to growth, which articulates itself in some key pillars.

The first pillar is related to internal consumption, which is meant to substitute investment and export as the main driver for growth, with the redistribution of wealth and the extension of social welfare as supporting strategies. More reliance on internal consumption will also stabilize growth and prices, making the whole economy less dependent to international market fluctuations.

The second pillar is linked to technology innovation and service industry, which are prioritized for sustaining job creation and raising internal income. The government recognized the necessity to shift to high value-added production, with higher creative and leading potential. The new economic growth model is grounded on a more socially and environmentally sustainable path.

The current transformation of the Chinese economical, institutional and social landscape under the New Normal is led by a set of policies, which define a number of mid- and long-termed targets, both at a general and at a sectorial level.

The main long-term targets fall under the denomination of two 100-year plans, by which the CPC assumes two symbolic dates (2021 and 2049, respectively, one hundred years from the foundation of the

CPC and one hundred years from the birth of the PRC) as two historical turning points. These two plans respectively aim at transforming China into a "moderately prosperous society," eliminating any extreme poverty by 2021, and to transform China into a fully developed country by 2049. (CESIF, 2016)

In the meantime, these goals are addressed by general and sectorial plans where environment plays a crucial role. The most important and comprehensive one is the 13th five-year plan (FYP 2016-2020). The plan covers many issues setting general targets for areas which range from the economy, infrastructure, social development and, of course, environmental protection. Three out of the ten main pillars of the Plan can be related to this last issue. They refer to: energy consumption (with the goal of keeping the energy consumption within the limit of the equivalent of 5 billion tons coal in 2020, compared with 4.3 billion tons in 2015); energy efficiency (to reduce by 2020 the energy consumption and the CO2 emission per each GDP point respectively by 15% and 18% compared to levels in 2015); air quality (to obtain at least a classification as "good" for the at least the 80% of the days in urban area, compared to the 76.7% rate in 2015); nuclear energy (increase the installed capacity from 28.3 GW to 58 GW by the end of the five-year period).

Specific measures set by the FYP for environmental protection confirm that the preservation of the environment and the anti-pollution measures are a fundamental part of the new Chinese model of growth. In fact, the FYP promote: more stringent policies for the protection of cultivated land and ensure grain safety; clean production and low-carbon industries, green finance and the establishment of a green development fund; inclusion of parameters related to natural resources protection in the appraisal of official performance; development of new energy vehicles and electric cars; nationwide real time online environment monitoring system, mapping all the emission spots; improvement in forest protection and reforestation, with the ban of commercial exploitation of forests.

Those general measures indicated by the FYP are articulated in

Table 1. Environmental Protection Plan 2016-2020 Targets

		2015	2020 Goals	Total
Air Quality	Air quality rate in Prefecture and Municipal Level Ranking as "Excellent" and "Good" (%)	76	>80	-
	Reduction of the concentration of fine particles in Municipal and Prefecture Level (%)	-	-	18
	Reduction of "Seriously" (and Above) polluted days in Municipal and Prefecture Level (%)	-	-	25
Water environment quality	Water surface quality ratio reaching Class III or better (%)	66	>70	-
	Class V water surface quality ratio (%)	9.7	<5	-
	Water standard rate of important rivers, lakes and water parks (%)	70.8	>80	-
	Underground water quality ratio (%)	15.7	Around 15	-
	Water quality in coastal in inhabited areas ranking as "Excellent" and "Good" ratio (%)	70.5	Around 70	-
Soil environment quality	Pollution free cultivated soil (%)	70.6	Around 90	-
	Pollution free soil usage ratio (%)	-	>90	-

Source: 13th Environmental Protection Five Year Plan, MEP (translation by the authors)

sectorial specific five-year plans. Specifically, the five-year plan titled 13th Environmental Protection Five Year Plan was released on November 24, 2016, and sets detailed environmental protection targets to be reached by 2020. Table 1 is extracted from the third section of the second chapter of the Plan. It summarizes the main targets and key performance indicators used to monitor the implementation of the strategy. The planning action is carried out also at a sub-sectorial level, with the issuance of ad hoc action plans.

Beside the FYP, many sectorial and specific plans set the guidelines for specific industries or social facets. As the new normal aims at boosting the innovation of industry as one of its main cornerstones, two plans deserve our attention. The first is the Made in China 2025 plan, launched in 2015 and geared to turning China into a *manufacturing power* by 2025. The term, manufacturing power, means that China should improve the quantity of its production (which is already characterized by a substantial overcapacity), but with value-added environmental sustainability of its industrial sector. The guidelines of this plan are developing an innovation-driven industry, focusing on quality rather than merely quantity and on environmental sustainability. This includes rebuilding national industrial layout as a whole and improving human capital.

Prioritized industries include clean energy transportation, along with IT, automatization, aerospace, navigation technologies and logistics, railways, agricultural machineries, new materials and bio-pharm.

China Environmental Protection: A New Legal Context

According to Shapiro (2016), industrialization, population increase and urbanization were the main drivers that led to environmental deterioration in China. Heavy industry is the first violator, because of the way by which manufacturing-related processes impact the environment as a whole. A study by Zhu, Pickles and He (2017) lists nonferrous metal mining, electricity and heating production and paper-making as the top-three pollution intensive industries in China. According to the same study, intensive pollution industries are located on the coastal regions of the country, following the pattern of economic development. Environmental regulations and their enforcement by authorities will influence the ultimate impact of pollutants and the consequences for the environment.

Since the Age of Reform, China's administrative pattern has been granting local governments with a high degree of autonomy in the implementation of environmental and economic development policies (Jahiel, 1998), with both diachronic and synchronic effects on the geography of pollution. On the one hand, during the first stages of economic reform, developmental purposes were often privileged over environmental protection. On the other hand, local government within less developed areas were more likely to compromise on environmental regulations. (Zhu et al., Ibidem)

The institutional point of view is therefore crucial for understanding China's pollution issue. This must be examined under legislative actions, which are addressed in the following paragraph, but also under the perspective of the political and sociological realities of China.

To have a clear understanding of the commitment of China in the protection of the environment, the analysis of the historical evolution of Chinese environmental law is essential. Three main periods can be highlighted.

Earliest Stage (1949-1977)

Regulations addressing environmental issues were sporadic and mainly originated by human health concerns (Bao, 2006), like the Plant Health and Safety Regulations (1956), which was a first attempt to regulate the plant wastes disposal. It was designed safeguard plant workers and nearby inhabitants. This included the Decision on Preventing Silica Dust in Mining Companies (1956) and the Drinking Water Health Regulations (1959).

After the chaos brought by the Cultural Revolution, in the wake of the Stockholm Conference (1972), in 1973 China issued the Regulation on Environmental Protection, which was the first comprehensive — although preliminary — environmental protection set of measures in the history of PRC (Bao, Ibidem).

The Environmental Protection Law (1978-2014)

In 1978, the National People's Congress amended the Constitution and included, for the first time, environmental protection, with the amended article 26. It stated: "The State protects and improves the living and the ecological environment, prevents pollution and other damages. The State organizes and encourages and protects forest trees." This article acted as the juridical basis for the country's environmental protection legal framework for years to come.

The first, fundamental step was the approval of the Environmental Protection Law (for Trial Implementation) in 1979. The same law was then re-affirmed on the occasion of its first amendment in 1989. The Law provided basic provisions for environmental protection, which acted as the basis for other specific laws.

The first act, which followed the Environmental Protection Law, was the Marine Pollution Law, in 1982 (revised in 1998), which addressed the protection of the marine environment and its resources from pollution and unsustainable exploitation.

In 1984, the Water Pollution Law was enacted (further revisions occurred in 1996 and 2008), with the aim of protecting the country's hydric resources and their safety (Art. 1 and Art. 2).

The Air Pollution Law was issued in 1988 (revisions were brought in 1995 and 2000) and targeted the prevention and the protection of air from atmospheric pollution. After the amendment and the confirmation of the Environmental Protection Law, in 1989, a second round of legislation began. In 1996 the Solid Waste Law (revised in 2004) covered the protection of the environment by solid waste pollution (Art. 1) of dry land, with exception of the seas, falling in the jurisdiction of the Marine Pollution Law (Art. 2). Clean Production Law was issued in 2002, with the objective of promoting cleaner production practices, with lesser impact on the environment and human health. The same year, the Environmental Impact Assessment Law was enacted, with the purpose implementing a pollution prevention framework with conditional environmental appraisal to be carried out before the implementation of programs and construction projects. In 2009, the Circular Economy Law, supporting the improvement of the circular economy and of resource usage efficiency, concluded the legal framework. Thanks to this law China became one of the first countries in the world to follow the

Table 2: Environmental protection legal framework

Pollution source	Marine Pollution Law Water Pollution Law Air Pollution Law Solid Waste Law Radioactive Pollution Law
Resource focused instruments	Grassland Law Forestry Law Water Law Fishery Law Land Administration Law Mineral Resources Law Wildlife Protection Law Water and Soil conservation Law Desertification Law
Management of environment-sustainability	Environmental Impact Assessment Law Circular Economy Law

philosophy of the circular economy.

In the same period, aside from these general provisions, a certain number of resource-specific measures have been issued in the same period: the Forestry Law (1984, 1998); the Grassland Law (1985, 2003); the Fishery Law (1986; 2000; 2004); the Land Administration Law (1986; 2000; 2004); the Mineral Resources Law (1986; 1996); the Water Law (1988; 1998; 2004); the Wildlife Protection Law (1988; 1989); The Water and Soil Conservation Law (1991); The Desertification Law (2001); The Radioactive Pollution Law (2003).

The above listed provisions can be classified according to their function and scope within the Environmental Protection legal framework (see Table 2).

The New Environmental Protection Law (2015)

After more than 25 years, and on January 1, 2015, a new amendment of the Environmental Protection Law (1979, 1989) came into force, providing the country with the most up to date and stringent provisions on environmental protection.

Important innovations included increased responsibilities and penalties for polluters; increased responsibilities for public authorities and their officers; increased information divulgation to the public; major role to be played by NGOs; and protection for whistleblowers. (Padoan, 2016)

The 2015 Environmental Protection Law (2015 EPL) states that environmental protection is a fundamental national policy, giving priority to protection and emphasizing prevention and integrated governance, with a major role to be played by the public and in particular by local governments, firms and citizens.

One of the most important innovations is the introduction of a daily-based fine system, which replaces the off-fine system disposed by the 1989 edition. Public bodies and related officers are evaluated also for their commitment to environmental protection and are punished with loss of income and criminal prosecution for their illicit acts and behaviors. The goal of a more integrated governance, with increased involvement of public actors, is pursued by improved measures on disclosure of monitoring data and environmental quality parameters, the protection of whistleblowers, and a major role recognized to registered and well established NGOs, which are allowed to bring legal actions against polluters.

The effects of the new law were positive during the first year of implementation, under the point of view of both enforcement and results. According to the Ministry of Environmental Protection (MEP) data, reported by Zhang et al. (2016), MEP inspected 1.77 million enterprises, with 191,000 prosecuted firms, shutting down 20,000 of them, and inflicting fines for total $87.5 million U.S. dollars.

Based on the same data, in the most important urban industrial districts, the air quality sensibly improved, with a reduction of main pollutants by 5 to 28%.

Environment and Well-being: The Link with Health and Food

Environmental problems in China had huge implications and consequences for two other extremely important domains that are strictly related to the socioeconomic sustainability of the Chinese growth model: healthcare and food safety.

Soil, water and air pollution heavily affected the Chinese territory with severe impact on risks associated to health conditions of Chinese citizens. The need to secure China's future with a sustainable growth model made it necessary to embrace parallel reforms to the healthcare system and to the food protection system as a part of the New Normal course, in line with the vision for a socialist-inspired harmonious society, as described by the 12th FYP (2011-2015) (Tung, 2011; Deloitte, 2011; WHO, 2012; Wong et al., 2014).

In the document "Essential points of the national Plan for the health system and healthcarc (2015-2020)," the Government formalized the commitment to extend to the whole population, basic healthcare service coverage in order to tackle the emerging issues of exacerbated environment conditions, aging population, and rapid urbanization. (Lv and Spigarelli, 2016)

At the same time, the demand for a better food safety environment has increased, as well as the attention devoted by authorities to food safety regulations and standards. The government has traced important policies aimed at ensuring the progress towards a better food safety environment. Chapter 18 of the 13th FYP, titled "Strengthen capacity for ensuring safety of agricultural products," focuses on the upstream processes in the food supply chain at the agricultural stage. It addresses six areas in which to intervene in order to improve the quality and safety level of agricultural production:

1) *Safeguards for grain production.* The Plan foresees the building of farmland irrigation systems and water conservancy infrastructure, restoration and reconversion of

lands to agricultural use, establishing functional zones and protected areas for the production of major agricultural products and grain crops:

2) *Agricultural structural adjustments.* The Government actively guides the adjustments to the production mix of agricultural products for the optimization of the supply chain and the quality control of each stage;

3) *Integrated development in the rural areas.* A well-balanced and sustainable integrated development model for rural areas is promoted, with the integration of primary, secondary and tertiary industries;

4) *Strengthening of product quality and safety to improve and implement agricultural standards along the whole value chain;*

5) *Sustainable agricultural development.* Pursuing "zero growth" in the use of chemical fertilizers and pesticides. China intends to implement demonstration projects for circular agricultural through integrated planting and breeding, as well as promotion to fight the agricultural pollution for non-point sources, in particular soil pollution;

6) *International cooperation, to promote international trade for stabilizing the demand and supply of quality food.* China intends to actively pursue all forms of agricultural cooperation aimed at establishing large-scale internationally competitive offshore centers for farm production, processing, and storage, transportation. Also, it promotes the bilateral and multilateral agricultural cooperation in technology transfer.

Food safety is also mentioned as an important target by the 60th Chapter, titled "Promote a Healthy China," specifically in its Section 8,

"Food and Medicine Safety." This section introduces a food safety strategy, which will pass through the following key points: improvement of safety laws and regulations, standards, focusing at the source; food enterprises are called to assume responsibility for food safety, exercise grid-based oversight, increase the frequency of inspections, carry out sample-based monitoring and achieve product traceability; and development of model food safety cities.

This strategy has been to strengthen by a sector specific plan of food safety released in 2017, titled "13th National Food Safety Plan." The plan establishes as its main objectives the following points:

1. Implementation of a national unified sampling-based inspection model, to be applied in each Province;

2. Decrease of agricultural source of pollution in order to reach at least the 97% of test compliancy rate for agricultural products quality;

3. Strengthening of on-site inspections by means of professional inspectors and standardization of enforcement procedures;

4. Improvement of national standards for food safety;

5. Improvement of food safety supervision and technical support capability; and import and export food inspection are harmonized to international standards.

Implications for Foreign Businesses

The evolution of the environmental protection regulatory framework presents enormous implications for foreign business. It opens new market opportunities, on the one hand, and new restrictions to economic activity, on the other hand. Investors will discover there are opportunities for foreign businesses approaching the green market in China. They will also discover challenges that are a consequence of the stricter environmental rules on the commodity market.

Thanks to greater attention on environmental protection and new regulatory framework, the green market in China is growing fast and big opportunities are attracting foreign companies, which can leverage their advanced know-how and technical capability to their competitive advantage. The Green market, which of course is highly structured in diverse sub-sectors, can be segmented into two bigger segments; on the one hand, machineries and devices, and on the other hand, plants and systems. (CESIF, 2016)

As for the first segment, the target customers are those industries that are now forced by the new regulations to monitor their emissions. The business model in this case is a traditional business-to-business (B2B) model, where the foreign firm sells its product to the Chinese customer. The second segment is represented by public administrations and industry networks that share the common need to develop centralized monitoring and processing systems. This is a more complex architecture of business, where foreign firms can find their opportunities by joining public-private partnerships[2] and by transferring their

---

2. Recently, China introduced new rules for Public-Private Partnership. The Chinese government is trying to organize the funding of infrastructure and utilities projects on a more market-oriented way, with increased involvement of private ventures. To this end, in 2015 the National Development and Reform Commission issued the Public Concessions Reform. The Reform brings relevant innovation to the relationship between public and private partners; the most important is that public government are no more allowed to guarantee a fix return from the investment, with the entrepreneurial risk being transferred to the privates, who are granted with the permission to set their tariff scheme to the end user, in accordance with their business model. (Padoan, 2016) The Reform applies to five sectors: energy, transportations, hydric resources, environmental protection, and urban public works. For the first time, the regulation defines the nature of the concession, which is granted by means of a written agreement to be signed between the public administration and the concessionaire, with clear indications about the execution, performance assessment, modifications and resolution of the agreement.

technology or know-how.

The green market, since the 12th FYP (2012-2016), which first placed environment protection at its core, is developing fast and its aggregate size is huge, (Padoan, 2016) with a forecast investment of 9.4 trillion CNY ($1,700 billion USD) for the implementation of the sectorial action plans (with 61% devoted to soil protection, 21% to water protection and 18% to air pollution control). Nevertheless, the green market, as its start-up is relatively recent, can hardly be said as mature. Industries and public administrations are only recently acquiring the needed technical knowledge and understanding, with low problem-solving capability. (Padoan, 2016)

Foreign firms can act as exporters, be involved in Public-Private partnership or invest in China directly. Exporting environmental protection and monitoring devices and machineries requires local certification, so that an episodic approach to the market is quite uncommon. As for the chance to take part in Public-Private partnership projects, the foreign company that wishes to operate in China in such a framework is required first to register as a Wholly Foreign Owned Enterprise (WFOE) or a Foreign Invested Commercial Enterprise (FICE), then obtain the relevant qualifications and certifications in relation to the scope.

The new environmental regulatory framework has also wider and indirect implications for foreign companies operating in China. Stricter environmental surveillance is heavily impacting the country's industrial landscape, markedly in the low-value added sectors. For instance, metalworking raw material prices have increased by an average rate of 115% from January 2016 to September 2017. In the plastics sector, the situation is even more serious, with companies claiming for critical raw material shortage.

The trend is not likely to come to an end. The Ministry of Environment is intensifying control over polluting firms, forcing them to comply with the new standards or close their business. Apart from sounding as a direct confirmation of the commitment by the Chinese government in enforcing the new environmental measures, this trend, if confirmed in the future, is likely to reshape the whole industrial system in China, with serious implications for the supply chain management for firms manufacturing and sourcing in China, which can be then pushed to recalibrate their strategy or delocalize their low-value added activities elsewhere.

Regulatory barriers described above can be deepened by cultural differences. Linguistic and cultural features are likely to impact business development strategies and exacerbate institutional gaps, especially in the green sector where public bodies and local government play a very important role. Here, the support by home country institutions is crucial in preparing the ground for business players, by providing them with needed information and relationship networking.

Business players, for their part, should not underestimate the importance of barriers and concentrate their efforts as much as possible in gathering all the information about the market, relating regulations and cultural habits. Choosing the right (local) partner can be a good solution for filling the cultural gap (even though to evaluate who is a good partner can be difficult for the same reason a partner is needed) as well as the financial gap.

Aside from partnerships in the local market, a growing willingness of Chinese firms to invest abroad could be a good opportunity for foreign firms to gain a direct access to the Chinese market.

Beyond opportunities related to green technology industries, there is also a growing demand for quality and safe food. This is counterbalanced by a more complex regulatory environment. Since its reform phase and, in particular, after its accession to WTO, China has been striving to align its food safety standards, management and technical capabilities to that of Western nations.

Fast-changing and more complex regulations, nonetheless, represent a potential barrier to foreign exporters and investors. Like many other foreign investment opportunities discussed in this book, operating policies and procedures are not always straightforward.

Conclusions

The Chinese environment has been negatively affected by the scale and rapidity of national economic development. Recently, China has been promoting strong economic and environmental policies and reforms to recover, at least partially, the damage to water, soil, and air quality in the country. (Spigarelli et al., 2016) Currently, and to its credit, China is the world's largest investor in clean energy worldwide and the leading country for renewable energy sources technology, especially in wind power and photovoltaic industries (Eyraud & Clements, 2012). China has also made huge technological progress and its image has changed "from that of a laggard on the environment, to a position of leadership in many instances" (China Greentech Report, 2011, p. 13).

Actually, environmental protection is one of the key strategic points of the transition towards the New Normal growth model. A better-quality environment is seen as not only the premise, but also the result of the general shift toward a sustainable economic, institutional and social development model.

On the one hand, along with the economic growth involving a large share of the population, people are asking for better quality of life. Chinese citizens have growing awareness about environmental issues, which reflects their increased — although still limited — involvement into the governance as stakeholders. On the other hand, with a more sustainable development model, China is moving away from low-value added and high pollutant industrial patterns, developing high-value added industries and service-reliant economy, with lower impact on the environment. While the environmental situation of air, soil and water is still alarming, the commitment shown the Government by means of legal development, regulatory reform and enforcement effort appears to be genuine and effective. There is still much work to be done to show the results the Chinese hope to achieve.

In this landscape, foreign companies are called to play a major role, leveraging their advanced technologies, know-how and technical capabilities. The market opportunities are by all means enormous but barriers and obstacles are very challenging. This is particularly true for small- and medium-sized enterprises, because of the high level of risk and complexity that entering an immature market like China implies. Environmental protection reform, moreover, is likely to affect also those firms which do not directly operate in the green market, because of the cross-cutting and massive effects that stricter environmental measures can bring into their operations and supply chain management.

References

Bao, M. (2006). The evolution of environmental policy and its impact in the People's Republic of China. *Conservation and Society* 4 (1).

CESIF (2016). La Cina nel 2016. Scenari e Prospettive per le Imprese. Fondazione Italia-Cina, a curi di Alberto Rossi e Filippo Fasulo.

Chen B, Hong C, Kan H. (2004). Exposures and health outcomes from outdoor air pollutants in China. *Toxicology*. 198(1–3):291–300.

China Greentech Initiative. (2011). *The China Greentech Report 2011. China emerges as a global greentech leader.* Available at: http://cgtr.china-greentech.com/CGTI-ChinaGreentechReport2011.pdf

Cohen AJ, Anderson HR, Ostro B, Pandey KD, Krzyzanowski M, Kunzli N, et al. (2005). The global burden of disease due to outdoor air pollution. *J Toxicol Environ Health* A. 68(13–14):1301–1307.

Deloitte (2011). China's pharmaceutical market: Summary and prospects. Available at http://www2.deloitte.com/content/dam/deloitte/ch/documents/life-sciences-health-care/ch_studie_pharmaceutical_China_05052014.pdf

Eyraud, L., & Clements, B. (2012). Going green-investment in environmentally friendly technologies is growing globally. *Finance and Development - English Edition*, 49(2):34. Available at: http://www.imf.org/external/pubs/ft/fandd/2012/06/eyraud.htm.

He, K, Wang, S and Zhang J. (2009) Blood lead levels of children and its trend in China. Sci Total Environ 407(13):3986–3993. Available at: http://apps.who.int/iris/bitstream/10665/69477/1/WHO_SDE_PHE_OEH_06.02_eng.pdf

Jahiel, A.R. (1998). The organization of environmental protection in China. *The China Quarterly* 156:757–787.

Kan, H. (2009). Environment and health in China: Challenges and opportunities. *Environ Health Perspective* 117(12): A530–A531.

Lu, P., and Spigarelli, F. (2016). The determinants of location choice: Chinese foreign direct investments in the European renewable energy sector. *International Journal of Emerging Markets* 11(3):333-356.

Ministry of Environmental Protection of China (2009). *The 2008 report on the state of the environment in China*. Available at: http://english.mepgov.cn/standards.reports/soe/soe2008/

Ministry of Health of China (2004). *Analysis report of national health services survey 2003* [in Chinese] Beijing: Chinese Academy of Medical Sciences Press.

Ni, H.G., Zeng, E.Y. (2009). Law enforcement and global collaboration are the keys to containing e-waste tsunami in China. *Environ Sci Technol.* 43(11):3991–3994.

Padoan, S. (2016). *Il Green Business in Cina. La rivoluzione verde cinese e l'evoluzione del mercato della Tutela Ambientale*. EEGEX - Energy Environment Glob-al Exchange.

Shapiro, J. (2016). *China's Environmental Challenges*. Cambridge: Polity Press.

Smith KR, Mehta S, Maeusezahl-Feuz M. (2004). *Comparative quantification of health risks*. Vol. 2. Geneva: World Health Organization. Indoor smoke from solid household fuels, pp. 1435–1493.

Spigarelli F., Arteconi A., Curran L. eds. (2016). *China and Europe's Partnership for a More Sustainable World: Challenges and Opportunities*, Emerald publisher.

Tung, A. (2011). Alliances form in growing pharmaceutical market. *China Daily*. Available at: www.chinadaily.com.cn/bizchina/2011-08/.03/content_13043302.htm

Who (2012). China. Available at: http://www.wpro.who.int/countries/chn/en/

Wong, J., Wu, C. and Xiam N. (2014). New rules for winning in China's pharmaceutical-calmarket. Available at: https://www.beg.com/publications/2014/new-rules-winning-chinas-pharmaceutical-market.aspx

Wu ,C., Maurer, C., Wang, Y., Xue, S., and Davis, D.L. (1999). Water pollution and human health in China. *Environ Health Perspect.* 107:251–256.

Zhang et al. (2016). China's new environmental protection regulatory regime: Effects and gaps. *Journal of Environmental Management*, 1-6.

Zhang, J.J., and Smith, K.R. (2007). Household air pollution from coal and biomass fuels in china: measurements, health impacts, and interventions. *Environ Health Perspect.* 115:848–855.

Zhang M, Song Y, Cai X, Zhou J. (2008). Economic assessment of the health effects related to particulate matter pollution in 111 Chinese cities by using economic burden of disease analysis. *J Environ Manage.* 88(4):947–954.

Zheng, Y. et al. (2017). Air quality improvements and health benefits from China's clean air action since 2013, *Environmental Research Letters*. DOI: 10.1088/1748-9326/aa8a32.

Zhu et al. (2017). *Going Green or Going Away. Geographical Dynamics and Firm Spatial Strategy in China*. Springer: 169-197.

Conclusions

By Gary Bonvillian

This book has attempted to point out not only the factors leading to and reinforcing China's current position in the world, but also the opportunities and challenges that present themselves for this massive and unique society and for foreign investors as well. The authors have taken the reader through a journey of discovery, beginning with a brief examination of China's history and its significant impact on decisions and actions in a modern world. Other topics in this book span a range of economic and social issues that the authors believe are essential for any would-be investor to understand before investing in China. The goal was to present the hard facts and to share some insight into what other educated and experienced professionals are saying about China.

National pride is one formidable variable at play in China's rapid rise in the world order. Those of us who have witnessed China's transformation first hand, and particularly advancements in the past twenty years, caution authors not to underestimate the power of national pride. There is a palpable determination among Chinese government officials to regain what many believe is a lost respect of their culture and heritage — purportedly at the root of all major government decision-making. Their goal is to raise the standard of living for all Chinese, to innovate rather than emulate, and to lead rather than follow among the great nations of the world, most of whom have become dependent upon one of the largest economic engines humankind has ever known. This determination has filtered down to the citizenry and the collective energy that is translating into rapid economic growth, rebuilding of archaic and inadequate social services, an explosion of educational opportunities, a mass migration to urban areas, and a rising military power.

Clearly there are many challenges but also opportunities for intelligent, foreign investors who are searching for the most productive avenue to capitalize on the transformation that is unfolding. There is no consensus on how China will ultimately fare in this transformation. The literature and testimony of many learned individuals presents conflicting opinions on timing, substance and outcomes. That said, what virtually everyone agrees is the fact that the sheer size of China and its influence on the world is undeniable. What has not yet fully played out is the question of where that influence will take China and the world.

China's Supreme Leader

This book and its messages would not be complete without reporting on what may be one of the most influential variables in attempting to predict China's future: Its leader. In March 2018, the Chinese People's Political Consultative Conference voted to change the nation's constitution to grant Xi Jinping what essentially amounts to a lifetime appointment as President. Xi will also continue as head of both the general secretary of the Communist Party and the military. China has not seen this movement toward a centralized power structure since the dictatorship of Mao, and many around the world are worried about the consequences. China's constitution, up until this vote, was crafted in

1982 precisely to prevent another situation where one person held such power. (Bodeen, 2018)

While there has been some internal criticism of President Xi's move to position himself as the supreme leader of China, it has been tepid at best. Critics outside of China believe President Xi has postured himself to control everything from the media to education and even to how the country will interpret and embrace its culture. (The New York Times, 2018)

In leading up to the historic vote recasting China's constitution, President Xi made it clear that he felt it was an imperative to allow for this stronger central governance authority in order to assure that the country could achieve its ambitious economic and social transformation. Indeed, an examination of only a few of President Xi's accomplishments might lead us to say he may be right. Xi's supporters feel strongly that the future is dependent on his "personal leadership," which has already led to China's claim over the South China Sea, the Belt and Road initiative, the reorganization of the military, the increase in domestic security, and the enforcement of ideological purity in schools and the media — all of which are part of "his vision of China as a prosperous, respected player on the world stage that stays faithful to its Communist and Confucius roots." (Buckley, 2018)

Not all economists see this historical action on the part of the Communist government as totally negative. As far back as 2007, when China's economic growth excelled beyond any world standard at the time, there were signs of problems to come. Those problems were labeled "structural" by Premier Wen Jiabao and encompassed what he saw as "unsteady, unbalanced, uncoordinated and unsustainable development." (NPR, 2018) Given what contributors of this book have identified, it is reasonable to conclude that this insight was on target.

At the center of this warning was the belief, which has proven itself to be accurate, that much of China's growth to date has benefited a small number of limited constituencies. Those constituencies include the higher echelon of government people and a relatively small circle of entrepreneurs. The average Chinese worker is still struggling to gain ground on what is needed to be a member of the consumer class. Xi entered the position of President in 2013 with full knowledge that he had to find a way to turn this tide. He has been credited for cracking down on corruption, particularly in the political circles of China. This has not gone unnoticed by the Chinese people, 49% of whom believe that "corrupt officials are a very big problem in the country." (Wike, 2016)

Limited time in office has been Xi's challenge. Michael Pettis, an economist at Peking University, has asserted that corrective action is needed now and must be carried out over a longer period of time than the President would serve with term limits. Pettis believes that this historical change to China's constitution allows more time for Xi to enforce the centralized power he has garnered since taking office and actually see the reforms all the way through to fruition. (NPR, 2018)

Even before this vote, Xi wielded his considerable power and authority. He has made it no mystery of his belief that a totally free market path cannot work in China. In recent years, Xi has made certain that the government involve itself in economic matters that have national implications. This has included monitoring and even restricting activities of China's private companies, insisting other world leaders provide China more access to their markets yet, at the same time, limiting opportunities for some foreign companies attempting to invest in China. (*The New York Times,* 2018) Of course, this has not gone unnoticed by other nations, including the President of the United States, Donald Trump. In March of 2018 he signed a bill that would impose significant tariffs on steel and aluminum shipped from China and other countries.

Like many other aspects of China's historical transformation, we really cannot predict the final implications of the decision to allow President Xi to remain in office indefinitely. While the initial reaction was one of great concern around the world, only time will tell what his actual policy influence and decisions will mean for foreign investors.

Demographics

Several chapters in this book have examined demographic changes with respect to selected initiatives. The following is shared to emphasize, even further, what this means for investors.

In the not too distant past, if we asked what was China's greatest asset, the answer could very well be its enormous population. This is less likely to be heard today as China is on the verge of a prodigious shift in the makeup and direction of its population. The directional change is clearly due to the one-child-policy, fully introduced under the Chinese leader Deng Xiaoping, and held mostly steady until only recent years. In reality, there were rising questions among subordinate leaders in China even at the end of Mao's position of power to curb population growth, which at the time, was in conflict with his own belief that China would prosper from its size.

This policy has been reported to prevent hundreds of millions of births over the past forty years in an effort to curb the already overwhelming challenge of attending to such a large population. What appears to be an error in judgment regarding the consequences of such a policy has resulted in the current predictions that China's population growth will end and reverse within the next several years.

In addition, the one child policy gave rise to a biased perspective that a male child was favored over a female. The consequences of this perspective also has long-term implications for China's future. This has resulted in a gender imbalance that has far reaching implications for families and businesses alike, not merely in the present but for decades to come. It is estimated that by 2030, at least one-fifth of China's male population will not be able to marry. (Chang, 2015) What those implications will be has given rise to more intensive study of this phenomenon.

The first implications of the reversal were felt in 2010, when the available working-age population of China actually fell. Estimations today suggest that China's labor force will decline from 761 million to 640 million by 2035. (Global Demographics, 2015) This implication is of no small consequence to the Chinese or any outside investor. As this book has illustrated, much of China's future is dependent upon its available workforce and the pendulum is about to swing in a different direction. It is estimated that within the next ten years India will overtake China in population and its available workforce. India's population is estimated to peak at a staggering 1.6 billion within the next forty years. (Chang, 2015)

Taken together, this data presents an even more powerful punch to China's ambitions than is readily apparent to the casual observer. By 2050 here is how that data translates:

- It is projected that India will have approximately 1 billion citizens of workforce age…or 130 million more than China
- The median age in China will be 46 years
- The median age in India will be only 37 years
- China's population over the age of 65 will be 23.9%
- India's population over the age of 65 will be only 12.7% (Chang 2015)

As can be seen, and in concert with the implications of workforce availability, the aging population of China will place even greater demand on social systems, as was aptly covered in Chapter 4.

What may be less obvious to an outsider, but worth mentioning at this point, is the impact these demographic realities are having on the family unit. Until this current one-child generation came along, the family unit was the stalwart of Chinese society. Several generations would live together under one roof, or at least within close proximity, with an understanding that the younger family members would attend to the needs of the older. Anyone who has done business with young professionals in China within recent years will report this has changed dramatically.

The young generation's necessary migration to the thriving business centers of China's mega-cities, in order to not just advance a career but merely to have one, has presented some odd situations for family life. A look at this data is revealing. In 2015, 56% of China's population lived in urban areas. It is projected that, in 2035, 78% of China's population will live in urban areas. (Global Demographics, 2015)

Many of us could share stories from our personal encounters in China of a young husband in one city doing his professional work, the spouse in another and their child in another being attended to by the grandparents. Even though such notions would seem unthinkable to some in the United States it is not as uncommon in China. This, and other reported consequences of national policy decisions and the reality of changing demographics, has surely played into the yet unknown future of China.

This data, examined from a different perspective, also presents obvious opportunities for foreign investors. Just one data point is quite revealing. In 2015 China's urban population accounted for 79% of household expenditures. That figure is estimated to increase to 90% by the year 2035, and the income of this population will more than double. (Global Demographics, 2015) The increasing buying power of a concentrated and easily identifiable market segment in China should be attractive to foreign investors.

It is worth mentioning in this closing section that much of Asia, and not just China, will be experiencing dramatic demographic shifts that are most certainly going to influence the economic clout of that region of the world. Gordon Chang (World Affairs, 2018) points out that the Total Fertility Rate (TFR), the number of births per woman per lifetime, is low in a number of Asian nations. This includes China, where TFR is between 1.5 and 1.6; Japan, 1.4; South Korea, 1.3; Taiwan, 1.1; Hong Kong, 1.2; and Macau, 0.9.

China's Intentions and Soft Power

China's rise in worldwide prominence has not been lost on its citizenry. A notable research group recently reported the following regarding China's view of themselves:

- 75% say China is playing a more important role in world affairs than it did 10 years ago. Only 10% believe that they are a less powerful player in the global arena;
- 60% believe their country's involvement in the global economy is a good thing; only 23% think this is bad for China;
- 77% of the public believes that their way of life needs to be protected against foreign influence, and such sentiment is up 13 percentage points since 2002;
- 52% believe the U.S. is trying to prevent China from becoming as powerful and 45% see U.S. power and influence as a major threat;
- Just 22% of Chinese say their country should help other nations deal with their problems. (Wike, 2016)

The data and other recent reports would further suggest that China has little interest in world domination. Such a notion is quite contrary to what appears to be the genuine agenda of self-reliance. This is often misunderstood by foreign publics, who question China's motives. But to date there is no substantive evidence that China is using its military for anything other than defense.

President Xi has on numerous occasions expressed, at least publicly, that his desire is to be a partner with other great nations to advance China's interest. We could point to many examples of his outward gestures to make this apparent. The January 2017 World Economic Forum in Davos is a good recent example. There were and still are skeptics, particularly in Washington D.C. However, his words could very well lead some, including this writer, to believe that there are genuine opportunities to listen and act on Xi's outward gestures.

Xi's speech clearly left open the prospect for the United States to take a step toward accepting his apparent willingness to work together on many social and economic fronts. Proceeding with caution would certainly be prudent. However, in his speech Xi said, "We came to the conclusion that integration into the global economy is a historical trend … it has proved to be the right strategic choice." (Mazaar, 2017) Many believe that the time is now to take President Xi at his word.

What is often mistaken as aggressive expansion, some have called simply exercising soft power. (The Economist, 2014) A good illustration of soft power is China's reach into colleges and universities around the world to include many in the United States. That reach includes outright financial gifts as well as funding the Confucius Institutes that have numbered as many as 500 around the world. There has been much written about China's assertion of soft power in just the past few years. For some it is intimidating as China has not really been subtle about its intentions with the use of this tactic to influence the world. The question really comes down to what exact harm can be done by China's public relations initiatives related to soft power. It may not be as much as China critics contend.

China made a $4.1 million donation to Stanford University in the United States in 2010 to provide funding for a new Confucius Institute and to create an endowed Professorship. (Bauman, 2018) Understandably, there are many who have and continue to question China's real agenda with these Institutes. You really do not have to look far into the media reporting over the past ten years to discover that agenda.

In 2010, the then Minister of Propaganda in Beijing, Liu Yunshan, made it clear in a leading media publication read by the Chinese citizenry, as well as foreign visitors, that "with regard to key issues that influence sovereignty and safety, we should actively carry out international propaganda battles against issuers such as Tibet, Xinjiang,

Taiwan, human rights and Falun Gong ... we should do well in establishing and operating overseas cultural centers and Confucius Institutes." In 2011 a high ranking official in the Beijing's Politburo publicly stated, "The Confucius Institute is an important contribution toward improving our *soft power*." (Epstein, 2018)

Notwithstanding the undercurrent of controversy and contention that the presence of Confucius Institutes on American campuses has caused for some, it would seem the strategy of gaining soft power is working. Some would argue that the general public should not overreact to China's assertion of soft power, as this is a tactic Western nations have utilized for much of their existence as world leaders.

Due to the controversy that surrounded the election of the United States President Donald Trump, accusations of Russian interference in the American voting process, and a real awareness that China could pose an economic threat to the United States, Confucius Institutes again came under question within the higher education community in 2018. However, the degree of rising concern at the time was hardly noteworthy. While it is true that some Confucius Institutes have closed, reportedly due to lack of interest on the campus, there is no evidence of wholesale abandonment of the partnerships that exist between China and American colleges and universities. In 2017, there were still 103 Confucius Institutes operating in the United States.

Contributors to this book would decidedly lean toward a more tempered view of Confucius Institutes than its reported critics. The reason is quite simple. There is no harm in being cautious about the true, and sometimes, hidden agendas of foreign powers. However, in the world that we have created it is far more fruitful to understand our friends and competitors around the world than it is to shut them out. Ignorance is the real danger, and for foreign investors weighing the risks of venturing into unknown markets, knowledge is the first and most important tool for making sound decisions. What better place to start than in the colleges and universities of the United States, which still enjoy the envy of the rest of world when it comes to advanced higher education opportunities.

Predicting the Future

Many things have been written in recent years by academicians, business leaders, politicians and commentators about China's future. While some projections are based on valid and defensible data, such as the tidal wave of change occurring within China's demographics, for the most part we really do not know as of yet what will happen. Nonetheless, it is worth revisiting select elements of the predictions as we close out this body of work.

We conclude this section by sharing what many believe to be a unique and fascinating approach to telling China's story and taking at least a glimpse into the future. While somewhat dated by the time of this publication, Henry M. Paulson Jr., former Chairman and Chief Executive Office of Goldman Sachs and then as Treasury Secretary under George W. Bush wrote a book published in 2015 with parts that still resonates with many of us.

In a world that changes so rapidly, including the political and economic forces of great nations, it is time for people throughout the world to recognize that change is the only constant. Just look at the American Presidency as an example. Hardly anyone, with the exception of a largely silent constituency that came alive in the 2015 campaign and then in the 2016 elections, was predicting that Donald Trump would become President of the United States. Not only did he become President, his sweeping legislative changes during his first year in office, bolstered by a Republican dominated House and Senate, made it virtually impossible to stop the agenda he promised to put into place if elected — and that agenda, like the changes President Xi has introduced in China, has taken their respective countries by storm.

Paulson, among things, is credited for having been the most influential foreign figure in opening up China. His unique talent for both personal and professional engagement of the Chinese, opened the doors for others to follow in exploring the real potential that presented itself for all nations. An overarching message to Paulson's readers, which many would still argue today, is that all nations benefit from cooperative efforts, even if that means assisting what some may see as a rival, in resolving their internal problems. The reason for this belief is really quite simple: hardly any nation, and certainly not the most powerful ones that direct world affairs, can be ignored. Their issues carry over to the rest of the world as has been illustrated throughout this book. According to Paulson, President Xi understands and would support this assertion. In a conversation with Xi, the President said, "There has been a pattern of suspicion leading to fear, which in turn leads to hostility. This is the kind of logic we need to prevent. We need to identify where our common interest lie." (Paulson, 2015) Therein might be the most important lesson for all nations as a new world order continues to unfold.

In the end, the decision to venture into China with investments in mind will come down to personal and corporate tolerance for risk and an understanding that there is no certainty of the results. However, the uncertainty can be tempered through open-mindedness, research, education and a healthy awareness that all entrepreneurial ventures incur a degree of risk. Contributors to this book are hopeful that our readers will recognize these factors but also move forward to be a part of the new world order-not based on political ideology but rather on mutual respect and willingness to work with others whose history, culture, and unique perspective of life does not conflict but rather enhances our own.

References

Bauman, Dan (2018, March 9). Confucius Institutes Face Renewed Skepticism. *The Chronicle of Higher Education,* LXIV(26), A36.

Bodeen, Christopher (2018). China Cites Support for Ending Presidential Term Limits. *The Washington Post*, Retrieved from www.washingtonpost.com/ The Savvy Investor's Guide to Doing Business in China 211 world/asia_pacific/china-cites-support-for-ending-presidential-term-limits/

Buckley, Chris, Bradsher, Keith. China Moves to let Xi Stay in Power by Abolishing Term Limit. *The New York Times*, Retrieved from https://www.nytimes.com/2018/02/25/world/asia/china-xi-jinping-html

Chang, Gordon G. (2015). Shrinking China: A Demographic Crisis. *World Affairs*, Retrieved from http://www.worldaffairsjournal.org/article/ shrinking-chinademographic-crisis

China's Demographic Future (2015). Retrieved from www.globaldemographics. com/Chinas-demographic-future

Epstein, Ethan. (2018). How China Infiltrated U.S. Classrooms. *Politico*, Retrieved from https://www.politico.com/magazine/story/2018/01/16/ how-chaininfiltrated-us-classrooms-216327

Mazarr, Michael J. (2018, February 15). China's Opportunity and Ours. *U.S. News and World Report*. Retrieved from https://www.usnews.com/ opinion/worldreport/articles/2017-02-15/the-us-should-view-chinas-davos-speech-on-world-order-as-an-opportunity

NPR. Some Economists See a Plus Side in Eliminating Term Limits for China's Xi Jinping. Retrieved from https://www.npr.org/sections/parallels/2018/ 03/17/593841022/some-economists-see-a-plus-side-in-eliminatingterm-limits-for-chinas-xi-jinping

Paulson, Henry M. (2015) *Dealing With China: An Insider Unmasks the New Economic Superpower.* Hatchette Book Group. New York.

Wike, Richard (2016). Chinese Public Sees More Powerful Role in World, Names U.S. as Top Threat. *Pew Research Center,* Retrieved from http://www.pewglobal.org/2016/10/05/chinese-public-sees-more-powerful role-in-world-names-u-s-top-threat/

What China Wants (2014). *The Economist.* Retrieved from www.economist.com/ news/essays/21609649-china-becomes-again-worlds-largest-economy-it-wants- respect-it-enjoyed-centuries-past-it-does-not-know-how-to-achieve-or-deserve-it

Xi Jinping Dreams of World Power for Himself and China (2018). *The New York Times*. Retrieved from https://www.nytimes.com/2018/02/27/opinion/xijinping-power-china.html

About the authors

Dr. Roland Bardy is owner of BardyConsult in Mannheim, Germany, where he mainly engages in management education, and he serves as Executive Professor of General Management and Leadership at Florida Gulf Coast University. Born in Vienna, Austria, he received a B.Sc. in chemistry there in 1964, and his M.B.A. degrec in 1969. His Ph.D. degree (1974, in econometrics) is from Heidelberg University, Germany. He worked in Finance and Administration at BASF SE, the German multinational chemicals manufacturer, for about thirty years until 1999. Then he took up teaching and consulting at Goizueta Business School (Emory University), at Fachhochschule Worms (Germany), and in various Swiss and Austrian MBA-programs. His areas of expertise are accounting, supply chain management, leadership and business ethics. He promotes the philosophy and implementation of responsible development, accountability and sustainability through a working group of the UN PRME initiative and through the Wittenberg Center for Global Ethics (www.wcge.org). Residing both in Mannheim, Germany, and in Naples, Florida, he is privileged to experience both U.S. and European developments in business and academia. He has published, in English and in German on management accounting, leadership and business ethics. He can be reached at <rbardy@t-online.de> and more information is available at <www.bardy.de>.

Dr. Gary Bonvillian is a consultant for an international education group in the People's Republic of China. He taught business courses at five different universities over four decades, and in his last position served 10 years as President of Thomas University in Thomasville, Georgia. His research, teaching and consulting focus has been primarily in the areas of International Business, Management, Leadership, Leading Change, Organizational Development, Total Quality Management, Organizational Behavior and Higher Education Leadership and Strategy. He continues to teach both Leadership and International Business. Dr. Bonvillian led the development of international partnership programs for two universities that resulted in the largest foreign providers of higher education in China in business and later in nursing. He has published works in two books and has contributed invited chapters in four other books and numerous refereed journals and other publications. Dr. Bonvillian earned his Ph.D. from SUNY Buffalo. He can be reached at <garyb101749@gmail.com>.

Dr. Daniel Borgia is the Dean at Bryant Zhuhai, a Sino-foreign academic joint venture between Bryant University and the Beijing Institute of Technology Zhuhai, China. Previously, he was Dean of the School of Business at Canisius College in New York, Associate Dean of the school of business at the University of Idaho, and Associate Dean at Nottingham University Business School in China. From 1997 to 2010, Dr. Borgia was a professor of finance at Florida Gulf Coast

University (FGCU). During that period, he was a China Fulbright Scholar at Nanjing University, a founding Director of the FGCU Institute of Chinese Studies, a founding Director of the Southwest Florida Chinese Language School, a vice president of the Southwest Florida Chinese Association, and a vice president of the Speaker's Assembly of Southwest Florida. Dr. Borgia received a B.S. in Business Management from Cornell University in 1981, an MBA from Gannon University in 1986, and a Ph.D. in Finance and International Business from Kent State University in 1991. Dr. Borgia has a broad publication record, writing on topics that include international business and finance with reference to China, working capital financing, entrepreneurial finance, and financial education. He can be reached at <daniel.borgia@zhuhai.bryant.edu>.

Dr. Jorge L. Díaz-Herrera became the 19th President of Keuka College on July 1, 2011. Prior to this appointment, he was professor and founding Dean of the College of Computing and Information Sciences at RIT in Rochester, NY (2002-2011); professor of Computer Science and Department Head at SPSU in Marietta, GA; Yamacraw project coordinator with Georgia Tech, Atlanta, GA; senior member of the technical staff and associate professor of software engineering at Carnegie Mellon's Software Engineering Institute; associate professor of software engineering and department chair at Monmouth University in NJ; assistant professor of computer science at George Mason University and at SUNY Binghamton. Dr. Díaz-Herrera has conducted extensive consulting services with a number of national and international firms and government agencies. He has served on various national and international technical advisory committees and governing boards. He has chaired several national and international conferences and has been a technical reviewer for the National

Science Foundation, the American Society for Engineering Education, and several conferences and journals. He is currently the Editor-in-Chief *Journal of Applied Sciences and Art*. He has more than 100 publications. He completed his undergraduate education in Venezuela and earned both a Master's and Ph.D. in Computing Studies from Lancaster University, UK. He completed two graduate certificates in Leadership in Education from Harvard University's Graduate School of Education in 2007 and 2011. He can be reached at <jorgediazh@keuka.edu>.

Dr. Sandra Figueira is a casual professor at the University of Queensland, Australia. She earned a master's in Sociology from Instituto Universitário de Lisboa in Portugal and a Doctorate in Business Administration from Grenoble Business School. Her research focuses on innovation, business systems, ethics, corporate governance and corporate social responsibility with a focus in Asian countries. She can be reached at <s.figueira@business.uq.edu.au>.

Dr. Jonathan Francesco Marano studied International Relations at the Oriental Studies University of Naples. He earned a master's degree at ISTAO Business School in Ancona, then enrolled as an Executive Ph.D. student in International Law at the University of Macerata (awarded in 2018), where he had the opportunity to deepen his academic and professional expertise on China affairs and business development strategies in the Far East Asia. His research

is conducted in cooperation with Chinese institutions, including Beijing Normal University and the Shanghai East China University of Political Science and Law. As a professional, he accounts for several experiences in the field of business development, having cooperated with several important Italian companies and brands, such as Brosway, Nava Design Milano, Ora Office and others. He currently holds the position of Sales Area Manager for Simonelli Group S.p.a. He can be reached at <jona.marano@gmail.com>.

Dr. Attilio Mucelli is associate professor of Management Accounting at the School of Economics "Giorgio Fuà," Polytechnic University of Marche, where he teaches Business Administration and Management Control and Cost Analysis. He also is member of the scientific board of the Ph.D. program of "Business Administration," held by the Schools of Economics of the Marche Region, and is a faculty member of the ISTAO Business School. He is visiting professor at the Florida Gulf Coast University (USA). He has been visiting professor/scholar at University of Heilbronn (Germany), Rollins College (USA), Toulouse Business School (France), Capital University of Economics and Business (P.R. China), Beijing Normal University (P.R. China). He has coordinated several national and international research projects with a special focus on the cooperation opportunities between Europa and China. He also has been CEO, member of the board of the directors, the board of auditors and consultant for Strategic Planning & Management control activities for public and private Companies. In this period he is also the General Manager of an Italian Medium sized company, in the fashion industry (Simonetta S.p.a.). He can be reached at <a.mucelli@staff.univpm.it>.

Dr. Rui Torres de Oliveira is a lecturer at the Queensland University of Technology, Business School. Previously, he worked as EY research fellow at the University of Queensland, was an assistant professor at the College of Saint Benedict/St. Jonh's University and an invited professor at Pontificia Universidad Católica del Peru. Prior to becoming an academic, Dr. Oliveira worked in the industry for more than fifteen years, including seven years in China, where he was the Managing Director of Multinational European firms. He earned an MBA from Catholic University, a master's in Civil Engineering from Oporto University in Portugal, and a doctorate in Business Administration from Manchester Business School, UK. His research interests include innovation, firm internationalization, business systems, strategy and M&A with a specific focus in Asia. He can be reached at <rui.torresdeoliveira@qut.edu.au>.

Dr. Arthur Rubens is professor emeritus and former professor of Management in Lutgert College of Business (AACSB Accredited) at Florida Gulf Coast University (FGCU) in Fort Myers, Florida. He is also currently a Fulbright Scholar at City University, School of Management, Bratislava, Slovak Republic. At FGCU, he taught in the B.S. MBA and Executive MBA programs and was actively involved in executive professional education and international educational programs. Dr. Rubens also has held multiple visiting professor positions, as well as short-term teaching assignments at varied universities throughout the world, including France, Italy, China, Denmark, New Zealand, Slovak Republic, and Germany. Dr. Rubens primary teaching areas are in business strategy, international management, leadership, and quality management. His primary research interests are in leadership, ethics, international management, sustainability/sustainable development, economic development, entrepreneurship, and quality management. Dr. Rubens is an accomplished scholar and has many peer-review publications, book chapters, and books to his credit. Professionally, Dr. Rubens has more than 28 years experience in the management field as an educator, consultant, researcher, and administrator. He earned a doctorate from the University of Pittsburgh and has MPA (Public Administration) and MSH (Health Services and Counseling) degrees. He can be reached at <arubens@fgcu.edu>.

Dr. Raymond Saner is Titular Professor at Basle University (Trade & Development) Switzerland and teaches at University of Luneburg, Germany (environmental science). He was a member of expert groups which drafted scientific contributions to the Sustainable Development Goals (SDGs), and a member of the editing teams that drafted the Global Sustainable Development Report. He is a founding partner of Organisational Consultants Ltd, Hong Kong, and co-founder of CSEND, Geneva. He co-authored the first ever publication on Business Diplomacy and his current research focuses on factors of successful Public Private Partnership in leveraging the opportunities of SDG development. He can be reached at <saner@csend.org>.

Dr. Lichia Saner-Yiu (EdD.) is president and co-founder of the Centre for Socio-Eco-Nomic Development (CSEND) in Geneva, Switzerland, a think tank with ECOSOC accreditation and special consultative status. She specializes in transformative technology and institutional development and has designed institution development and change strategies to enable public administrative reforms in China, Slovenia, Russia, and Bolivia. She also developed a standard framework on high performance learning systems. She has been member of the executive board of the Management Education and Development Division/Academy of Management and publishes extensively in academic and professional journals and teaches as visiting professor at universities in Taiwan, Switzerland and the United States. More recently her work focuses on sustainable cities and circular economy. She can be reached at <yiu@csend.org>.

Dr. Gary Smith has been a professor of management in the Division of Business and Management at Keuka College since 1994. He has held various college leadership positions, including Division Chair, Associate Dean, and Associate Vice President before becoming Vice President in 2010. He was nominated for the Teaching Excellence Award in May 2017, received the Academic Achievement Award in May 2016, appointed to the Fulbright Specialist Roster spring 2016, and named AGB Fellow for International Initiatives 2015-2016. He earned his Doctorate of Education from Saint John Fisher College in Rochester, New York, and his M.B.A. in Finance from the State University of New York at Buffalo. He holds undergraduate degrees in Business and Human Resource Management. His research interests include entrepreneurial leadership and international higher education. Dr. Smith has been instrumental in leading the creation of Keuka College's off campus programs in New York, overseas, and online. He has worked extensively throughout Asia as well as in the Middle East and South Africa. He also is an entrepreneur and has owned several hospitality related businesses. He continues to provide business consulting services to both public and private organizations, domestically and abroad. He can be reached at <gmskeuka@gmail.com>.

Dr. Francesca Spigarelli is associate professor of Applied Economics, at the University of Macerata, where she also serves as Vice Rector for Entrepreneurship and Technological Transfer and Director of the China Center. She is coordinator of LUCI- Laboratory for Creativity and Humanism, and of the CreaHub, incubator and co-working space, at University of Macerata. She is or has been coordinator of several EU funded projects (7° program framework or Horizon 2020) focused on China. Her main teaching areas include International business, applied economics, and microeconomics. She is author of papers published in international journals and books on the topics of multinational enterprises from emerging countries, China, and internationalization strategies of enterprises. She can be reached at <spigarelli@unimc.it>.

Dr. Yang Zhao has been involved in international higher education on multiple fronts over the past twenty years. She has served different institutions as a faculty member and administrator in China and the United States, working with higher education partners from around the world. Dr. Zhao earned her first master's degree in economics from Dongbei University of Finance and Economics in China. She was recognized as an Outstanding Young Professor and Excellent Teaching Researcher while working in China. She earned her second master's degree in management and a doctorate of education in the United States. Dr. Zhao has worked closely with the National Economics Teaching Association in the United States and has presented papers at its annual conferences. In 2017, she was appointed to the Fulbright Specialist Roster by the U.S. Department of State's Bureau of Educational and Cultural Affairs and World Learning. In 2018, Dr. Zhao completed a certificate program in Business Strategy from Cornell University. Dr. Zhao's entrepreneurial activities over the past decade have included several hospitality related businesses. She continues to provide business consulting services to both public and private organizations domestically and abroad. She can be reached at <yangzhao29@yahoo.com>.

Index

J

K

L

M

N

O

P

Q

R

S

T

U

V

W

X

Y-Z